Research and Higher Education

The United Kingdom
and the United States

Edited by
Thomas G. Whiston and
Roger L. Geiger

The Society for Research into Higher Education
& Open University Press

Published by SRHE and
Open University Press
Celtic Court
22 Ballmoor
Buckingham
MK18 1XW

and
1900 Frost Road, Suite 101
Bristol, PA 19007, USA

First Published 1992

British Library Cataloguing-in-Publication Data

Research and higher education: The United Kingdom
and the United States. – (SRHE/Open University
Press series)
    I. Whiston, Thomas G.   II. Geiger, Roger L.
    III. Series
    378.007

ISBN 0-335-15641-X

Library of Congress Cataloging-in-Publication Data

Research and higher education: the United Kingdom and the United
    States/edited by Thomas G. Whiston and Roger L. Geiger.
        p.   cm.
    Includes bibliographical references and index.

ISBN 0-335-15641-X
    1. Research – United States.   2. Research – Great Britain.
3. Education, Higher – United States.   4. Education, Higher – Great
Britain.   I. Whiston, Thomas G., 1938–   .   II. Geiger, Roger L.,
1943–   .
    Q180.U5R382   1991   91-21336
    004.1'0973 – dc20   CIP

Typeset by Rowland Phototypesetting Limited
Bury St Edmunds, Suffolk
Printed in Great Britain by St Edmundsbury Press Limited
Bury St Edmunds, Suffolk

Contents

Part 3: Prospects for Academic Research

List of Contributors

Harry Atkinson, a physicist, is a director of the Science and Engineering Research Council, the organization which supports most areas of basic research in United Kingdom universities and polytechnics. He has been chairman of the European Space Agency and has been on the governing bodies of many international science organizations, in Europe and elsewhere. He has recently published, with Philippa Rogers and Richard Bond, *Research in the United Kingdom, France and West Germany: A Comparison*, in two volumes.

Sir Christopher Ball, previously Warden, Keble College, Oxford, and Chairman, National Advisory Board for Public Sector Higher Education in England, has published extensively on a range of educational issues.

Burton R. Clark is Allan M. Cartter Professor of Higher Education and Sociology and Chairman of the Comparative Higher Education Research Group, University of California, Los Angeles. He has published extensively in areas of Higher Education in a cross-national setting. In 1979 he received the American Educational Research Association–American College Testing Program Research Award for his studies of American universities and colleges. In 1988 he became the first recipient of the Distinguished Research Award of Division J, Higher Education, American Educational Research Association. In 1989 he received the Outstanding Book Award of the American Educational Research Association for his book *The Academic Life*.

Irwin Feller is Director of the Graduate School of Public Policy and Administration and Director of the Institute for Policy Research and Evaluation and Professor of Economics at Pennsylvania State University. His research has centred on the diffusion of innovations, university–industry–government collaborative R&D agreements, the commercialization of academic research, and federal–state science relationships. His articles have appeared in numerous economics and policy journals; he is the author of *Universities and State Governments*. He is a member of the American Association for the Advancement of Science's Committee on Science, Engineering, and Public Policy. He has served as a consultant to many federal, state and not-for-profit organizations including the President's Offices of Science and Technology Policy, the National Science Foundation, the Ford Foundation, the National Governors Association, and the National Conferences of State Legislatures.

Mary Frank Fox is Associate Professor of Sociology and Women's Studies at Pennsylvania State University. Her research focuses upon women and men in organizations and occupations, especially scientific and academic ones. Her current research projects are a study of publication productivity in four fields, and a study of the participation and performance of women in doctoral education in science. Her works include the books *Women at Work* (Mayfield, 1984) and *Scholarly Writing and Publishing* (Westview, 1985) and articles in fifteen different scholarly journals and collections. Fox is past Associate Editor of *Gender & Society* and is a member of the editorial boards of *Work and Occupations*, *The American Sociologist*, and *Journal of Vocational Behavior*. She is a member of the Publication Committee of the American Sociological Association (ASA) and Council Member of the ASA Section on Science, Knowledge, and Technology.

Roger L. Geiger is Professor of Higher Education at Pennsylvania State University. An historian, he has written extensively on the history and current conditions of university research, including *To Advance Knowledge: The Growth of American Research Universities, 1900 to 1940* and a forthcoming sequel, *Research and Relevant Knowledge: American Research Universities Since World War II*. Until 1987 he was at the Yale Institution for Social and Political Studies, where he wrote on topics in comparative Higher Education, including *Private Sectors in Higher Education: Structure, Function and Change in Eight Countries*.

Michael Gibbons is Professor of Science and Technology Policy at the University of Manchester. His texts include *Science, Technology and Society Today*; *Science and Technology Policy in the 1980s and Beyond*.

Mary Henkel is a Lecturer in the Department of Government at Brunel University. Her research relates to policy evaluation; and the relationship between policy and the organization and development of knowledge. She has recently published *Government, Education and Change* (Jessica Kingsley, 1991). She is also co-author (with Maurice Kogan) of *Government and Research: The Rothschild Experiment in a Government Department* (Heinemann Education, 1983).

Maurice Kogan is Professor of Government and Social Administration at Brunel University. He has written extensively in various areas relating to educational administration, politics, health and the social services. For fourteen years he was at the Department of Education and Science where he was Private Secretary to Sir Edward Boyle and also Secretary to the Plowden Committee.

R. Eugene Rice recently became Dean of the Faculty and Vice-President of Antioch College. He moved to Antioch from the Carnegie Foundation for the Advancement of Teaching (Princeton, NJ) where he was Senior Fellow and Program Executive engaged in a national study of faculty scholarship. In

1989–90 he was also Visiting Professor of Higher Education, Teachers College, Columbia University. During the major part of his career, Dr Rice has been Professor of Sociology and Religion at the University of Pacific, where he served as Chairperson of the Department of Sociology. His teaching and research focus on the sociology and ethics of the professions and the workplace. Rice has been Research Director (with Ann Austin) of 'The Future of the Academic Workplace Project' sponsored by the Council of Independent Colleges, Washington, DC. Articles on his research on faculty morale have appeared in a number of publications and will be reported on in full in the forthcoming book *A Good Place to Work*.

Robert M. Rosenzweig is a member of the 'Financing Higher Education in the 1990s' panel. He has been President of the Association of American Universities (AAU) since 1983. Before taking the helm of AAU, he was Vice-President for public affairs at Stanford University. In his twenty-one years of service at Stanford, Rosenzweig also served as adviser to the President, Director of the Center for Research in International Studies, and Associate Dean of the university's Graduate Division. The author of *Research Universities and Their Patrons* and *The Federal Interest in Higher Education*, Rosenzweig was cited by *Business Week* in 1989 as one of twelve key policy-makers in American science and technology.

Bruce L. R. Smith has been a Senior Staff Member in the Center for Public Policy Education of the Brookings Institution since 1980. Since 1983 he has been a professional lecturer at the Johns Hopkins University School of Advanced International Studies. In addition, he lectures widely on the quality revolution in US manufacturing, recent trends in US science policy, and government–business relations. He is the author of *American Science Policy Since World War II* (Brookings, 1990). He serves as Associate Editor of *Minerva*, a journal of higher education, science and learning.

Martin Trow is Professor of Sociology in the Graduate School of Public Policy at the University of California, Berkeley. He has written widely on topics in comparative politics and Higher Education, and is currently working on a comparative history of British and American Higher Education.

Thomas G. Whiston is Senior Fellow at the Science Policy Research Unit (SPRU), University of Sussex. Previously he was Lecturer in Psychology, University of Manchester. His research studies focus upon Higher Educational policy issues in relation to technical and social change, areas in which he has published extensively. He has undertaken numerous policy reviews for UNESCO, ICSU, OECD and UK Research Councils. His texts include *Management and Assessment of Interdisciplinary Training and Research* (UNESCO, 1986); *The Uses and Abuses of Forecasting* (Macmillan, 1979); *Managerial and Organizational Integration* (Springer, 1991).

Preface

The Society for Research into Higher Education (SRHE) was involved in convening two international seminars on 'Quality in Higher Education' at Oxford in December 1986 and at Princeton, New Jersey, in September 1987. The discussions at those meetings – attended by senior academics, administrators and others actively involved in policy-making – focused upon the undergraduate level. They related to problems of quality in undergraduate education and of access to higher education. Experience of these seminars indicated the need for a third international seminar which moved beyond 'The Undergraduate Level to Graduate Education and the Relations between Research and Higher Education'.

The papers which comprise this volume are one of the outcomes of the third Anglo-American Conference held at Derwent College, University of York, in the autumn of 1989. Papers (and other contributions) given at the conference related to several European countries and to the USA. The present volume includes only the British and American contributions. They yield interesting and informative comparisons relating to the central theme of Research and Higher Education. The individual papers are not meant to provide an *exhaustive* overview of the myriad of factors, problems or developments presently confronting research in general. Rather, the aim is to provide informed accounts from individuals who have spent many years 'researching the field' and who possess their own particular specialities of knowledge and expertise. In so doing the editors believe that not only is the resultant text 'greater than the sum of the parts' but also the heterogeneity of style and perspective is in itself stimulating and rewarding to the wider readership.

Although each section includes contributions both from the UK and the USA the intention is *not* to make formal comparisons; indeed authors often chose to emphasize different aspects. Further, such international comparisons would seem, at this stage, to be invidious and unwarranted in a formalistic sense. Nevertheless, as readers progress through the volume they will no doubt form conclusions, or be provoked to make further comparison, or demand further detail regarding various issues pertinent to Research, Higher Education and the prevailing British and American systems.

If that is so then the wider purpose both of the Conference and this volume will have been achieved. For on both sides of the Atlantic there is much ferment and the need of continual discussion regarding all of the topics considered here. Despite the obvious difficulties of cross-cultural transference (what holds or may take shape or flower in one country is by no means automatically transferable to another) there is much to be gained by observing, analysing and signalling the best, indifferent and worse features in either system. In so doing a more absolute or universal rule-book may ensue.

Having made the above qualifications it is inevitable that the sections into which the text is divided is necessarily somewhat arbitrary, for many of the contributors touch on areas relevant to topics discussed in more detail by their peers. This reflects the interdisciplinary nature of the topics under discussion. However, that interdisciplinarity can be placed into a useful pedagogic context. Therefore the structure we have chosen here is as follows.

In the first part we consider the national systems (in as much as they may be classified as such) under three subthemes:

1. The 'historical moment': where we are now and some of the dynamics and forces which led to the present scene.
2. Issues in funding research (the second paper in that section provides a useful comparative commentary on the UK, France and West Germany).
3. The connections between academe and industry and their relevance to the research function of higher education.

The second part considers what we refer to as the 'institutional dimension', and is subdivided into research environments; teaching and research interactions; and graduate education and research training.

In the third part there is a final discussion of 'prospects for academic research'. This is not intended to be a summary or conclusion derived from the earlier papers; for neither in the UK nor in the USA is it possible or desirable to indicate broad consensus of opinion relating to the future of the research-function in higher education. The purpose of the final papers is to signal issues, now on the debating table, which will require much fuller research and discussion in their own right if Research and Higher Education are to evolve in a way satisfactory to the pluralistic requirements and demands of governments, industry, academe and society at large.

The editors

List of Abbreviations

AAAS	American Association for the Advancement of Science
AASCU	American Association of State Colleges and Universities
AAU	Association of American Universities
ABRC	Advisory Board for the Research Councils
ACOST	Advisory Council on Science and Technology
AEC	Atomic Energy Commission
AFRC	Agriculture and Food Research Council
AIDS	Acquired Immune Deficiency Syndrome
AMA	American Medical Association
AMT	Advanced Manufacturing Technology
ASA	American Sociological Association
AUT	Association of University Teachers
BFP	Ben Franklin Partnership Program
BID	Bureaux, Institutes, Divisions
BMFT	Federal Ministry of Research and Technology (Germany)
CAD	Computer-assisted design
CAM	Computer-assisted manufacturing
CAT	College of Advanced Technology
CCUC	Committee of Chairmen of University Councils
CEA	Atomic Energy Commission (France)
CERN	European Centre for Nuclear Research (France)
CEST	Centre for Exploitation of Science and Technology
CNRS	National Centre for Scientific Research (France)
COMETT	Community in Education and Training for Technology
CVCP	Committee of Vice-Chancellors and Principals
DES	Department of Education and Science
DFG	German Research Society
DHSS	Department of Health and Social Security
DNA	Deoxyribonucleic Acid
DOD	Department of Defense (USA)
DOE	Department of Energy (USA)

DRG	Divisions of Research Grants
EC	European Community
EPST	Établissement public à caractère scientifique et technologique (Public Establishment of Scientific and Technological Character)
ESA	European Space Agency
ESO	European Southern Observatory
ESPRIT	European Strategic Programme for Research and Development in Information Technology
ESRC	Economic and Social Research Council
FE	Further Education
FFRDCs	Federally Funded Research and Development Centers
FhG	Fraunhofer Society (Germany)
FTE	Full-time equivalent
FY	Financial year
GBAORD	Civil budget government R&D appropriations
GDP	Gross domestic product
GFE	Grofforschungsceinrichtungen (overall specific research directives)
GNP	Gross national product
GOVERD	Government intramural expenditure on R&D
GUF	General university funds
HE	Higher Education
HEI	Institution of Higher Education
HERD	Higher education expenditure on R&D
HMI	Her Majesty's Inspectorate
ICSU	International Council for Scientific Unions
IES	Industrial Extension Service
INRA	Institut national de la recherche agronomique (National Institute for Agricultural Research)
INSERM	Institut de la santé et de la recherche médicale (National Institute for Health and Medical Research)
IOM	Institute of Medicine
IPR	Intellectual Property Rights
IRC	Interdisciplinary Research Centre
IT	Information technology
MEN	Ministry of National Education (France)
MIT	Massachusetts Institute of Technology
MPG	Max Planck Society (Germany)
MRC	Medical Research Council
NAB	National Advisory Board
NAE	National Academy of Engineering
NAO	National Audit Office
NAS	National Academy of Sciences
NASA	National Aeronautics and Space Administration
NERC	Natural Environment Research Council

NIH	National Institutes of Health
NIMBY	Not In My Back Yard
NSF	National Science Foundation
NVQ	National Vocational Qualification
OECD	Organization for Economic Co-operation and Development
ONR	Office of Naval Research
ORUs	Organized Research Units
PCFC	Polytechnics and Colleges Funding Council
PennTAP	Pennsylvania Technology Assistance Program
PNP	Private non-profit
PPP	Purchasing Power Parity
R&D	Research and development
RANN	Research Applied to National Needs
RSE	Research scientists and engineers
S&T	Science and technology
SDI	Strategic Defense Initiative
SERC	Science and Engineering Research Council
SPRU	Science Policy Research Unit
SPSG	Science Policy Support Group
SRHE	Society for Research into Higher Education
SRI	Stanford Research Institute
SSC	Superconducting Supercollider
UCLA	University of California at Los Angeles
UFC	University Funding Council
UGC	University Grants Committee
UNESCO	United Nations Educational, Scientific and Cultural Organization
USR	Universities' Statistical Record
VC	Vice-Chancellor

Part 1

The National Systems

1

The Dynamics of University Research in the United States: 1945–90

Roger L. Geiger

Research economy and research capacity: two faces of the system

The major American universities have changed vastly since the Second World War in terms of size, composition of enrolments, and the mix of activities encompassed. Nowhere has change been so far-reaching, however, as in their research role.[1] Driving this transformation was an abundance of external support, primarily from the federal government, available for university research. The proper utilization of these funds, however, required a substantial enhancement, largely using their own resources, of the capacity of universities to perform research. Underlying the evolution of the university research system of the United States since the Second World War has been a dynamic interrelationship between these external and internal conditions for research.

American colleges and universities developed historically as teaching institutions. The primacy of the teaching mission, particularly undergraduate teaching, has been reflected perhaps more in the organizational realities of the university – in its departmental structure and in its patterns of finance – than in the behaviour of individual faculty. This situation has meant that resources intended exclusively for research have generally had to come from outside of the institution. Since the end of the First World War, a steady and recurrent flow of such resources has been made available from, first, foundations and private industry, and, starting with the Second World War, from the federal government (Geiger 1986; 1990a). This pool of resources outside of the university that is available for research inside constitutes the 'university research economy'.

Universities compete for the funds available in the research economy, and these funds are largely distributed according to the capacity of institutions to conduct fruitful research. The complement of the research economy, then, is the 'research capacity' of universities – the capabilities of faculty, the nature and quality of facilities, and the presence of research staff and graduate students. To a large extent, the research capacity of a university depends upon the resources that it can generate and, implicitly, its willingness to devote them to research-related purposes. There is an obvious interrelationship between the research economy and university research capacity. External funds, for example, routinely provide for the purchase of equipment or support for graduate students, thereby enhancing internal capacity. But the research economy and research capacity represent conceptually distinct spheres of activities, and their historical development has been distinct as well.

The relationship between the research economy and American universities has been characterized by four qualities: from the standpoint of research funders, the university system presents a high degree of *decentralization* and, concomitantly, *competition* among performers. From the standpoint of universities, the research economy has exhibited considerable *pluralism*. The combination of multiple sources and many eager recipients has tended to encourage *adaptability* in universities. Although the American system of academic research is notable in these four respects compared with most other nations, the nature and extent of these qualities has varied at different points in time.

The development of the university research system since 1945 has occurred through changes in the research economy, in the research capacities of universities, and in the nature of their interrelationships. The first of these, the research economy, has been monitored since 1953 by the National Science Foundation (NSF), which has recorded the volume of research and development (R&D) expenditures of colleges and universities, their distribution between basic and applied research and development activities, and the sources of those funds.[2] It will be argued here that the character of the research economy is significantly determined by a quality less easily measured – the motives of funders, whether they be to further the 'disinterested' advancement of knowledge, or to produce 'programmatic' knowledge with an identifiable utility for the sponsors.

The research capacity of universities is similarly not subject to direct measurement, but in research universities it is closely related to the overall financial strength of the institution. One measure of long-term fluctuations in core financial strength is provided by the instructional budget. This figure comprises the expenditures of academic departments, and largely reflects faculty salaries and support. It stands as a rough proxy, then, for the capability of an institution to assemble a distinguished – and highly paid – faculty suited to perform first-rate research. A second financial requirement is the capital needed for research facilities. Public universities depend upon their respective state legislatures for such capital, while private universities look to their donors. Only in the case of special facilities for 'Big Science' projects have research patrons normally been willing to assume capital costs. The financial requirements underlying a university's research capacity have thus been a limiting factor in the university research system. As a result, only a slowly growing number of institutions have qualified as 'research universities'.[3]

The well-developed research capacities of institutions combined with continuity of purpose among research patrons have imparted considerable stability and inertia to the system. The characteristic form of change has accordingly been through growth – selective growth to be more precise. Few activities have been terminated, but those finding favour in the research economy have grown disproportionately; in a few cases entirely new patrons have emerged. The post-war evolution, then, has largely occurred through incremental changes in the balance of ongoing activities due to the selective expansion of favoured modes of research.

The post-war era: 1945–57

Academic science demonstrated its usefulness to the United States during the Second World War, and it was continued usefulness that was demanded from universities by the federal government in the years following the war. Prior to 1940, the only significant amounts of federal support for university research were directed to the agricultural extension stations. Afterward, such aid was joined by four other distinct channels of support, which together then comprised the federal component of the university research economy.

1. Military research continued to be supported on a broad range of subjects, with the largest amounts going toward research related to radar and electronics, fuses, and rocket propulsion.
2. The Atomic Energy Commission (AEC) assumed the mantle of the Manhattan Project, and with it control over all research involving radioactive materials.
3. The Public Health Service assumed the outstanding contracts of the wartime Committee on Medical Research and began building the National Institutes of Health (NIH) empire.
4. Last and certainly least was the implicit government responsibility to support basic university research for the advancement of knowledge. This mission was advanced as the central purpose of a national research foundation, proposed by Vannevar Bush in his blueprint for post-war policy, *Science: The Endless Frontier* (1944). But, unlike the other channels, Congress failed to pass the enabling legislation during the crucial summer of 1946. Instead, the Office of Naval Research (ONR), with far more funds and fewer constraints, became the chief patron of basic university research during the remainder of the 1940s and well into the 1950s (Sapolsky 1990). The National Science Foundation was belatedly enacted in 1950 (England 1982), but would not overshadow ONR as the patron of disinterested academic research for another decade.

In the early 1950s (when somewhat reliable figures first became available) the university research system had a definitely applied cast. In a university research economy of $255 million (1953), $138 million (54 per cent) were provided by the federal government. Federal agencies also supported an additional $121 million of research at large, semi-autonomous federal contract research centres that were nominally managed by universities. At the universities proper, federally funded research was only 53 per cent basic, versus 47 per cent applied research and development. At contract research centres, these latter activities comprised 73 per cent of research funds.

These figures do not fully reflect the extent to which academic research was dominated by its patrons. The actual state of affairs was disturbing to many scientists and university leaders. Harvard President James B. Conant, for one, argued that the distinction between basic and applied research was not really the crucial issue; rather, the system had become dominated by programmatic research – 'a research program aimed at a specific goal' – to the neglect of 'uncommitted' or disinterested research, aimed at advancing knowledge without respect to ulterior goals (Conant 1951: viii). The problem facing the university research system was that, while all applied research was programmatic in nature, much of the basic research being supported was as well. The principal federal supporters of basic research – NIH, AEC and even the much-lauded ONR – all had practical missions. There seemed to be comparatively little support for the kind of unfettered investigations that had long been regarded as the true mission of the university.

The dominant presence of the federal government in the post-war research economy thus produced a research system that was heavily skewed toward programmatic ends. Some fields flourished, particularly in physics and engineering; while for others research funds remained difficult to obtain. Funds were also lacking to 'grease the wheels' of science by supporting fellowships, exchanges, meetings and publications. Probably most serious was the absence of funds to support the strengthening of the research capacities of universities.

Despite the lack of federal assistance, universities generally managed some increase in research capacity. In the immediate post-war era the universities were tossed by cross-currents. The influx of students as a result of the GI Bill partially revitalized institutional finances after the ravages of the Great Depression and the deprivations of the war years. For universities in general, the decades of the 1930s and 1940s had been ones of low investment in physical capital. The 1950s brought first the uncertainties of the Korean War, accompanied by renewed inflation. Not until the mid-1950s was higher education able to benefit from a strong economy and a normal financial environment.

State and private universities were affected somewhat differently by these conditions. The public research universities expanded in order to accommodate the influx of veterans, and then largely retained their gains as enrolments subsided. By 1955 they had considerably increased their instructional spending and expanded their faculties. Private universities generally suffered from the diminished purchasing power of their endowment income and from a dearth of capital for growth. Voluntary support, on which they depended for capital, did not surpass the levels of 1928–31 in real terms until after 1955. Improvements in research capacity prior to 1955 were made from exceedingly low levels, except perhaps for the strongest of the research universities. Thus, even in the mid-1950s faculty were grievously underpaid and virtually every university had a long wish-list of badly needed facilities. The situation was epitomized in the medical schools, where there was an abundance of research funding, while the schools themselves were on the brink of insolvency. This financial weakness of institutions, together with the concentrated nature of the research economy, combined to produce the characteristic qualities of the university research system in the post-war era.

Immediately after the war there was an intense, and not altogether healthy, competition for the services of scientists, especially atomic physicists. They naturally tended to cluster at the leading universities, which offered them the most propitious conditions for research. At the same time, the continuation of wartime laboratories assured that certain fields would be planted at certain institutions. These two factors alone were sufficient to account for the concentration of post-war research in relatively few universities. In fact, the concentration of research funding has declined rather steadily from the post-war years to the present. In 1952 the first ten universities received 43.4 per cent of federal research funds (not including federal centres); whereas their share currently is less than half that figure (Table 1.1).

'Decentralization' was a concept that applied only in part to the post-war university research system. Agencies that supported 'Little Science' through modest, short-term grants – ONR, NIH and later NSF – distributed their funds fairly widely, even considering the concentration of research talent. Elsewhere, however, the system was characterized by quasi-permanent relationships between large university laboratories (and especially contract research centres) and their mission-agency patrons. These latter relationships accounted for the vast bulk of funds in the research economy during this era.

The obverse of this last condition would be that pluralism of funding was limited as well. The research economy appeared to be fairly pluralistic, if one took into account the several federal patrons, including the independent research programmes of the armed services; however, the funding possibilities for individual fields were often quite circumscribed. The post-war statesmen of science – Vannevar Bush, James Conant, and Massachusetts Institute of Technology (MIT) President Karl Compton, among others – had been concerned to preserve the pluralism of American university research by maintaining viable private alternatives to federal funding. In the natural sciences, though, just what they had feared came to pass. The overweening presence of federal support caused private foundations to withdraw from the field. In the life sciences the picture was more mixed. The foundations committed to this area were gradually overshadowed by the growth of NIH, but private funders remained and sought out unfilled niches. Only the social sciences continued to rely upon the private foundations for research funding, although the

Table 1.1   Concentration of funding: federal R&D obligations to top ten universities (%)[4]

1952	1958	1968	1978	1988
43.4	37.0	27.7	23.0	21.5

dominance of the Ford Foundation in this area by the mid-1950s might also be considered a limitation of pluralism (Geiger 1988).

The attitudes of universities toward the swollen post-war research economy varied from apprehension to exasperation, but in hindsight their actual adaptations reflected pragmatism and flexibility. The arrangements for accounting for organized research, which had been quite casual before the war, had to be regularized and eventually confided to a separate administrative unit. The most prominent organizational difficulty was created by the hypertrophy of research in selected areas of the university. As research became an end in itself, with its own continuing financing and separate staff, the complementarity of teaching and research, upon which the academic departments were predicated, was superseded.

Three kinds of adaptations were evident. In medical schools and sometimes in physics departments, regular faculty positions were decoupled from the instructional budget: permanent faculty were hired on 'soft' money. In other areas the demands of research were often met by creating Organized Research Units (ORUs). Such units were not entirely new, but the extensive reliance upon them was (Geiger 1990a). The universities that had the largest amounts of research funding – notably MIT and Berkeley – also had the most ORUs. The federal contract research centres were a direct outgrowth of the war. For at least a decade a sorting process took place, which tended to isolate weapons-related research in this kind of institutional quarantine (e.g. Lawrence Livermore Laboratory of the University of California, Berkeley, the Lincoln Laboratories of MIT, and the Applied Physics Laboratory managed by Johns Hopkins). For a time it appeared that the contract research centres might serve programmatic federal purposes better than university research proper, but after the 1950s they grew much less than university research. The dynamics of these centres reflected government needs for research in the particular fields in which they operated. Their relationship with their respective universities, however, was in most cases tenuous.

The Sputnik era: 1958–68

The transformation of the university research system began in the mid-1950s. Prosperity brought a marked expansion of the research economy: expenditures for research in universities proper grew by 60 per cent from 1954 to 1958, that is before the effects of Sputnik were felt. Increases were roughly comparable in both federal and non-federal funding, but within the federal component two opposed tendencies were evident. Funding from the armed services became decidedly more pragmatic as military budgets came under some unaccustomed pressure. The result seems to have been greater use of Federally Funded Research and Development Centers (FFRDCs) in preference to research in universities proper. In the other federal channels of the research economy, however, trends favoured academic research. Of greatest quantitative importance, the NIH began a prodigious expansion of its extramural grants programmes after 1956. The AEC also increased its funding of university research, and the NSF finally became a significant patron. With these changes, the proportion of basic research in the university totals rose to 70 per cent.

These years also witnessed a dramatic improvement in university research capacity, particularly at the major private institutions. In general, public research universities made some relative advances in instructional spending before 1955, and then registered further progress driven by enrolment growth thereafter. Private universities, capitalizing on propitious financial conditions and considerably higher levels of voluntary support, registered impressive advances in the decade after 1955. Because of changes in the research economy, university research became less concentrated. Whereas in 1954 only eleven universities expended more than $5 million on separately budgeted research (not including agriculture and federal centres) twenty institutions had crossed that threshold by 1958.

In the years prior to Sputnik, the university research system was evolving away from the cast that it had taken immediately after the war. It was encouraged in this respect by a campaign extolling the virtues of basic research that was orchestrated by NSF, and conducted by university scientists and administrators. This trend was impeded by the frugality of the Eisenhower Administration and the increasingly pragmatic orientation of the armed services. Sputnik resolved this uncertainty in favour of basic research. Within a few years the system was transformed into the antithesis of what it had been in the post-war era (Geiger forthcoming).

The USA responded to Sputnik with new and substantial commitments to Space, Science and Education (McDougall 1985). New programmes in each of these areas redounded to the benefit of the research universities. The preoccupations with space resulted in the creation of NASA (National Aeronautics and Space Administration). Although the ultimate thrust of NASA was toward Big Science and engineering, it forged numerous links with university research during the 1960s. As a newcomer agency, eager to build a network with academic science, it was in a position analogous to ONR in the late 1940s. It provided generous funding on lenient terms to scientists at a wide group of institutions. By 1966 NASA was supplying almost 10 per cent of federal funds for academic research; some thirty-six universities were receiving more than $1 million from the agency.

The National Defense Education Act 1958 was the beginning of regular federal support for graduate students, foreign languages and area studies. The federal government thus undertook to support the research role of universities in ways other than the funding of research. The most spectacular gains were nevertheless made in precisely this last area. The federal government committed itself unequivocally to supporting basic research in the universities for the sake of advancing knowledge (and also besting the Soviets). From 1958 to 1968 federal funds for basic university research rose from $178 million to $1,251 million – a sevenfold increase during a decade of relatively stable prices. This was by far the most significant component of growth in an expanding research economy. Moreover, it tilted the balance of the nation's basic research

Table 1.2   Post-Sputnik changes in the role of university research

	Gross national product	National basic research	% GNP	Total univ. R&D	% GNP	Basic univ. res.	% Nat. basic	% Univ. res.
	A	B	B/A	C	C/A	D	D/B	D/C
1953	364,900	441	0.12	255	0.07	110	25	43
1960	506,500	1,197	0.24	646	0.12	433	36	67
1964	637,700	2,289	0.36	1,275	0.20	1,003	44	79
1968	873,400	3,296	0.38	2,149	0.25	1,649	50	77
1986	4,291,000	14,163	0.33	10,600	0.24	7,100	50	67

into university laboratories: the national budget for basic research grew by $2,400 million during these years; university-based research accounted for $1,400 million of this increase; federal funds comprised $1,100 million of that. Whereas universities expended 32 per cent of the funds for basic research in 1958, they spent 50 per cent of the total in 1968, and thereafter (Table 1.2). In retrospect, this would appear to have been a golden age for academic science.

The expansion of the research economy was accompanied by the recognition of the need to strengthen the infrastructure for university research. A committee of the President's Science Advisory Council (Seaborg Report) recommended in 1960 that the number of research universities in the nation should be doubled – from 15–20 to 30–40. The Ford Foundation had already begun a programme of upgrading selected universities, and federal programmes eventually followed at the principal agencies supporting university research. During the 1960s for the first time the federal government provided substantial support to enhance the research capacity of universities. By 1968 the government was supplying almost one-third of the capital funds expended by universities (which compares to a proportion of about one-eighth in the 1980s).

Federal support for infrastructural needs, together with greater financial support from other sources, rectified one of the conditions that lay behind the substantial concentration in the university research system, namely the restricted research capacity of all but a few institutions. The growing abundance of funds for research, especially investigator-initiated projects, ended another limitation. Finally, as the graduate schools turned out an increasing number of research-oriented PhDs, the number of university researchers greatly increased. By 1968, forty-one universities were receiving more than $10 million in federal R&D obligations, and the share of the total claimed by the first ten had declined to 27.7 per cent.

By the mid-1960s the post-Sputnik accretions to the research economy had overgrown the configurations of the post-war-era research economy.

Comparing 1958 and 1968, the *additional* funding to NIH and NSF, plus the net addition of NASA, comprised more than 60 per cent of federal support for university research. By the latter year it appeared that an 'Academic Revolution' had taken place, that the values of the graduate school had gained ascendancy in American universities (Jencks and Riesman 1968). The domination of investigation by disciplinary paradigms even became the object of criticism: a crisis of 'relevance' was perceived in the university curriculum, and perhaps in the conduct of research itself. Meanwhile, much of the programmatic research sponsored by the Department of Defense was deemed unfit for university campuses and opposed by anti-war students and faculty.

The 'new' federal funds in the research economy were spread far more widely than the 'old' funds had been, thereby furthering the decentralization of the research system. This, in turn, enhanced competition. University leaders and academic scientists greeted the new regime with alacrity. The emphasis given to basic research allowed them to do what they felt universities ought to be doing, and without the misgivings about secrecy, continuity, or external control that had plagued them during the preceding era. Thus, universities readily adapted by increasing their emphasis on research and its attendant values. They aggressively recruited productive scholars and scientists, and devoted their own discretionary funds to building research capacity. This was the rational course. For perhaps the first time in university history, research seemed to be a remunerative activity for a substantial number of institutions. Not only did the federal government stand ready to assist universities to meet the high overhead expenses associated with efforts to maintain and extend research capacity, but also that capacity could now assuredly generate a continuing flow of project funds and indirect-cost reimbursements.

In this heady environment, few expressed real concern over the attenuation of pluralism. The Seaborg Report had declared that the federal government, and only the federal government, was responsible for expanding the university research system. During the 1960s each discipline in turn defined its absolutely indispensable research needs, and then, in effect, presented the bill to the public in quasi-official reports published by the National Academy of Sciences (Greenberg 1967: 151–69). The federal contribution to academic R&D rose from 53 per cent in 1953, to 63 per cent in 1960, to a peak of 74 per cent in 1966; it then remained above 70 per cent for the remainder of the decade (Table 1.3). Private contributions to university research (industry and nonprofits) fell as low as 8.6 per cent (1967–9). At this juncture universities finally were forced to face the consequences of overdependence on a single source – the condition that had worried university leaders during the preceding postwar era.

Table 1.3 Federal dependence: university R&D supported by federal funds (%)

1953	1960	1966	1976	1989
53	63	74	67	59

The stagnant decade: 1968–78

The momentum imparted to academic science by the reaction to Sputnik lasted for ten years. The year 1968 represents a kind of apogee for the university research system in terms of real expenditures and federal support for research. This was not solely a university phenomenon; research expenditures for the country as a whole peaked in 1968 as well. The university research economy remained roughly stable in real terms for the next seven years, through 1975, while the national R&D economy actually declined by nearly 10 per cent. Significant growth in university research did not occur again until 1978. The system thus experienced a decade of stagnation, which in some cases brought outright retrenchment.

Despite the abrupt transition from expansion to stagnation, the university research system changed only slowly during this decade. The federal contribution to university research fell somewhat to 67 per cent. Applied research fared somewhat better than basic, so that the proportion of the latter declined from 77 per cent (1968) to 69 per cent (1977). Still, despite evident dissatisfaction with the supposed irrelevance of academic research, there was limited movement toward a more programmatic orientation. NSF was forced to adopt a programme on 'Research Applied to National Needs', and the NIH was directed to conduct the 'War on Cancer'; but universities seemed disinclined to pursue programmatic funding. Both NIH and NSF altered their policies by devoting significantly larger proportions of their funds to actual research. These steps protected the pool of project funds, but had an additional, adverse impact on universities. During the 'Stagnant Decade' federal support of the kind that bolstered university research capacities was severely curtailed. Funds for R&D plant peaked at $126 million in 1965, but averaged just $35 million annually during the 1970s (current $). Federal fellowship support reached a high figure of $447 million in 1967, but stood at only $185 million a decade later. Universities were asked to do more on their own to sustain their research roles, and they were hard-pressed to meet this challenge.

These years were difficult ones for university finances. The private universities, in general, had tended to overcommit themselves during the late 1960s, and as a result were compelled to concentrate on putting their budgets back into the black during the early 1970s. State research universities came under increasing pressure during the early 1970s to justify their high costs to egalitarian-minded legislators. From about 1968 it was virtually taken for granted that a major new federal programme would have to be initiated in order to rectify the financial conditions prevailing in higher education. When it came in 1972, however, Congress provided expanded forms of student financial aid instead of institutional aid that would have been of immediate succour to the research universities. Under these conditions, few institutions were able to augment their instructional budgets in real terms during the 1968–77 period. Their problems were not only with income, which in most cases continued to rise, but also with the rapid growth in non-instructional expenses, such as energy costs, administrative requirements, and the necessity of meeting federal regulations. Research was in fact severely crowded as an institutional priority by other concerns, and few institutions sought to advance their research capacities to any significant extent.

The 'State of Academic Science' well into the decade of stagnation was carefully monitored in a study conducted by Bruce Smith and Joseph Karlesky (1977). One of the striking conclusions that they reached was that the secular trend toward decentralization of university research was about to be reversed. The proportion of federal research funds received by the top ten universities had actually declined from 29.1 per cent in 1967 to 25.8 per cent in 1975. It seemed, however, that the stagnation in research funding and the persistent financial difficulties facing universities would now favour the leading institutions. As the competition for research funds became more intense, the advantage of those universities with the highest peer-rated faculties ought to have become more pronounced. Sustaining a research commitment also seemed to demand a larger investment of institutional funds. At the second-tier research universities, however, a de-emphasis of research seemed apparent. In so far as institutions were adapting to this situation, they appeared to be contemplating a withdrawal from research commitments – either to turn toward undergraduate and professional teaching, or to abandon broad research/graduate programmes for more specialized undertakings. The authors did not feel that the United States could sustain as research universities the number of institutions that had aspired to that status in the 1960s.

The Smith/Karlesky prognosis was predicated upon an extrapolation of existing trends. Specifically, they foresaw federal funds for university research keeping pace with inflation but exhibiting no real growth, and they assumed that federal funding would be the limiting factor for the system as a whole. This view reflected the loss of pluralism that had occurred during the expansion of the previous era. It furthermore indicated that although the federal portion of university R&D had declined, there was not yet any perception of greater pluralism. One somewhat hopeful development in this direction was apparent to the authors. Links between industry and university research seemed to have reached their nadir in the early 1970s. Since then several positive developments seemed possible harbingers of constructive co-operation between the two sectors. The authors nevertheless, in language typical of the period, hedged their hopes with warnings of the 'obstacles' to improved relations. Moreover, they held it 'unlikely that industry [would] retake the position it held before 1955', when it supported more than 7 per cent of academic R&D (Smith and Karlesky 1977: 76).

Revitalizing the university research system: 1978–90

The Smith/Karlesky prediction of greater stratification in the university research system did not come to pass. This point merits consideration not to chide the authors, who made a very reasonable assessment of the situation circa 1976; but rather because the explanation why the system developed differently illuminates important changes that occurred largely in the 1980s.

Instead of continued stagnation, the university research system renewed its secular expansion in 1978. In ten years (1979–89) it grew by 73 per cent in real terms – not a bad showing for a mature system that experienced little growth in students or faculty. Moreover, in a largely unforeseen development, support for the increase in research came disproportionately from non-federal sources. Federal funds for university R&D increased by ten percentage points less than the average, while non-federal sources grew by twenty points more. The fastest growing single source of university research support was private industry, which contributed 6.6 per cent of the 1989 total. That figure, in fact, understates the rising importance of university–industry ties. A portion of non-profit support of academic research comes from corporate or industry-related foundations; some state support is now directed toward subsidizing university–industry linkages. Directly and indirectly, industry accounted for about 10 per cent of academic research – roughly double the level of fifteen years earlier.

The expansion of research support from non-governmental sources has increased the actual and perceived pluralism of the system. No longer are the research universities considered to be wards of the federal government: when Robert Rosenzweig and Barbara Turlington wrote of this in 1982 they deliberately referred to 'The Research Universities and their Patrons'. In 1989 the federal share of support for academic research fell below 60 per cent for the first time in thirty years.

The current decade has been reasonably prosperous for the research universities generally; their instructional budgets grew by roughly 30 per cent in real terms (1974–6 to 1984–6). This figure most likely understates the improvement that has taken place in their financial positions. The trend toward privatization in university income is almost certainly more pronounced than is the case with just research funds. The great gains of the 1980s have come from increased tuition (the delayed pay-off from the expansion of student aid) and donations. Without a doubt, many universities have used gifts in particular to enhance research capacity; but it has probably been more common to bolster disproportionately those aspects of the university that most directly affect its ability to attract students and raise money – admissions, development, student aid, and perhaps those structures that most appeal to students and alumni. Unlike the 1960s, universities have acted conservatively toward creating new faculty lines or enlarging curricular commitments.

The financial conditions of the 1980s were especially beneficial to the leading

research universities. They have well-established channels for raising voluntary support and a surplus of applicants with little sensitivity to price. Despite
these factors, and despite the continued stiff competition for federal research
funds, the leading research universities have by and large seen their shares of
the research economy diminish. The proportion of federal R&D funds received
by the ten largest recipients had declined below 22 per cent by 1989.

The twenty-five universities with the highest academic rankings (Jones *et al.*
1982) generally fared poorly in terms of their shares of the research economy.
Between 1974–6 and 1984–6 just six of them increased their shares, while
nineteen registered declines.[5] The implication of this trend is that research
capacity has been developing far more widely among universities, enhancing
decentralization and competition within the system.

The institutions that have done most to improve their share of the research
economy would seem to include many state institutions from Sunbelt states
where, at least until recently, economic growth has provided the underpinning
for increases in enrolment and state support. California, in particular, was
conspicuous for its generous public funding of universities throughout the
1980s. Also prominent among advancing institutions are public and private
universities with close ties to industry, especially engineering schools. For the
advancing state universities, the old formula of more students and higher
appropriations seems to have translated into greater research capacity. For
the engineering schools, links with the fastest growing segment of the research
economy, defence and industrial research, produced above average growth.
More generally, this pattern would indicate that the growth in the research
economy during the 1980s has been due substantially to the initiative and
adaptation of individual institutions.

The research enterprise in American universities is far more vigorous at the
start of the 1990s than it was at the beginning of the 1980s. To be sure,
serious problems are present, but if anything should be clear from a historical
perspective, it would be that they always are. High on the current roster of
concerns are the continuing inadequacy of support for university infrastructure
and uncertainty about recruiting sufficient numbers of new scientists to maintain a healthy expansion. More deep-seated worries stem from the federal
budget deficit and its dampening effect on federally supported research, erod-
ing state support for public universities, and a looming economic recession.
Over all, there is deep concern that academic science is currently underfunded
in relation to the rising costs of research and the expanding size of the research
community (Lederman 1991).

The positive aspects of the current situation, however, should also be evident
from a long-range view. They would be, first, the continued decentralization of
the university research system. More universities continue to develop sufficient
research capacity to participate meaningfully in the research economy.
Second, these institutions have done this in part by adapting to the research
needs of their environments. The expansion of research in the private sector,
public policies aimed at fostering technology transfer, and the eagerness
of universities to provide research services have all worked to enhance the

pluralism of the research economy. The research universities today may be more responsive to the needs of society than at any time since the Second World War. It is, of course, possible to perceive a danger in this situation. If James Conant were alive today, he might well lament a diminished autonomy for academic scientists, for, just as in the post-war era, the university research system of the 1980s has assumed a decidedly programmatic cast. That is the bargain which has been struck: service to society is the price that academic science has had to pay for renewed growth since the 1970s and for its current vigour. So far, this has not seemed too high a price to pay.

Notes

1. This chapter summarizes material covered in greater depth by the author in a forthcoming study, (1992). *Research and Relevant Knowledge: American Research Universities Since World War II*. New York: Oxford University Press.
2. All data on research expenditures and federal appropriations (obligations) to academic science are from National Science Foundation sources, published in various series: See (1989). *National Patterns of R&D Resources: 1989*. Washington, DC: National Science Foundation.
3. Different criteria may be employed to determine which institutions are 'research universities'. The term was given official currency by the Carnegie Commission on Higher Education, *Classification of Institutions of Higher Education*, first published in 1970. In the first classification, fifty-two institutions were designated 'Research Universities I' (RU-Is) and another forty, 'Research Universities II' (RU-IIs). The latest edition (1987, Carnegie Foundation) lists seventy RU-Is and thirty-four RU-IIs. The Association of American Universities has been the organizational arm of research universities since 1900: it currently has fifty-eight members. In terms of quantity of research funding, in 1989 sixty-nine institutions performed more than 0.5 per cent of academic R&D.
4. Research expenditure data after 1978 have been adjusted to remove amounts for the Applied Research Laboratory at Johns Hopkins University. Formerly a federal contract research centre, its totals were included in the university's after 1978. Without such an adjustment, the Laboratory constitutes almost 3 per cent of academic R&D.
5. These data are drawn from a doctoral dissertation in progress at Pennsylvania State University: Jennifer Krohn, 'Advancing research universities of the 1970s and 1980s'.

References

Bush, V. (1944). *Science: The Endless Frontier*. Washington DC: Government Printing Office.
Carnegie Foundation for the Advancement of Teaching (1987). *A Classification of Institutions of Higher Education*. Princeton, NJ: Carnegie Foundation.
Conant, J. B. (1951). *'Forward': First Annual Report of the National Science Foundation, 1950–51*. Washington, DC: National Science Foundation.

England, J. M. (1982). *A Patron for Pure Science: The National Science Foundation's Formative Years, 1945–57*. Washington, DC: National Science Foundation.

Geiger, R. L. (1986). *To Advance Knowledge: The Growth of American Research Universities, 1900–1945*. New York: Oxford University Press.

—— (1988). American foundations and academic social science. *Minerva* **26**: 315–41.

—— (1990a). The American university and research. In *The Academic Research Enterprise within Industrialized Nations: Comparative Perspectives*. Washington, DC: National Academy Press.

—— (1990b). Organized Research Units – their role in the development of university research. *Journal of Higher Education* **61**: 1–19.

—— (forthcoming). What happened after Sputnik? Universities and federal research policy, 1958–1968. In Reingold, N. and van Keuren, D. (eds) *Science and the Federal Patron*. Chicago: University of Chicago Press.

Greenberg, D. (1967). *The Politics of Pure Science*. New York: New American Library.

Jencks, C. and Riesman, D. (1968). *The Academic Revolution*. Chicago: University of Chicago Press.

Jones, L. V., Gardner, L. and Coggeshall, P. E. (eds) (1982). *An Assessment of Research-Doctorate Programs in the United States*, 5 vols. Washington, DC: National Academy Press.

Lederman, L. M. (1991). *Science: The End of the Frontier?* Washington, DC: American Association for the Advancement of Science.

McDougall, W. A. (1985). *. . . the Heavens and the Earth: A Political History of the Space Age*. New York: Basic Books.

President's Science Advisory Committee (Seaborg Report) (1960). *Scientific Progress, the Universities, and the Federal Government*. Washington, DC: Government Printing Office.

Rosenzweig, R. M. and Turlington, B. (1982). *The Research Universities and their Patrons*. Berkeley: University of California Press.

Sapolsky, H. M. (1990). *Science and the Navy: The History of the Office of Naval Research*. Princeton, NJ: Princeton University Press.

Smith, B. L. R. and Karlesky, J. J. (1977). *The State of Academic Science: The Universities in the Nation's Research Effort*, 2 vols. New York: Change Magazine Press.

2

Research and Higher Education: The UK Scene

Thomas G. Whiston

A broad overview

There is a temptation to delay writing this background chapter almost until the day of publication. Events change weekly – if not daily – and they are not of a trivial nature in terms of the future structure, governance, circumstance and quality of British higher education. Thus within a short time of writing we have witnessed, for example, a partial rejection of Morris's call for the total merger of the five British Research Councils; arguments for an increased participation rate in higher education over the next few years; suggestions for a national system of two-year rather than three-year degree courses as a means of increasing the 'throughput of students'; an encouragement by the University Funding Council (UFC) of 'competitive bidding' for the allocation of teaching funds (and subsequent demise of that initiative) . . . and so on. Any one of these developments could herald the most traumatic effects upon the UK higher education scene. Instability, and hence ephemeralness relating to any policy analysis of the underlying issues and structural changes, might therefore be attributable to this topic. (For explanatory notes on topics covered in this chapter see pp. 22–3.)

This is not necessarily so, however, since dominant trends, governmental and centralist tendencies are not that obscure. A broad strategy emerges from an examination of the events of the past decade or so. It is the ultimate consequences of the changes we are witnessing which are uncertain and fraught with anxiety. Indeed, that anxiety pertains not only to the conditions of academe, but also to the disbenefit which may in the long run accrue to industry, commerce and the state at large. (To take but one example, the policy shifts regarding the allocation of resources to 'basic', 'strategic' or 'applied' research are not clearly to the benefit of industry; short-term interests may compromise generic robustness; similarly, 'concentration' though always necessary, to some degree implies opportunity costs and the logic of selection leaves much to be desired.)

What then is this 'broad strategy which emerges over the past decade or so' and what issues, policy dilemmas, concerns and uncertainties does it require us to consider?

If we were to cast our minds back to the conditions prevailing in the late 1970s, we would encounter a more confident (and possibly arrogant) higher education (HE) system: fifty or so major institutions each expecting to grow; five Research Councils sure of their territory; a University Grants Committee (UGC) (and later a National Advisory Board – NAB) prepared to face government; a dual-support system which had not yet failed; a binary-divide which had some semblance of logic other than academic elitism and self-interest; and cutting across all a gentle, if unstated, assumption of the importance and social relevance or value of independence of mind, liberalism, tenure, as pillars of HE wisdom and constructive social critique. Much of this had been reinforced by the post-war years of growth, an increase in participation rate (though poor in international comparative terms), the institutional expansion following Robbins, the transition of 'CATs' (Colleges of Advanced Technology) to universities; the growth of 'Big Science' and an insufficiency of self-critique regarding the importance of the applicative.

So much for yesterday. The pattern of the 1980s fell into a series of events which now characterizes today and determines tomorrow: first, the changed funding regarding overseas students' subsidies and a policy of 'level funding' for home students (Sizer 1987); second, a rationalization of participative contraction based on arguments of demography (Whiston 1979); third, in the early 1980s the introduction by the UGC of institutional selectivity with regard to block-grants which resulted in wide differential cuts to British universities (Bath 2.1%; Cambridge 3.7%; Aston 18%; Salford 27.5%). All of this on top of the cessation of the quinquennial system of funding (given up in 1974) . . . making forward planning that much more difficult.

Against that backdrop further moves aimed at restructuring, concentration, selectivity, in order to focus the use of more limited financial resources flowed year by year. The rationale for such a programme was later provided by the Advisory Board for the Research Councils (ABRC 1987) and an epistemological requisite indicated by the Science Policy Support Group (SPSG) (Ziman 1987). Thus it was recognized by the former that lack of success in obtaining more funds from government clearly necessitated selective allocation according to agreed priorities (national and scientific), while Ziman in *Science in a 'Steady State'* pointed to an inevitable limit to growth, a plateauing of funding and the structural importance of interdisciplinary endeavour.

Superimposed upon, or fitting into, this broad framework we have witnessed either calls for, or actual implementation of, a range of fundamental policies which are seen as synergetic to that scenario:

1. Restructuring and selectivity in relation to the organization of staff, departments and institutes within the HE sector (Whiston 1988a).
2. Increasing reliance on the development of review and evaluation techniques in order to legitimize selective allocation of funds (CIBA 1989).
3. Calls for the tiering of universities (or disciplines) according to more

specialized and concentrated research and teaching functions (ABRC 1987; UGC 1987).

4. Greater reliance on 'directive programmes' (e.g. in Biotechnology, IT, New Materials, Advanced Manufacturing Technology (AMT)) on the part of Research Councils rather than reliance upon the responsive mode; increased reliance on 'Corporate Planning' by Research Councils in part reflecting the ABRC position (Whiston 1987).

5. Calls for the total merger of the five Research Councils into one body in order to obtain greater coherence of research strategy (Morris Review). This also permits greater governmental control of national research strategy.

6. A significant programme geared to reliance upon Interdisciplinary Research Centres (IRCs). (Again fitting in with the directive mode and centralization/concentration/critical mass views pertaining to research.)

7. Transition of the UGC into UFC (with greater industrial membership); NAB into PCFC (Polytechnics and Colleges Funding Council); which may lead to greater central control.

8. Creation of new strategic policy bodies, e.g. Advisory Council on Science and Technology (ACOST); Centre for Exploitation of Science and Technology (CEST); increasing emphasis upon industrial–academic linkage through a wide variety of programmes (Whiston 1988b).

9. New terms and conditions for university staff (tenure rights; contractual obligations; Intellectual Property Rights (IPR) issues, etc., arising from the recent Education Reform Bill).

The overall policy thrust embracing the above (and much else) can be categorized in relation to a perceived governmental need to limit public spending; concentrate and select overall research priorities; increase control of and accountability of the HE sector; increase the strategic relevance of academic research; introduce a much greater directive mode between the Research Councils and HE (mainly the universities); increase or improve academic–industrial collaboration. Whether or not such policies achieve their aims, compromise quality of research and teaching, are socially or economically legitimate, present significant problems regarding future social, scientific or academic development (e.g. deter academic recruitment; induce institutional stratification; stifle or kill initiative; compromise scholarship; fail to facilitate sufficient generic research; or encourage new forms of institutional and regional rigidities) remains an ongoing debate. Empirical validation and legitimization of many of these subpolicies remains very much on the agenda. Within that context I signal below some examples of policy questions which require much examination.

Some policy questions pertaining to the quality of research

1. Is overall quality of research being compromised due to an impoverished HE sector? How might this be usefully measured?
2. Much of the policy debate (and initiative) has focused upon the 'science side': how relevant is this to the Arts? What alternative models (and policies) are required?
3. What international policy comparisons might be made and to what good purpose?
4. Concentration, selectivity, increased monitoring and evaluation have several positive virtues (and, it can be argued, responds to a deeper political and economic reality). Are we, however, sufficiently cognizant of, and responsive to, the unwanted negative features (e.g. regional and institutional stratification; loss of motivation and confidence; recruitment problems; stifling of initiative; encouragement of false indices of performance; over-centralization; conceptual rigidity and the introduction of a new conformity)?

One might argue (see Whiston 1988b) that scientific and artistic creativity is closely intertwined with academic independence; that unwarranted certainty regarding future science and technology (S&T) trajectories may compromise 'flexibility' in the future; and that the optimum 'scale' to achieve a 'critical mass' requires much fuller social, managerial and empirical examination before unwarranted commitment is made. A fuller examination may well reveal that greater pluralism is required in policy initiative, institutional structures, and so on: a much wider and richer exploration of policy initiatives is therefore justified.

Understandably, considerable criticism of contemporary policies abounds. The spectrum is wide. There are those who argue for a significant increase in resource allocation plus a large increase in student participation rate; others point to inconsistency in policy, faulty implementation, too rapid change (see National Audit Office 1985; Jarratt Report 1985; Merrison Report 1982). Thus Merrison (then Chair of the Committee of Vice-Chancellors and Principals – CVCP) noted:

> the rate at which they want to run the universities down will inevitably ensure a drastic deterioration of the quality of what remains, which is even more important. We cannot believe that this policy has been arrived at with any kind of consideration of the social, economic or scientific consequences. (Merrison 1982)

This begs several important questions: what is meant by quality and how we measure it; what social, economic and scientific goals and achievements are expected of the HE sector; who should 'decide' upon those aims; and what administrative, selective, monitoring and analytic procedures can best assist in the achievement of those aims or sense of purpose? New structures are being put into place, but they await testing. The papers which comprise this volume examine or provide perspectives to related issues from both sides of the Atlantic; some of the issues I have signalled above are given fuller treatment at a later stage. Undoubtedly at the time of writing there are insufficient empirical data available with which to draw unchallengeable conclusions as to the best institutional structures which must serve a nation's disparate needs. Selection has to be made. The more that that selection is subject to inquiry, debate and international comparison, the greater is the confidence that the newly emerging educational structure will be able to satisfy those needs.

Explanatory notes

The general reader (and especially the US audience) may be unfamiliar with some of the terms referred to in the text. I give below brief notes relating to some of the more important items.

1. The *'Binary-Divide'*: British higher education is split into two parts – the universities (nearly fifty) and the polytechnics (and other colleges). The latter group are seen as in the 'public sector', the former possess a quasi-independence but are primarily dependent upon state funding.

2. The *University Funding Council* (UFC) replaces an earlier body (the University Grants Committee – UGC) which acted as a 'buffer' between government and the individual university bodies. The UFC is now a smaller body and has a greater industrial representation. The equivalent body for the public sector is the Polytechnics and Colleges Funding Council (PCFC) which replaced the National Advisory Board (NAB). The individual polytechnics now possess 'corporate' status and related Charters thereby providing them with more individual autonomy. By far the greater proportion of the nation's higher education research budget is directed towards the university sector.

3. The *'Dual-Support' System* refers to the two main sources of funding allocated to universities. Of the two streams of finance, the first comes via the UFC and provides for salaries, various faculty support costs and finance for 'the well-found laboratory'. Level of support is related to student numbers and unit-of-resource. In recent years various selectivity formulae have been explored. The second source of funding comes via the five Research Councils in relation to specific research awards.

4. There are five *Research Councils* at present (although studies have been undertaken examining the desirability of various forms of merger). These are the Science and Engineering Research Council (SERC); the Medical Research Council (MRC); the Agriculture and Food Research Council (AFRC); the Natural Environment Research Council (NERC); and the Economic and Social Research Council (ESRC). Some councils maintain their own Research Institutes of permanently supported units in addition to providing funds to the universities.

5. The availability of *Research Funds* coming from the government through the Research Councils (in part on advice from the Advisory Board for the Research Councils – ABRC) might be seen to fall into two broad categories: responsive- and directive-modes. The former (responsive) mode as the name implies is made in relation to peer-judged applications from academia. The 'directive-mode', though again judged and evaluated by a variety of mechanisms, tends to conform to more centrally decided research-priorities. In recent years there has been a significant increase in the funds allocated to the directive-mode. Also there is ongoing debate as to the relative allocation of funds between the two arms of the dual support-system (the UFC and the Research Councils). While the proportion given to the latter *may* increase, the absolute value may decline.
6. The 'binary-divide' referred to above may incur a certain degree of erosion in a variety of ways in future years.

References

ABRC (1987). *A Strategy for the Science Base*. London: Advisory Board for the Research Councils.

CIBA (1989). *The Evaluation of Scientific Research – Ciba Foundation Conference*. Chichester: Wiley.

Jarratt Report (1985). *Report of the Steering Committee for Efficiency Studies in Universities*. London: Committee of Vice-Chancellors and Principals.

Merrison Report (1982). *Report of a Joint Working Party on the Support of University Scientific Research*. Cmnd 8567. London: HMSO.

National Audit Office (1985). *Report by the Comptroller and Auditor General. DES: Redundancy Compensation Payment to University Staff (Gordon Downey)*. London: HMSO.

Sizer, J. (1987). Universities in hard times: some policy implications and managerial guidelines. *Higher Education Quarterly* **41**(4): 354–7.

UGC (1987). *Strengthening University Earth Sciences (Oxburgh Report)*. London: University Grants Committee.

Whiston, T. G. (1979). Population forecasting: social and educational policy. In Whiston, T. G. (ed.) *The Uses and Abuses of Forecasting*. London: Macmillan.

—— (1987). *The Production and Effectiveness of the AFRC Corporate Plan*. Confidential Report to AFRC. University of Sussex.

—— (1988a). *Restructuring and Selectivity in Academic Science*. SPSG Concept Paper no. 5. London: Science Policy Support Group.

—— (1988b). Co-ordinating educational policies and plans with those of science and technology: developing and Western developed countries. *Bulletin of International Bureau of Education* **247**: 1–139.

Ziman, J. M. (1987). *Science in a 'Steady State': The Research System in Transition*. SPSG Concept Paper no. 1, London: Science Policy Support Group.

—— (1989). *Restructuring Academic Science: A New Framework for UK Policy*. London: Science Policy Support Group.

3

Strengthening the US University Research System

Bruce L. R. Smith

The nation's universities have been a source of great strength in the post-war period. Widely recognized as the world leaders in numerous scientific fields, American university scientists and engineers have continued to enjoy extraordinary successes even in the periods of intense industrial competition. By measures such as Nobel Prizes, or publication rates, the American research universities appear to enjoy continuing strength. A recent OECD (Organization for Economic Co-operation and Development) report, as illustrated in Table 3.1, depicting rates for publications per unit of research for two capital-intensive fields of science, shows the apparent strength of the American research system.

Experienced observers have continued to worry, however, about potentially erosive forces that threaten the long-term vitality of the university research

Table 3.1 Average expenditures for 1980 and 1982 and publication outputs in 1984 in two 'Big Science' subfields for six OECD countries. (Expenditures in millions of constant 1982 dollars, outputs in publication counts)

		United States	Japan	Germany	France	United Kingdom	Netherlands
Astronomy and astrophysics	Expenditure	128.5	68.2	81.2	69.3	72.8	30
	Output	1,584	112	215	141	375	85
	Numbers of publications per million dollars (outputs/ expenditure)	12.3	1.6	2.6	2.0	5.1	2.8
Nuclear and particle physics	Expenditure	450.1	113.2	224.1	297.6	112.1	48.6
	Output	1,242	160	373	181	156	69
	Number of publications per million dollars	2.8	1.4	1.7	0.6	1.4	1.4

Source: OECD (1988). *Science and Technology Policy Outlook 1988.* Paris: OECD, p. 84, Table 5.

system. The health of the entire national research effort is at issue since the universities play a critical role for the system as a whole. The concerns have centred around a number of broad questions: has there been inadequate investment in physical infrastructure and in the institutional base (somewhat akin to the neglect of investment in American industry)? Have the universities played an adequate part in the technology development concerns of the economy? Can the nation continue to be a world leader in science and engineering in the face of striking weaknesses at lower levels of the educational system affecting the quality and supply of the future scientific work-force? Are 'politics' undermining the integrity of national decisions on resources for science and technology?

Infrastructure needs

Recent reports and studies have called attention to the neglect of the physical infrastructure, including buildings, equipment and supporting resources, upon which the university research effort depends.[1] How to maintain the institutional base for university research was not systematically thought out in the early post-war years, but the expansion and rapid growth of higher education as a matter of course included considerable capital funds. Federal programmes, state policies and philanthropy each played a part in supporting institutions in the growth years (along with research support). When the growth of research funding slowed in the late 1960s, federal support for R&D plant dropped dramatically. While research funding for colleges and universities picked up at the beginning of the financial year 1977, no such increase occurred in plant and equipment. Meanwhile, state legislatures were also retrenching with respect to capital facilities in higher education. The 'crisis' of infrastructure has been the predictable result of these trends.

The universities have been able partly to cope with the problem through such devices as borrowing, revenue bonds and covering costs of maintenance and repair through higher indirect costs on research grants. Universities have also become much more aware in their accounting, planning and general management practices of the importance of capital needs. But much more remains to be done. The federal government, the states, private philanthropy and the universities themselves, all need to assume greater responsibilities in protecting the capital base for university research.

The federal government cannot merely 'buy' particular research projects from the universities without concern for the health of the institutions themselves. This point is generally conceded at least at the theoretical level. This general awareness, however, has typically not led to concrete programmes to remedy the situation. Even in a time of fiscal constraint, investment needs rather than merely support of operating programmes must be accorded a high priority. For this to happen, the universities themselves will have to plan for the future even at some potential cost to current research output. That this will be a very difficult challenge at a time of intense competition for research funds, and when overhead staffs have grown more sharply than the research and teaching staffs, hardly requires elaboration.

Beyond federal policy and university action, clarification of the role of state governments in the financing and upkeep of capital facilities will be significant. Industry, stimulated in part by recent legislation,[2] has increased its collaborative research with universities. This has resulted in increased industry funding of university research facilities. Traditional philanthropy plays a lesser role in capital support than it did when the scale of expenditures was smaller. Private philanthropy funded most early medical research in the United States. This pattern is unlikely to be repeated, but philanthropy can continue to play a highly useful role in innovative projects in universities (e.g. the funding of the Whitehead Institute and MIT, the gift of a $75 million optical telescope to be operated by the California Institute of Technology, and the grants by the Hughes Medical Institute in selected fields).

Block, project and formula funding for research

The American system has never been a 'pure' case of small-scale individual project support only. Rather, it has been a mix of block, project and formula grants (projects varying in size from the very small to the large project involving a team). The funds have originated, of course, from a variety of public and private sources. The issue has always been how to achieve the best balance among the different kinds of funding. For the universities the project grant has been the typical mode of support (though centres and institutes are also common, as are large-scale facilities in some fields and fellowship support). Government and industrial laboratories typically have operated on a larger scale of research effort than universities, and in more clearly targeted areas.

Universities have been thought to be highly creative because of the close linkage between teaching and research, the intense competition for research funds, and the tendency for individuals to develop earlier in their careers the habits of being independent investigators. The US and the UK university systems appear generally alike in this respect, whereas the continental European pattern tends to rely more on block funding to research institutes. These may often be separated from or be only loosely attached to universities.

Individual project support to a principal investigator cannot, however, by itself provide for a healthy, ongoing university research effort. While the research base is inadequate to permit firm judgements on the point, the nation may have relied too heavily on the individual project grant in recent years. The NSF has maintained data that enable one to detect trends among different categories of research support. A steady climb in the proportion of project support to total NSF support took place in the period 1971–9, rising from 50 per cent to 70 per cent. This change reflects primarily the decrease in institutional support that occurred from 1970 to 1976 and the phase-out in the Research Applied to National Needs (RANN) programme in the late 1970s. Fellowship support over the period has been under pressure since the early

1960s. With the adoption of its National Science Foundation (NSF) engineering centres initiative in the Reagan administration, the support for centres has climbed to 8 per cent of NSF outlays.

The most striking change is absence of institutional support, which was a major part of NSFs rapid growth during the 1960s. During the 1960–8 period, institutional support accounted for 20–25 per cent of the NSF research budget. The seemingly stable support for facilities is deceptive. The growth in the 1960s can be attributed to the rapid build-up in support for astronomy observations, large-scale field projects, oceanographic ships and computing facilities. Facilities support contracted sharply during the 1959 budget crisis; one programme alone – university computing facilities – dropped from $61 million to $39 million in a two-year period. The increase in 1972 and afterward largely reflects several programme transfers from the Defense Department, notably the National Magnet Laboratory. The only other significant increase in the modern period resulted from the advanced computing centre programme, begun in 1985.

Many factors have to be weighed in assessing the significance of these trends. Still, the total absence of institutional support by NSF suggests some of the shortcomings of the present system: too much reliance on projects, exacerbated by short time periods of grants; a shortened time horizon for investigators, particularly the young scientists who must achieve a quick pay-off to justify continued support and to gain tenure; the sheer weight of evaluating proposals, carried on in a context of resource constraint, leads to heightened career tensions among university scientists and anything but a tranquil life; and possible loss of 'critical mass', in attacking some problems. That is excessive dispersion of intellectual energies may result from the relatively passive role on the part of agency funding officials and university administrators when the entire scientific effort is left up to 'proposal pressure' from individual investigators.

Most importantly, perhaps, the project emphasis has focused on what is required to get the immediate job done. Along with resource limits, this has reduced incentives for vital 'by-product' aspects of research support, for example fellowship and research assistantship support, laboratory modernization – precisely the components that nurture the 'technology base' in NAS's terms or Ergas's concept of 'diffusion-oriented' strategies.[3] Agency officials and university administrators need to think in terms of 'system' needs. That is they need to balance personnel and human resource support, facilities, coherent research clusters, small-scale support for the individual investigator, and areas of comparative advantage for a particular institution, region or department.

There is no universal recipe for all federal agencies. Agencies will vary in their own style of operation, whether they will place their research bets on fewer and larger grants or distribute them widely in a larger number of smaller grants. No one formula is 'correct' for all programmes of research support. What is critical is that the needs of the system of higher education and advanced training be considered as well as the capacity of particular universities, departments or investigators to advance the research goals in question. At various times and in various agencies the goals of coherent policy have been more nearly realized.

Perhaps the NIH in the late 1950s and early 1960s under Director James Shannon was one of the conspicuous successes of reconciling system maintenance needs with efficient use of finite resources.[4] The NIH was able to combine institutional, block and project support along with fellowship, traineeship, facilities and construction grants and contract support to produce the modern health research empire. The system also combined in a high degree scientific choice of research directions with a broad base of public and congressional support and understanding. More recently, resource pressures have limited fellowship and traineeship support, potentially tilting the system toward shorter-term goals. The NIH has also encountered some pressures in maintaining support for centres in the light of the growing demand for resources to maintain an adequate number of new investigator-initiated project awards; the portion of support for centres has dropped from 22 per cent to 18 per cent over the 1978–87 period. Otherwise, the NIH has adapted to resource constraint by cutting in half the proportion of support for R&D contracts relative to total research support.

At the opposite pole from the individual project is the 'Big Science' field, that is a field dependent on a large investment in a particular scientific instrument or set of technologies, typified by the Superconducting Supercollider (SSC), the Space Station, and the human genome project. Such massive efforts, and the enormous resources they entail, pose strikingly different challenges: the displacement of individual creative energies into one all-consuming task, the potential 'crowding out' effect on finite resources available for alternative scientific endeavours, the difficulty of weighing the productivity of the many research teams involved in the effort. The 'Big Science' activity reflects the mission orientation, which emphasizes the achievement of a few goals at the expense of gradual diffusion of technological awareness throughout the society and economy. Some fields, of course, can be pursued only as Big Science. Ways must be found to share costs internally on the large-scale projects, to avoid premature commitment to particular research technologies, and to weigh the impact of mega-efforts on the human resources and the funding base of other scientific fields.

An area where this issue is now acute is in the calls for the mapping and sequencing of the human genome, a major issue confronting the biomedical research community. The magnitude of such an effort is suggested by the fact that scientists would seek to determine the order of 3 billion base pairs in the DNA.[5] The need to do so is defended on scientific grounds and on economic grounds in that success may confer an advantage in information processing and in the manipulation techniques essential to genetic engineering. Critics contend that more numerous teams pursuing different approaches will offer a better chance for scientific advance and for building a strong industrial base across the biotechnology and genetic engineering disciplines. This argument cannot be resolved here, but it would appear that science cannot progress solely through numerous small individual projects or through one mega-project. The 'mid-level' of strategic thought in science is perhaps the most demanding, but potentially also most rewarding, for universities and their patrons in government and industry.

University–industry links

A persistent criticism of the United States' research universities is that they are closed-loop systems, driven by internal incentives of publication and recognition for high-science activities which bear little or no relation to wider social and economic needs.[6] A contrary image, which sometimes coexists in the mind of the critic along with the foregoing criticism, is that universities are populated with shameless charlatans who blow with the winds of current funding fashions and who exaggerate the practical applications of their work. There is some truth to both criticisms. The research universities have not generally sought, or played, an effective role in technology transfer and economic development. Agriculture is an exception. The land-grant institutions have brought knowledge to farmers as an important part of their mission (they have done less well in the promotion of the 'mechanical arts'). Partly for the reason that they have emphasized diffusion of knowledge rather than generating new knowledge, the agriculturalists have often been second-class citizens in the universities. Some few exotic technologies have attracted the interest of leading scientists and engineers, but usually at a stage far removed from product development. Certain aspects of biomedicine have witnessed a merging of basic inquiry and product development, thus propelling universities and their medical centres into a significant role in economic development in some instances.

Broadly, the university contribution to economic development can be viewed from two perspectives: as the source of advanced training and research, the university system as a whole should be oriented toward its long-range goal of laying the basis for future development and advancing the goals of a civilized and learned society. Under this conception, any short-term contribution to economic development would be an incidental by-product from the university system's principal function. If society accepted this paradigm, academic science would not be supported at the levels it aspires to – the doubling over five years of the NSF budget, for example, as part of a national competitiveness strategy would not be a logical policy. Society may wish, for reasons of high culture, to support academic science generously, but not on the expectation of short-term contributions to economic growth, job creation or industrial competitiveness.

The alternative perspective is that the university research system should be more directly and fully engaged in the economic development process and in achieving related societal goals – and that the institutional 'culture' both in the universities and federal grant-making agencies be modified to reflect this perspective. Engaging the universities in short-term goals without explicitly altering incentive structures is, in this view, merely to invite disillusion when the goals are not met – to replicate, once again, the nation's experience with the theory that basic research leads more or less automatically to commercial applications. Federal officials should pay more attention to applied research and demonstration projects (the reverse of actual trends since the late 1970s). Universities should encourage and reward scientists and engineers who have applied research interests. Greater selectivity in the support for basic science in the system as a whole is urged as well as within individual universities. Shapley and Roy are vigorous exponents of this view:

> The postwar science system has spread basic research thinly around many institutions and has made university scientists working on applied problems unhappy. A greater concentration of basic science effort may be needed. Perhaps only the twenty top-ranked universities should remain striving for world-class basic science at the frontier. . . .
>
> We would bring about a value shift . . . to remove the tilt towards basic-science-is-best which has been overlaid on the universities for the past 30 years. For the main middle block of universities would continue some basic research, as overhead for their main work, which would be purposive basic science, applied science, and engineering.[7]

The MIT Commission on Industrial Productivity has also called for changes in the universities with the aim of educating students 'to be more sensitive to productivity, to practical problems, to teamwork' and has urged that 'the federal government's support of research and development should be extended to include a greater emphasis on policies to encourage the downstream phases of product and process engineering'.[8]

Gradually, events seem to have moved the universities toward greater involvement with practical problems. Universities have sought closer collaboration with private industry and with local economic development authorities, partly to sustain research funding and partly because university researchers have been attracted to the popular cause of rebuilding the USA's industrial competitiveness.[9] Within the scientific community, engineers and applied scientists have asserted themselves and created a more vocal presence. The National Academy of Science has become the National Academy of Science–National Academy of Engineering–Institute of Medicine (NAS–NAE–IOM) complex as a symbol of the engineers' insistence on co-equal status with their scientific colleagues.

It is probably unrealistic, however, to expect that the research universities will become prominent instrumentalities of technology transfer – at least not for the myriad smaller companies so important to economic health. For these companies, the community colleges are a more likely source of training on computer use, statistical process controls, and management. Certainly, research institutions are unlikely to be prominently involved in near-term product development even as they move gradually toward focusing their attention and resources to a greater degree on the applied sciences.

Nor should there be any single pattern for all universities. The universities, as varied in their strengths and orientations as the nation's economy, can render service to their communities, regions and country in multifarious ways. The pressure of local circumstance and the logic of decentralized choice will and should continue to shape the evolution of university research and teaching efforts. Institutions may increasingly 'target' their scientific opportunities in light of a mixture of theoretical and practical concerns. But this should not be disturbing, for good science has always involved choice of fields, methodology and research strategy. University–industry linkages will evolve in various patterns across the country, and will blend the broad diffusion of knowledge with the search for new knowledge in equally diverse ways.

Peer (or merit) review

A persistent issue that has troubled the government–science relationship in the USA is the status and effectiveness of peer review (or merit review, in the NSF terminology). Recently, the use of 'pork barrel' amendments in the area of scientific facilities and construction has been highly controversial, raising fears that the whole structure of objective judgement of scientific proposals could be undermined. Even some scientists have grown discouraged at what appears to be a loss of congressional confidence in peer review and have quietly urged their colleagues to begin considering alternatives. The conclusion reached by this observer is that, despite its imperfections, the peer review system remains a critical and indispensable element in the nation's research system. Particularly in a time of resource constraint, the notion of a fair and objective process to allocate resources and to produce the most efficient outcomes deserves affirmation by all those with a stake in the system – scientists, administrators, politicians, and citizens alike.

The reality is that approximately 80 per cent of all citations in the scientific literature are accounted for by 15 per cent of the publishing scientists.[10] Science is, in this sense, an elitist activity. Ways must be found, therefore, to see that support is channelled to those who can use the resources most productively. But this cannot be done in a fashion that incorporates a privileged status for any institution or principal investigator. The USA is precluded, by virtue of our political culture, from seriously considering some alternative funding mechanisms that make sense in the context of other countries. The concept of the Max-Planck Society, for example, where a sizeable fraction of the Federal Republic's basic science expenditures goes to distinguished senior scientists who allocate the resources within the institution, is virtually impossible for the USA. This is not to say that block funding is unknown here, but even these funding mechanisms depend on (and may be indirectly tied to) the investigator's performance in peer review competition. Peer review of individual proposals is the only practicable way, in short, to reconcile the elite character of science with the norms of American democracy. The peer review system is, furthermore, a self-correcting and evolving procedure, not a static and rigid formality.

The concept of peer review dates back at least to the seventeenth century, when the Royal Society of London established a board of editors to evaluate reports submitted for publication in its *Proceedings*.[11] Peer review procedures for federally supported research in the United States were initiated in 1902, when the Fifty-seventh Congress established a scientific advisory board of non-governmental scientists to assist the Surgeon General in the administration of the Hygienic Laboratory (renamed the National Institute of Health in 1930). In 1937 the National Cancer Act (PL 75-244) created a legal basis for the award of grants through the mechanism of an advisory council, and these procedures were extended to grants and fellowships in all health research areas when the Public Health Service Act was passed in 1944. Two years later, the NIH Director created the Division of Research Grants and the initial review groups (or study sections). The study sections would provide the initial review of proposals and would then pass them on with ratings and recommendations for approval or rejection – essentially the modern form of peer review still in use by the NIH.[12]

The NSF peer review system was developed in the 1950s and has been modified on a number of occasions over the intervening period. The essentials of the system are set out in NSF Manual 10, Subsection 122, Use of Peer Review, and in NSF Manual 1 (Administrative Information Manual), Subsections 310–390, External Peer Oversight. Under procedures adopted by the National Science Board at its 188th Meeting on 17–18 March 1977 and amended at its 251st Meeting on 15–16 March 1984, the NSF is required to submit an annual report to the Board on its use of peer review during the preceding year, including recommendations for change or reconsideration of the Foundation's policies on peer review. Other agencies making extramural research grants use variations on the systems employed by the NSF and the NIH, sometimes broadening the role of the programme officials within the agency and relying on fewer formalities in soliciting external advice.

One is astounded, looking at the NIH and NSF peer review systems, at the number of studies, examinations and external and internal reviews of the peer review policies. In addition to the annual NSF study of its peer review policies submitted to NSF Director Erich Bloch on 3 March 1989,[13] and the extensive eighteen-month study completed by the NIH in December 1988,[14] various congressional committees,[15] external review committees mandated by Congress[16] and independent studies[17] over the years have examined the operational and administrative aspects of peer review, studied the recurring issues, and documented the strengths and weaknesses of the system. While several important changes have resulted from their recommendations, the various reviews, including the most recent NSF and NIH studies, have found the system to be generally sound, and have upheld its validity and its essentiality to the overall system of research support in the USA.

The traditional criticisms of peer review can be grouped under several headings:

1. the system is unfair, dominated by an 'old boy' network, and displays favouritism
2. the paperwork burden is excessive and the process is too time-consuming
3. there is an inherent bias toward conservatism against 'high-risk' proposals, including those that do not fall neatly within established disciplinary categories.

As to the first criticism, the studies do not support the contention of systematic bias. Membership on the peer panels has generally become more diverse in recent years. For example, for the NIH the proportion of women on panels increased from 19 per cent to 21 per cent from 1977 to 1987; the proportion of MDs declined slightly; and representation of minority investigators grew from 5.7 per cent to 16 per cent.[18] The average age of NIH study section members, approximately 45, has remained relatively constant over the years; in 1987, only 19 per cent of section members were older than 50. The distribution of section members geographically has remained highly proportional to the research efforts in the various regions of the country (which is also the case for the NSF).

For both the NIH and NSF, competition has grown more intense. Priority scores to achieve success have been higher, fewer awards relative to the total number of applications have been made, and service on review panels or study sections does not appear to have a marked effect on success ratios.[19] For the NSF, state, region or affiliation with a 'prestige' university appears to have little effect on success ratios; 'renewal' applications fare better in some NSF divisions than others; new female principal investigators are treated equally to new male principal investigators.[20] About 11 per cent of 135,000 science and engineering faculty members in the USA apply to the NSF each year (13 per cent of chemists, 10 per cent of mathematicians, 4 per cent of economists, 20 per cent of earth scientists, 14 per cent of electrical engineers, 16 per cent of computer scientists) and NSF declines approximately two-thirds of the applications.[21]

As an indication of the competitive nature of the overall research support system, while the top twenty universities over the period 1967–84 continued to receive 42 per cent of total federal research funds (down from 45 per cent), there were four new universities represented in the top twenty institutions in 1984.[22] The data contained in Roger Geiger's paper in this volume (Chapter 1) show convincingly that the US university research system has remained pluralist, open and competitive over the past decade. The top ten research universities have never regained the proportionate share of the federal research support that they enjoyed in the early 1960s.

The sense of fairness with which university researchers view the peer review system is difficult to assess precisely, but a recent NSF survey of 14,200 principal investigators (9,500 or two-thirds responded) casts some light on the issue. Overall, 62 per cent of those who responded were satisfied with the process, or were neutral; 38 per cent were dissatisfied. Unsurprisingly, Table 3.2 shows that the more successful researchers tended to view the system in

Table 3.2   Survey of attitudes of principal investigators toward NSF peer review system (%)

	Satisfied	Neutral	Dissatisfied
Consistent declinee (28% of applicants)	27	16	57
One-time declinee (13% of applicants)	36	21	44
Frequent declinee (14% of applicants)	40	16	44
Frequent awardee (26% of applicants)	61	11	28
Consistent awardee (13% of applicants)	83	5	12
One-time awardee (5% of applicants)	87	7	6

Source: NSF, *Annual Report on the Foundation's Use of Peer Review* (Washington, NSF, 1989).

more favourable terms. Perhaps surprisingly, however, 56 per cent of frequent declinees and 57 per cent of one-time declinees were either satisfied or neutral. Even 43 per cent of the constant declinees were either satisfied or neutral.

Second, both the NIH and NSF have been conscious of the paperwork burden of the peer review process, and have taken steps to alleviate the weight of submissions and to streamline the process consistent with the goal of maintaining fair and orderly procedures.

The NSF in the financial year 1988 received 24,161 proposals which involved 140,994 requests for written reviews (of which 114,312 were actually received).[23] The NSF has some 170,000 reviewers in divisional files, of which 55,999 were asked to review in the financial year 1988 either as *ad hoc* reviewers or part of standing panels; there is an approximate one-third turnover in reviewers annually.[24] The NIH's Divisions of Research Grants (DRG) had sixty-eight chartered study sections, some with subcommittees meeting separately, for a total of ninety-two groups with approximately 1,500 reviewers in the financial year 1987; an additional forty review groups existed under the programme heading of Bureaux, Institutes, Divisions (BID); in total, they awarded an estimated 21,000 research grants of all kinds (continuing and new centres and projects) in the financial year 1988.[25] Each year from 1980 to 1987 the NIH has awarded new competing grants in numbers fluctuating from a low of 4,785 in 1980 to a high of 6,446 in 1987 out of a gradually increasing number of applications which reached a decade high of 19,119 in 1986 (and fell off by 649 in 1987).[26]

To address the considerable burden of work these numbers represent, both the NIH's and the NSF's most recent reviews of peer review recommended steps to streamline further their respective procedures. Both agencies recommended further use of electronic submissions, and improved agency computer data bases on proposers, reducing the amount of 'boilerplate' in applications, simplifying some requests from investigators, and other steps. Each agency has instituted small prizes and special awards for young scientific investigators which are less onerous.

The NIH decided, after its previous major review of the award process, that extending the duration of the grant would be a major improvement inasmuch as it would allow more time for research and reduce the number of proposals that would have to be submitted and reviewed each year. In 1988 the average length of award had increased to 3.92 years from 3.15 years in the late 1970s.[27] Programmes developed to extend grant duration include the Javits Award of the National Institute of Neurological Disorders and Stroke and the Outstanding Investigator Grant of the National Cancer Institute.

The NSF's Engineering Division in mid-1988 initiated a new programme of 'Expedited Awards for Novel Research' which eliminated external review and which sought to stimulate creative, innovative work. As of February 1989, 239 grants had been awarded. The programme was limited to one-time grants in the Award of up to $30,000 and overall was not to exceed 5 per cent of the Division's research budget. There is a similar mechanism Foundation-wide encouraging small grants for exploratory work up to $50,000 and again limited to 5 per cent of the programme's budget.

The third traditional criticism of peer review – that it leads to conservatism and a 'play safe' approach – was the issue that gave the evaluators the most difficulty. The exceptional investigator awards, the new scientist programmes, the expedited review effort just noted, and others represent administrative actions to combat a conservative bias in research support. Both agencies have attempted to encourage a climate of support for 'risky' research, but officials concede that there is no perfect solution. The exploratory grants, however, partly meet the need for ventures into emerging areas, novel research crossing traditional programme boundaries, and for experienced researchers to shift fields. Multidisciplinary research requires exceptional care in the review procedures employed and in the nature of things is more difficult to evaluate than traditional disciplinary research. Despite the problems of identifying the 'peers' for the review, informed, objective weighing of the merits of proposals continues to play a vital role.

In spite of its flaws, there is simply no substitute for the peer review process as it has evolved in the American research support system. It is flexible and can accommodate to new concepts; it provides the sense of due process which makes the unequal allocation of resources acceptable in a democratic society. There is no elite in religious, political, business or scientific terms in American society that is entitled to benefits without competition. The logic and the basic precepts of the whole research support system in the USA depend upon the evaluation and support of individual projects. The structure of law, and more importantly the set of norms underlying the political support for the system, relate to individual projects. Consider, for example, Section 301 of the Public Health Service Act (as amended in 1950) which specifies that

> the Secretary is authorized to make grants-in-aid to universities, hospitals, laboratories, and other public or private institutions, and to individuals for such research projects as are recommended by the advisory council to the entity of the Department supporting such projects.[28]

Coherent area grants or awards to centres are also dependent on projects. No scientific investigator typically depends exclusively on the block grant for support. Rather, there is a rough proportionality between the additional research support which investigators get through peer-reviewed projects and the amounts they may receive from the block grant at the host institution or centre. Even institutional grants in the US context are partly dependent upon competition, often pegged in proportion to the amounts received in individual project competition or awarded to the institution on the basis of student enrolment choices. As one moves toward large-scale facilities, peer review no longer operates easily. But even here scientists have tempered the operation of 'pork barrel' considerations by assuring that sites selected have technical merit as well as political support.

The peer review system, in brief, is the only rational way to allocate resources in a highly pluralistic nation where resources are always insufficient to satisfy all claimants. As resources are stretched thinly, the criticisms of peer review will inevitably mount, but the neutral appraisal of proposals – and the efficient use of resources – will be all the more urgent. Avoiding the large mistakes will have a higher priority than ever. No peer review system can ever be perfect, and in particular no system can ever fully escape the tendency to follow prevailing orthodoxies. The answer to that problem is for the nation to continue to rely on multiple sources of support both public and private.

Notes

1. L. Wilson (1985). The capital facilities dilemma in the American graduate school. In B. L. R. Smith (ed.) *The State of Graduate Education.* Washington, DC: Brookings Institution.
2. The University and Small Business Patent Act 1980 (and the 1984 amendments thereto), the Small Business Innovation Development Act 1982, and the Technology Transfer Act 1986. See B. L. R. Smith (1990). *American Science Policy Since World War II.* Washington, DC: Brookings Institution, pp. 135–6.
3. See H. Ergas (1987). The importance of technology policy. In P. Dasgupta and P. Stoneman (eds), *Economic Policy and Technology Performance.* Cambridge: Cambridge University Press.
4. See S. P. Strickland (1972). *Politics, Science, and Dread Disease: A Short History of the United States Medical Research Policy.* Cambridge, Mass: Harvard University Press.
5. J. L. Heilbron and D. J. Kevles (1988). Finding a policy for mapping and sequencing the human genome: lessons from the history of particle physics. *Minerva* **26**(3): 299–314.
6. See, for example, D. Shapley and R. Roy (1985). *Lost at the Frontier: U.S. Science and Technology Policy Adrift.* Philadelphia: ISI Press.
7. Ibid., p. 152.
8. M. L. Dertouzos, R. K. Lester and R. M. Solow and the MIT Commission on Industrial Productivity (1989). *Made in America: Regaining the Productive Edge.* Cambridge, Mass: MIT Press, pp. 154, 157.
9. Thirty states spent $700 million in 1986 on technology initiatives, including research parks, incubator programmes and technological training. See National Academy of Engineering (1988). *Technological Dimensions of International Competi-*

tiveness. Washington, DC: NAE, p. 48. For general review, see B. Jones (1986). *State Technological Programs in the United States,* Governor's Office of Science and Technology, Minnesota Department of Energy and Economic Development, St Paul, Minnesota.

10. Similarly, 90 per cent of all scholarly citations appear in 10 per cent of the journals. For a general discussion of peer review see B. L. R. Smith (1990). *American Science Policy Since World War II,* Washington, DC: Brookings Institution, pp. 179–84.

11. S. Lock (1986). *A Difficult Balance: Editorial Peer Review in Medicine.* Philadelphia: ISI Press.

12. National Institutes of Health (1988). *Report of the NIH Peer Review Committee.* Bethesda, Md: NIH.

13. E. Bloch (1989). Director, Memorandum to Members of the National Science Board, *Annual Report on the Foundation's Use of Peer Review,* 3 March, NSB-89-33.

14. NIH (1988). *Report of the NIH Peer Review Committee.* Bethesda, Md: NIH.

15. US House of Representatives (1966). *Report of a Special Subcommittee of the Interstate and Foreign Commerce Committee* (Rogers Committee); (1964). *Report of the House of Representatives Select Committee on Government Research* (Elliott Committee); (1967). *The Administration of Research Grants in the Public Health Service* (Fountain Report).

16. (1966). *Biomedical Science and its Administration: A Study of NIH* (Wooldridge Report); (1966). *Report of the Secretary on the Management of NIH Research Grants and Contracts* (Ruina Report).

17. (1977). *Grants Peer Review,* Report to the Director, NIH; (1967). *Report of the Commission on Research* (Whittaker Report), Chicago: American Medical Association; Jonathan Cole.

18. NIH (1988). *Report of the NIH Peer Review Committee,* p. 30.

19. Ibid., pp. 30–3.

20. NSF, mimeograph material accompanying *1989 Annual Peer Review Report,* p. 11.

21. Ibid., p. 15.

22. General Accounting Office (1987). *University Funding: Patterns of Distribution of Federal Research Funds to Universities,* p. 14, Table 2.1.

23. NSF, mimeograph material accompanying *1989 Annual Peer Review Report,* p. 2.

24. Ibid., p. 3.

25. NIH (1988). *Report of the NIH Peer Review Committee,* p. 27; *NIH Fact Book, 1988,* p. 23, Table 17.

26. NIH (1988). *Extramural Trends, FY 1978–1987.* Division of Research Grants, p. 31.

27. NIH (1988). *Report of the NIH Peer Review Committee,* p. 23, Figure 10.

28. Ibid., p. 7.

4

Issues in Funding Research

Harry Atkinson

'He who pays the piper calls the tune'. Or does he?

The answer is almost always that he does not, when the payer is a government (through its general funding) and the piper is a researcher in a university (or other institution of higher education – HEI).

Indeed, governments (or anyone else) do not usually even know with any precision how much of their general funding goes into research and how much into teaching – let alone what research programmes they are buying. University research has been called a 'black hole' for government funding.

It would be foolish to pretend, however, that it is easy to tackle the first of these issues – the separation of the teaching and research functions – because the two activities are almost inextricably mixed, each feeding with benefit on the other (or so the accepted wisdom goes). Some governments are, nevertheless, increasingly introducing more accountability regarding their general subventions to HEIs, with a tendency towards separate funding of research and teaching (where that is not already done).

With these things in mind, this chapter tries to concentrate on some basic questions:

1. What resources, money and personnel really are devoted by HEIs to research?
2. Do the statistics generally available, notably those of the Organization for Economic Co-operation and Development (OECD), present a satisfactory picture of these resources (and do governments give satisfactory information to the OECD in the first case?)
3. How do the resources used compare between one country and another?
4. Indeed, what are the problems of making such international comparisons?
5. What research activities outside the HEIs proper should be taken into account in judging a country's expenditure on basic research of the university type, notably those in government-funded research institutes?

Another issue of great importance, which is only touched on here, is the extent to which the organization of research in a country, and the funding channels provided, allow researchers to make the best use of the overall funds. It is no good having large government research budgets if, for example, the best researchers cannot get access to the equipment they need, whether it be a small-scale instrument or a major facility.

With these questions in mind, published data on the resources devoted to research in the HEIs are reviewed; an outline is given of the organizational structures within which the HEIs operate in France, Germany, the UK and, to some extent, the USA; a number of key problems in understanding research statistics generally, and in making international comparisons, are discussed; the chapter ends with reference to some other important issues for which there is simply not space here.

OECD and other published data on HEIs' research resources

The most comprehensive statistical data on the resources for research performed in the HEIs are published regularly by the OECD as part of their *Main Science and Technology Indicators*. The data cover only the industrial countries in membership of the OECD and therefore exclude, for example, countries in the old eastern block, Asia (except Japan), Africa and South America. Studies of 'academic and academically related' research in six of the OECD countries – France, West Germany (as it was then), Japan, the Netherlands, the United Kingdom (UK) and the United States of America (USA) – have been published by Martin and Irvine (1986), and by Irvine, Martin and Isard (1990); a comparison of the organization of research and the resources deployed in France, West Germany and the UK has been published by Atkinson, Rogers and Bond (1990; 1991).

OECD data

The OECD data are unique and of great value. However, they are highly aggregated and the bare numbers alone can be misleading without some understanding of the structure of the research institutions in the countries concerned. The data must also be treated with caution because different countries can use different definitions in the data they submit, as recognized in the footnotes and text of the OECD publications.

The OECD's *Main S&T Indicators* are published every six months and give overall R&D data for each of its twenty-four member states. The data, covering money and personnel, are broken down into a small number of categories of R&D performer and R&D funder: industry, higher education and government. The data are supplied to the OECD by governments on the basis of national questionnaires. The responses to the questionnaires are supposed to follow definitions and procedures agreed within the OECD, in part expressed in the *'Frascati' Manuals* (OECD 1981; 1989). In practice, there can be problems, as indicated below.

For Japan, the OECD points out that the figures in many of the Organization's tables substantially overestimate the real position, especially for the higher education sector, regarding both the numbers of researchers and their costs, because the personnel data supplied by the Japanese authorities give the numbers of individuals (or 'physical people') but not their full-time equivalent numbers (OECD 1990). In this chapter, however, I use the OECD's adjusted figures for Japan (OECD 1990: Annex 3). As discussed in more detail later in this chapter, the OECD's figures for France are also misleading in their division of resources between the higher education and government intramural sectors; and those for the UK somewhat underestimate research expenditure in the HEIs.

Regarding the higher education sector, the data in the *Main Indicators* (OECD 1990) comprise the following, in which RSE stands for 'Research Scientists and Engineers' and FTE for 'Full-Time Equivalent':

- higher education expenditure on R&D (HERD)
- higher education total R&D personnel (FTE)
- higher education RSE (or university graduates) (FTE)
- General University Funds (GUF) as a percentage of Civil Budget Government R&D appropriations (GBAORD).

Also relevant are the following data, because they include other research at the basic end of the spectrum and activities which, though supporting research in the HEIs, are not counted as HERD (see later):

- GOVERD (Government Intramural Expenditure on R&D)
- government total R&D personnel (FTE)
- government RSE (or university graduates) (FTE)
- non-oriented research programmes as a percentage of GBAORD.

No data on basic research as such are issued by the OECD, although they now cover 'non-oriented research' as indicated above.

The OECD regularly publishes data on education personnel and finances, and on the output of graduates. However, the higher education sector forms a relatively small part of these publications, which are mainly concerned with primary and secondary education, the high spenders. Little information is given on such important issues as private sector or other 'third-party' funding, an increasingly important element in the finances of HEIs. In interpreting the data there are major problems in the definition of different types of HEI, and difficulties in comparing different university degrees, an important issue in assessing a country's output of trained personnel.

These data do not generally separate the costs of research and teaching in the higher education sector. Thus, the *Main S&T Indicators* form the OECD's main published data on HEIs' research in different countries: I now outline some key information which can be extracted from them.

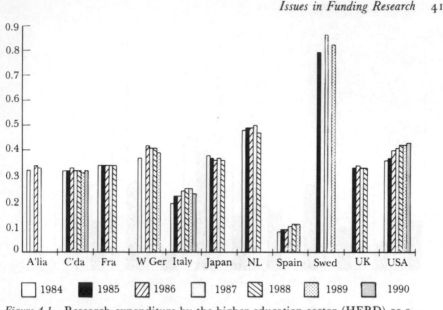

Figure 4.1 Research expenditure by the higher education sector (HERD) as a percentage of gross domestic product (GDP) for the years 1984 to 1990 (OECD 1990).

Research expenditure by HEIs

Figure 4.1 shows the value of HERD for eleven of the OECD countries as a percentage of gross domestic product (GDP) for the years 1984 to 1990. (Other ways of comparing research expenditures in different countries are discussed towards the end of the chapter.) Only in Sweden, the Netherlands, the USA and West Germany (by a whisker) does expenditure on HEI research exceed 0.4 per cent of the GDP. Japan is next, at a little more than 0.35 per cent. The UK hovers around 0.32 per cent, at about the same level as France (although the French data may overestimate the true position, and the UK data slightly underestimate it). Only in Italy, Spain and the USA did HERD rise significantly over the years concerned. (Note that data are not available for every year for every country.)

Sources of funds for research in HEIs

The *Main S&T Indicators* do not include information on the *sources* of funding of the research expenditure expressed in HERD. They do, however, give data for the estimated research component of General University Funds (GUF), which support much university research. However, it is important to recognize that the latter are *budget* figures – from governments' overall civil appropriations – and are not based on the actual costs of the research performed. It

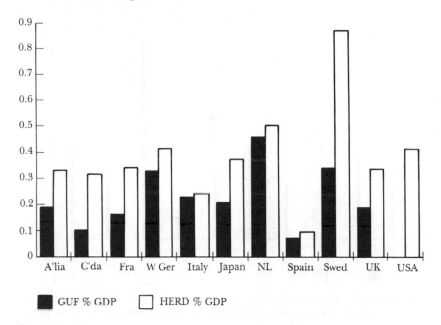

Figure 4.2 General university funds (GUF) and HERD as percentages of GDP for 1987 (OECD 1990).

is also important to recognize that GUF covers only *public* funding. As all who have looked closely at R&D statistics will know, budget figures are often substantially different from the expenditure statistics produced by the performers themselves (e.g. Atkinson *et al.* 1990).

Figure 4.2 shows the data for GUF for 1987 for ten of the eleven chosen countries, there being no OECD figures for the USA. It can be seen that government budgets in the Netherlands include over 0.45 per cent of GDP for research in the HEIs; West Germany and Sweden come next at something over 0.3 per cent. Italy and Japan just exceed the UK (about 0.2 per cent), while the governments of Spain and Canada contribute only about 0.1 per cent. Figures for HERD are also shown – to indicate roughly the contribution of GUF to HERD (while recognizing the dangers of comparing budget figures with those coming, or purporting to come, from the performers).

The OECD do not publish information on the *sources* of the funds which comprise HERD in a disaggregated form although they do seek such information from their member states.

However, for France, West Germany and the UK, the OECD secretariat has kindly supplied information on funding sources to the author (Atkinson *et al.* 1991: Table A3a). These data, for 1987, are shown in Figure 4.3 which gives the research expenditure by source of funds, as a percentage of the total expenditure on research in the HEIs of the country concerned. The sources are grouped into the following categories: industry, direct government (for example for research grants or contracts), 'GUF' (general university funds,

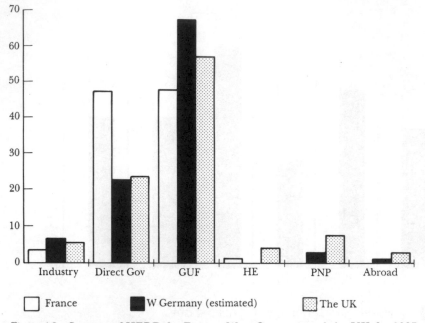

Figure 4.3 Sources of HERD for France, West Germany and the UK for 1987, as a percentage of HERD for the country concerned. The figures for Germany are estimated (see text). (Atkinson *et al*. 1991 from OECD private communication.)

see above), 'HE' (representing the income from the HEIs' own investments or sale of assets), 'PNP' (private non-profit, for example the medical charities) and 'abroad' (including funds from the Commission of the European Community). (Figures were not available in the last three categories for all the countries.)

For each of the three countries, government funding is the prime source of HEIs' research expenditure. This can be seen by taking the sum of 'Direct Government' and 'GUF' in Figure 4.3, giving government totals of about 95 per cent for France, 90 per cent for West Germany and 80 per cent for the UK. However, there are major differences in the way in which the governments provide their funds. Direct government funding, usually on a selective or directed basis, is particularly high for France, at nearly 50 per cent – more than twice the percentage for the other two countries. Correspondingly GUF, usually given without strings, is lowest for France and highest for West Germany. (Note: the figure for Germany provided by the OECD was for total government expenditure; the division of this into Direct Government and GUF is my estimate.)

The relatively low level of funding by industry of HEIs' research can be seen for all three countries, although France, at about 3.5 per cent is substantially lower than the other two (each at about 6 per cent). (The corresponding figure for the USA is thought to be about 7 per cent.) The UK has relatively more funding from private non-profit organizations than the other countries

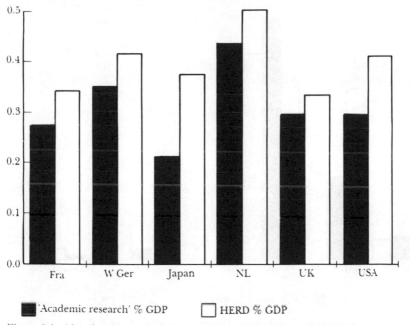

Figure 4.4 'Academic research' expenditure compared with HERD, as a percentage of GDP, for 1987 (Irvine *et al.* 1990; OECD 1990).

– mostly for medical research – and also gets the highest proportion from abroad and from the higher education sector itself (for example as income from an HEI's own investments, see above).

It is instructive at this point to compare the OECD's data for HERD and for GUF with the relevant data of Irvine *et al.* (1990) for the six countries they examined. Figure 4.4 compares Irvine *et al.*'s figures for expenditure on 'academic research' with figures for HERD, both for 1987, the data being expressed as percentages of GDP. ('Academic research' consists of research funded both from GUF and by public third parties.) For each country it can be seen that the figure for HERD is always greater than that for 'academic research'. Because HERD comprises funding from all sources, including the private sector, while 'academic research' covers only research funded from *public* funds, the former is bound to be higher than the latter. For Japan the difference between HERD and 'academic research' is particularly marked.

Figure 4.5 compares Irvine *et al.*'s figures for GUF with those of the OECD, again for 1987, as percentages of GDP. Apart from the UK, where Irvine *et al.*'s figure is greater than that of the OECD (probably because of the underestimate of the UK figure), the reverse obtains for the other countries. The data of Irvine *et al.* show a particularly low level of GUF for the USA, perhaps because much of the research in that country is in powerful *private* universities. (There is no OECD figure for GUF for the USA.)

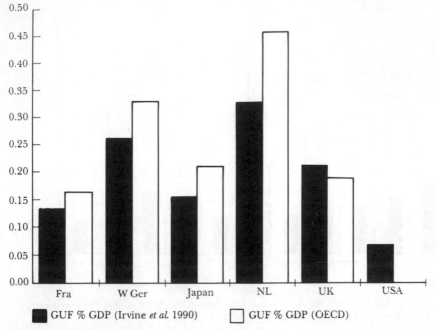

Figure 4.5 HEIs' research expenditure from GUF as a percentage of GDP for 1987: comparison of data of Irvine *et al.* and OECD (Irvine *et al.* 1990; OECD 1990).

Research manpower

Research is done by people and people cost money. The next few paragraphs look at the numbers of researchers in the eleven countries, and at aspects of their costs. First, some definitions. In the OECD's tables of R&D personnel, 'full-time equivalent' (FTE) numbers are given which take account of the proportion of time which the individual spends on R&D (rather than on some other type of activity). This is a particularly important factor for the HEIs, because academics are almost always employed both to teach and to do research. The tables give the numbers of FTE 'RSE (or university graduates)', never showing separately the numbers of RSE (research scientists and engineers). While for the higher education sector the numbers supplied by governments to the OECD, and therefore in the tables, are usually for RSE (or 'researchers') proper, in the case of government applied research establishments, the numbers submitted are usually those for university graduates, including many who are not researchers. In the text and figures I use the terms 'RSE' and 'researchers' interchangeably as shorthand for 'RSE (or university graduates)'.

Figure 4.6 shows the number of FTE researchers per 1,000 of the labour force in the HEIs of the country concerned, in 1987. This parameter has been chosen to allow satisfactory comparisons to be made between countries with

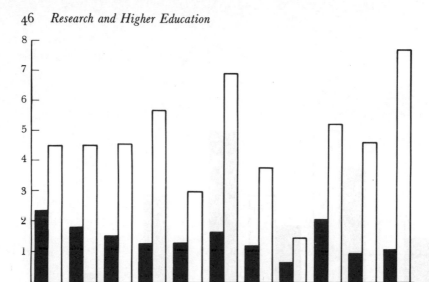

Figure 4.6 Researchers (RSE) per 1,000 of labour force for higher education sector and for country as a whole, for 1987 (OECD 1990).

widely varying overall populations. The figure also shows for each country the number of FTE researchers per 1,000 of the labour force for *all* R&D.

It can be seen that only the UK and Spain have fewer than 1 FTE researcher per 1,000 in the higher education sector. The USA has marginally more, but West Germany (1.25), France (1.51) and Japan (1.61) are substantially higher – though well exceeded by Australia, Canada and Sweden. (The figures for France, however, include researchers of the *Centre National de la recherche scientifique* (CNRS): see later.)

Figure 4.6 also shows figures for FTE researchers per 1,000 for *all* R&D in the country concerned. Here Japan and the USA lead with about 7 per 1,000; Germany has about 5.5, and France and the UK about 4.5. The figures for all R&D are consistently much greater than those for the higher education sector alone.

Expenditure per researcher

Atkinson *et al.* (1990) paid particular attention to the expenditure per researcher in their study of the UK, France and West Germany. Figure 4.7 shows such numbers for the eleven countries (in $US thousands) per FTE researcher, for researchers in HEIs and in government intramural research laboratories, for 1987. The conversion of national currencies to dollars has been made using 'Purchasing Power Parity' (PPP) rates, discussed near the end of the chapter.

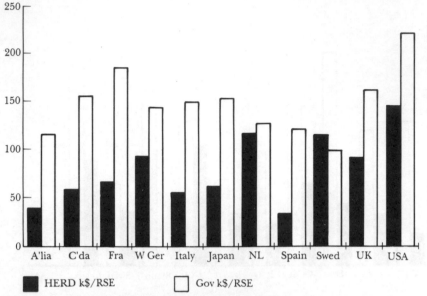

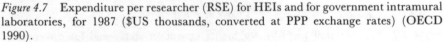

Figure 4.7 Expenditure per researcher (RSE) for HEIs and for government intramural laboratories, for 1987 ($US thousands, converted at PPP exchange rates) (OECD 1990).

A number of conclusions can be drawn. First, it can be seen that for every country, each researcher in an HEI receives substantially less support than his or her colleague in a government laboratory – except for Sweden and the Netherlands. (*Individual* academics have even less money at their disposal – leaving aside their salary – because each is both teacher and researcher, usually spending less than 50 per cent of their time on research, and therefore counting as less than o.5 FTE.)

Second, substantial differences can be seen *within* the higher education sector, the USA leading in resources per researcher (at $144,000). Worst off are researchers in Australia and Spain (each at about $35,000, figures so low that they should perhaps be questioned).

For researchers in government laboratories, the USA again leads followed by France, each with about $200,000 per FTE researcher; no country has a figure lower than about $100,000.

The cost per researcher includes the following elements:

- the cost of equipment
- the cost of support staff
- the researcher's own salary.

It is not easy to get data for each of these elements. However, the *number* of support staff per FTE researcher can be calculated from the OECD statistics. The resulting numbers (for 1987) are shown in Figure 4.8. From this it can be seen that FTE researchers in a university are again apparently less well supported than their government colleagues. However, these figures do not

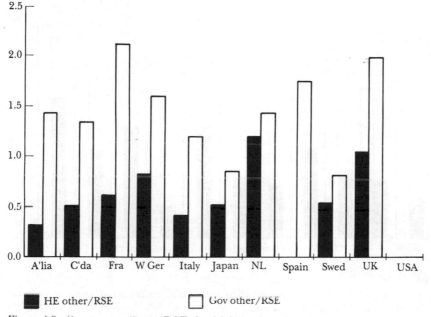

Figure 4.8 Support staff per RSE for higher education sector and for government intramural laboratories, for 1987 (OECD 1990).

always include research students, a major factor discussed near the end of the chapter.

Regarding the individual countries, the number of support staff per FTE researcher in the higher education sector exceeds 1.0 only for the UK and the Netherlands, while it is about 0.5 or less for many countries. (No figure is given for overall R&D staff numbers for the USA.) In government laboratories, the UK and France are high at about 2.0 (perhaps reflecting a high defence R&D activity requiring relatively more support staff) while Japan and Sweden are both below 1.

Organization of research in HEIs and in related institutions, and the channels for research funding

Data on research funding and personnel have real meaning only if something is known of the structure of research in the country concerned. I therefore set out below brief outlines of the organizational structures within which the HEIs operate in each of four countries – France, West Germany, the UK and the USA. For each, an indication is given of those public organizations outside the higher education sector which provide in-kind support for researchers in the HEIs – or which themselves perform basic research; and for each the funding channels are identified. It will be seen that each country has its own, very distinctive arrangements.

France

French HEIs comprise the universities and the *grandes écoles*. Traditionally, the latter have done little or no research, but this is now changing. The basic funding of the universities comes from the Ministry of National Education (MEN), covering both salaries and buildings. For the *grandes écoles*, some are funded by the MEN, while the remainder receive their prime support from other ministries.

Research in French HEIs is largely dominated by the CNRS and the other *grands organismes* (such as that for medicine, Institut de la santé et de la recherche médicale (INSERM) and that for agriculture, Institut national de la recherche agronomique (INRA)) – because French academics largely depend for their research on laboratories of these organizations. A substantial number of the laboratories (the 'associated laboratories') are set up jointly with an individual university. Essentially the only university research activity outside the ambit of the *grands organismes* is that of the 'recommended teams' (*équipes recommandées*) supported by the MEN from a relatively small central fund.

An overview of research in each university is provided by a mechanism in which the MEN and the university concerned enter into a four-year contract. The contract takes account of all the research programmes of the university, including those associated with the CNRS; however, for the latter, the quality of the research is not assessed by the MEN but by the CNRS. The general approach is thus centralized, through the CNRS on the one hand and the MEN on the other. Much of the basic research in France is performed by CNRS staff in CNRS laboratories, and by the staff of the Atomic Energy Commission (CEA) in the CEA's laboratories.

Researchers both of the HEIs and of the *grands organismes* have access to major facilities, national and international. The national facilities are usually provided by the CNRS or the CEA (e.g. synchrotron radiation and neutron beam sources). The international facilities are sometimes provided jointly by the CNRS and the CEA (for example the *Institut Laue-Langevin* and the European Synchrotron Radiation Facility) and sometimes by the Ministry of Foreign Affairs – for the European Centre for Nuclear Research (CERN) and the European Southern Observatory (ESO).

The overall balance of R&D expenditure and of FTE researchers, by type of performer, is shown in Figures 4.9 and 4.10, which indicate clearly the strength of government-type laboratories. In the figures I have divided the latter into two groups: on the one hand, the CNRS and other *grands organismes* (called Établissement public à caractère scientifique et technologique (EPST) in French government publications) and which I have called 'research councils'; and, on the other, the rest, which I have called 'government intramural'. (The data are based on French government statistics, Atkinson *et al.* 1991; some are substantially different from those of the OECD, see below.)

West Germany

In West Germany the HEIs comprise mainly the universities (*Hochschulen*) and the *Fachhochschulen* (which are more vocationally oriented). Little research is currently done in the latter. Each university is the responsibility of the state or *Land* in which it is sited.

For research, West German universities are funded along similar lines to those described below for the UK, the basic funding being provided by the government (of the *Land*), and selective funding by the German Research Society (DFG). Universities also receive support for specific projects from federal and *Land* ministries, from foundations and from private industry.

Basic research is also carried out in a wide variety of other organizations: the institutes of the Max-Planck Society (MPG), the big research centres (or Großforschungseinrichtungen (GFE), such as KFA Jülich and KfA Karlsruhr), the laboratories of the Fraunhofer Society (FhG), the so-called 'blue list' institutions and others. Each of these has its own funding arrangements. Overall, the German research system is very dispersed.

Major research facilities are provided in a variety of ways: by a big research centre or university, primarily for the use of its own researchers; by a big centre for national use (e.g. the accelerators of DESY at Hamburg, which also have strong international use); and through international organizations (for example, CERN, the European Space Agency (ESA) and ESO), usually with funding from the Federal Ministry of Research and Technology (BMFT).

Figures 4.9 and 4.10 show the strength both of the HEIs and of the research institutions outside the higher education sector. I have divided the latter into two groups: the *Private inländer Institutionen ohne Erwerbszweck* (private non-profit institutions, though not PNPs in the OECD sense); and the intramural institutions of both the Federal government and the *Länder*. I have called the former 'research council intramural', perhaps somewhat arbitrarily.

United Kingdom

In the UK, basic research is almost entirely the province of the higher education sector, which is made up of the universities and the polytechnics (and colleges). About 90 per cent of the research in the HEIs is done in the universities. The universities receive most of their money from public sources – primarily through the University Funding Council (UFC), which provides about 50 per cent of their overall income for teaching and research (Atkinson *et al.* 1991). Somewhat similar arrangements obtain for the polytechnics. The funding of the universities is becoming increasingly selective, particularly regarding the research element.

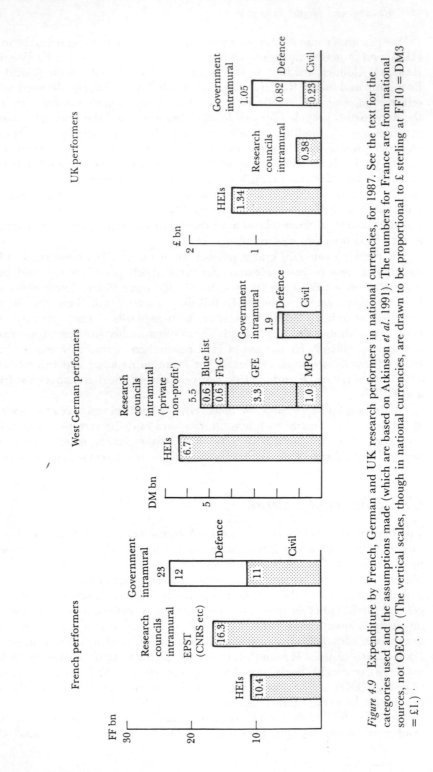

Figure 4.9 Expenditure by French, German and UK research performers in national currencies, for 1987. See the text for the categories used and the assumptions made (which are based on Atkinson *et al.* 1991). The numbers for France are from national sources, not OECD. (The vertical scales, though in national currencies, are drawn to be proportional to £ sterling at FF10 = DM3 = £1.)

Five research councils play an important role both in funding research in the HEIs, and in performing research intramurally. The Science and Engineering Research Council (SERC) is the biggest of the councils; both it and the Economic and Social Research Council (ESRC) are primarily devoted to the selective support of the HEIs under the 'dual support system'. In this, the universities provide the 'well-found laboratory' and the research councils provide top-up funding, usually through three-year grants, for specific research projects on a highly selective basis. Apart from this income from grants, the HEIs are increasingly seeking and winning research contracts from other 'third parties', for example from industry, government departments and the Commission of the European Community. The other research councils – the AFRC (for agriculture and food), the MRC (for medicine) and the NERC (for the natural environment) – have their own substantial research institutes as well as supporting research in the HEIs.

The research councils' grants provide funds for the HEI concerned to buy equipment and to hire research assistants (both post-doctoral and post-graduate) on a fixed-term basis – usually for three years. These assistants form a major element of the HEIs' full-time research staff. The councils also provide research studentships to cover the living costs of many research students. In addition, the SERC funds – and often builds and operates – major facilities specifically for the use of HEI researchers (subject to peer review), both nationally and internationally: for example national and international synchrotron radiation and neutron sources, astronomical and space facilities, and CERN.

Figures 4.9 and 4.10 show the relatively low levels of resources for research in the research councils' own laboratories, and in the government's civil laboratories, when compared with those of the higher education sector. A more detailed breakdown of the main elements of the latter sector is given later.

United States of America

The higher education sector in the USA comprises a huge number of institutions. There are about 4,000 universities, both 'state' (funded by the state in which they are located) and private. Relatively few – the major state, and big private 'schools' – have substantial research programmes.

Although much of the infrastructure is provided by a university from its general funds (whether from the state, or from private sources including the university's own endowments), research is largely dependent on winning grants or contracts from a variety of federal government agencies, notably the National Institutes of Health (NIH) – by far the biggest federal agency funding university research – the National Science Foundation (NSF), the Department of Energy (DOE), NASA and others. The Department of Defense (DOD) also provides substantial funds for university research.

A notable feature of the US system is that universities usually pay their academics for nine months' work only (essentially for teaching): the academics

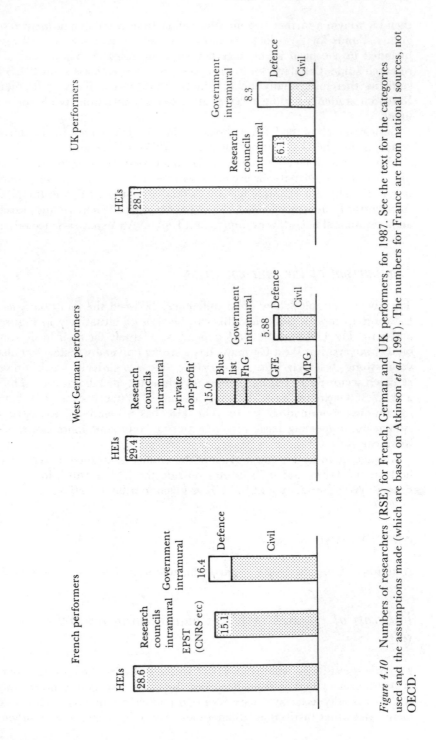

Figure 4.10 Numbers of researchers (RSE) for French, German and UK performers, for 1987. See the text for the categories used and the assumptions made (which are based on Atkinson *et al.* 1991). The numbers for France are from national sources, not OECD.

then try to win a further two months' salary from those giving them research grants. Funds for post-doctoral and other fixed term research staff are also included in a typical grant, together with the research component of each research student's salary, for his/her work as a 'research assistant'. (US R&D statistics therefore usually include the bulk of the cost of research students.) Research students seldom receive any other support from public or central funds.

Basic research in the USA is almost exclusively carried out by the university sector, as for the UK, but not for France or West Germany.

Major research facilities are provided in a variety of ways: by an individual, big, 'research' university for use of its own researchers; by a group of universities; nationally (for example telescopes funded by the NSF, and the National Accelerator Laboratory funded by the Department of Energy); and, rarely, on an international basis (for example, joint ESA–NASA space science missions).

Comparison of the four countries

The above examples show great differences between the four countries. For the three European countries, this can be seen quantitatively in Figures 4.9 and 4.10. The UK and the USA depend very largely for their basic research on the universities. West Germany has a strong university sector, but also has very strong research institutes. France has a relatively weak university research sector *per se*, but has strong government-type laboratories. The USA and West Germany have the most dispersed systems: note that both are federations of individual states. The UK has a relatively well-structured system for supporting basic research, but no country is more centralized in its research than France.

A rough quantitative comparison of the totality of 'academic' type research both in the HEIs and in institutes outside the higher education sector for France, West Germany and the UK is given in a later section.

Specific topics

A number of specific issues of particular importance are now addressed.

Full cost of research in HEIs and teaching/research split

The first question is: what is an HEI? Universities are the most familiar type of institution in higher education, but there are also polytechnics, medical schools (usually associated with hospitals and clearly involving clinical treatment) and other institutions. Sometimes, research by institutions other than the universities proper is simply ignored by the countries responding to the OECD's questionnaires. (For example, the data supplied by the UK has omitted the costs of research in the polytechnics, even though UK polytechnics do substantial research.)

The full economic cost of research in a university comprises, or at least includes, the following. (The term 'university' is used below, in part because the assessment of research in other parts of the higher education sector is even less well developed, and in part because most research in this sector is, in fact, done by universities.)

1. That part of the university's total expenditure which, using full costings, is actually spent on research. (The university's income, which covers this expenditure, comes from a variety of sources, both public and private, and often includes income from the university's own endowments and investments.)
2. 'In-kind' support through
   - laboratories not charged to the university (for example CNRS laboratories in France)
   - major science facilities, national and international
   - equipment and staff on loan from other organizations, without charge.
3. Subsistence payments to research students, whether from private or public funds (for example from the SERC in the UK). (Here I exclude students supported by university funds and those on specific posts.)

Of these, only the first (dealt with in some detail in the following paragraphs) is usually seen as contributing to HERD, even though the other two also give substantial support to the research activities of HEIs.

In Europe, at least, few universities account separately, and fully, for the costs to their overall budgets of their research and their teaching activities; and the national authorities, in submitting their returns for HERD to the OECD, appear to do no more than make, centrally, an overall estimate (or informed guess?) about the costs of research in their universities and, sometimes but not always, in other HEIs. (I understand, however, that the NSF obtains returns on research performed directly from each university in the USA, a system which other countries should emulate.)

Few countries seem to publish their detailed methods for estimating the costs of research in the HEIs. It may be assumed that they start with an overall single budget figure for both teaching and research, and then try to estimate the cost of the research component by estimating the proportion of time spent by academics (and other research staff) on research, and assigning other costs, *pro rata*.

It must be said, however, that calculations of the time spent by academics on research are bound to be somewhat arbitrary, because the teaching and research functions are so intimately linked. For example, in doing the sums should the proportion of time spent on research relate to a forty-hour week, or to a much longer one? Should the time of an academic as a member of, say, a peer review committee be counted as teaching or research? Indeed, should the research element be costed as a by-product of teaching, or should teaching and research be counted as functions of equal status?

I discuss below in some detail the costing of HEIs' research in the UK, in part to indicate the elements which need to be taken into account. I then turn briefly to France and West Germany.

Cost of HEIs' research in UK

In the UK, the estimates for the national submissions to the OECD for HERD are made by the Universities Funding Council, mainly on the basis of the so-called 'diary exercise' of the late 1960s (CVCP 1972), in which academics kept a diary of the time they spent on teaching, research and on other activities (such as administration). The UFC's figures, published each year in the UK Government's Annual Review of R&D (*Annual Review* 1989) are for *public* funding only, and do not include the cost of research in the polytechnics.

Atkinson *et al.* 1991 have attempted a more complete estimate of the costs of research in the HEIs, on the basis of Clayton's figures for staff time spent on research (Clayton Report 1987), and of the methods of Martin and Irvine 1986. Clayton showed, *inter alia*, that in most subject areas, academics spend on average between about 30 per cent and 40 per cent of their time on research.

The results of Atkinson's *et al.*'s calculations are shown in Figure 4.11, which divides expenditure broadly into

1. Academic departmental expenditure, comprising
   - *general* (mainly the research component of the salaries of all staff working in specific departments, and paid for out of general university funds)
   - *specific* (mainly research grants and contracts from 'third parties', which cover temporary research staff, special equipment and, for contracts, a charge for overheads)
2. Central expenditure, consisting of the research component of the infrastructure provided centrally – such as buildings and their maintenance, libraries, central computers and central workshops – and the salary costs of those providing these services.

Two important conclusions may be drawn:

1. the total cost of university research is higher than may at first be thought by looking only at the total income from research grants and contracts: at £1,427 million the estimated cost is about 50 per cent of total university expenditure – £2,948 million in the same year (1987–88)
2. the costs of salaries of staff in academic departments (mainly teacher-researchers funded from general university funds) form a relatively small part of the total real cost of the research.

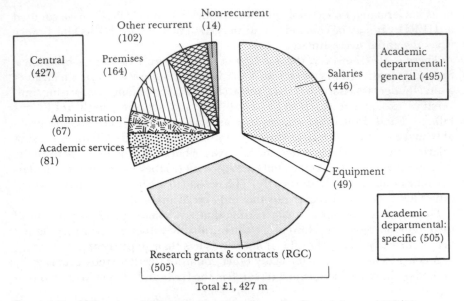

Figure 4.11 UK universities' research expenditure for financial year 1987/88 (£ millions) (Atkinson *et al.* 1991).

When account is taken also of the estimated costs of research in the polytechnics, the overall cost of research in UK HEIs is found to be £1,543 million. This is to be compared with the figure of £1,340 million for 1987, submitted by the UK government, and therefore the official OECD figure for HERD. In this chapter I have generally used the official figure. Note that both figures exclude the costs of in-kind support and of research studentships described above.

Cost of HEIs' research in France

The OECD's published figure for HERD for 1987 (FF18.19 billion) is that submitted to them by the French authorities. However, an official French government publication (*Rapport Annexe* 1989) gives the cost of research in the HEIs for 1987 as FF10.4 billion. The difference between the two figures seems to assume that the bulk of the costs of the CNRS – about FF10 billion per year – are counted as if they were part of the Higher Education sector.

There is no doubt that the CNRS gives substantial in-kind support to university research, for example through the 'associated laboratories' mentioned previously (although perhaps the reverse process should not be forgotten, the contribution of university academics to the research of CNRS through the same laboratories). Nevertheless, it seems unreasonable to attribute so much of the CNRS's costs to the higher education sector. (Note that the intramural activities of the research councils in the UK and similar organizations in Germany, for example the Max-Planck Society (MPG) are *not* counted as HERD.) It may be concluded that the OECD's figure for HERD for France is a substantial overestimate.

There is also, however, the question of how the figure of FF10.4 billion has been calculated. A hint comes from Table C9 of Atkinson *et al.* 1991, which gives a total 'budgetary effort' for HEIs' research of FF8.664 billion (comprising 'universities, ex-action research' at FF7.090 billion; and 'action research' at FF1.574 billion). Funds from other sources such as local authorities and industry probably make up the difference. However, most of the FF8.664 billion is for staff salaries; thus, it is not clear that the full costs of buildings and other parts of the infrastructure have been taken fully into account (as they have been in calculating, for example, HERD for the UK). (I have had to use both budget and expenditure figures above, because no other data are available.)

Finally, note that these totals assume that academics spend 50 per cent of their time on research. However, this is probably rather an arbitrary figure: before the early 1980s, the official figure was less than 40 per cent.

A conclusion is that, as for many other countries, further study seems to be needed of the cost of performing research in the HEIs and related institutions in France.

Cost of HEIs' research in West Germany

Aspects of the methodology used by the German authorities to calculate HERD are given in BMFT (1988) at part VII. Although relatively little detail is given, care has clearly been taken in estimating the fraction of their time which German academics spend on research, with figures varying between 45 per cent (for science, mathematics, engineering and medicine) and 30–35 per cent in the arts subjects.

In-kind support for research in HEIs

Reference has already been made to the in-kind support of research in the HEIs. Such support is not usually costed or counted by countries in their returns of HERD to the OECD – although for France, the CNRS's activities are thus counted, as already mentioned. However, *no* country seems to include in HERD the relevant parts of the costs of major national and international facilities.

I have made a rough estimate of the costs of providing major scientific facilities (ranging from telescopes and synchrotron radiation sources to CERN) for three European countries. This gives the following estimated figures expressed as annual 'cash flows' in 1989. They are not sums to be neglected. (The figures in brackets are the costs in pounds, following conversion at approximate market exchange rates.)

France	FF1,800 million (£180 million)
West Germany	DM1,200 million (£400 million)
United Kingdom	£130 million

Cost of academic and related work: basic research

Because of problems of definition, it is also interesting to look beyond 'HERD' to a country's expenditure on all research of the academic or basic type, irrespective of the institution in which it is performed. This is particularly important for countries (including West Germany and France) in which substantial 'academic' type work is done in research institutes outside the higher education sector. Such a study has been made by Atkinson *et al.* (1990) for 'basic and strategic research' in France, West Germany and the UK; in this, the costs of major facilities, national and international, and of research paid for by the private sector, are included. Irvine, Martin and Isard (1990) have also taken a wider look at 'academic and academically related' research, as already mentioned.

Table 4.1 compares figures for HERD with those for 'basic research' for the above three countries (taking as 'basic research', Atkinson *et al.*'s figures for 'basic and strategic research'). For France, two figures are given for HERD: that published by the OECD, and that drawn directly from the national source mentioned above.

The UK is seen to have the highest fraction of basic research performed in the higher education sector. (The figure would be about 80 per cent if HERD were calculated according to Atkinson *et al.* 1991, as outlined above.) The true figure for France presumably lies between 40 per cent and 70 per cent according to the proportion of CNRS attributed to the HEIs.

Table 4.1 Expenditure on R&D in the higher education sector (HERD) and total expenditure on 'basic research' in the country concerned

	HERD	*'Basic research'*	*HERD as % of basic research (national currencies in millions: 1987)*
France (OECD)	18,193	25,962	70%
France (national)	10,400	25,962	40%
West Germany	7,110	10,185	70%
United Kingdom	1,340	1,731	77%

Cost of research students

Research students make a major contribution to the performance of research in the HEIs for at least a proportion of their time. Indeed, it may be said that one of the main aims of universities is to train young people in research. Nevertheless, the subsistence costs of research students are often not included in the overall cost of HEI research – unless the student holds a post and is paid a regular salary, as is usually the case in the USA. Further study is needed of the way in which research students are (or are not) included in the statistics of a country's resources for research.

International financial comparisons

The straightforward way of comparing the costs of research in two or more countries is to express the expenditures as percentages of GDP, the approach generally taken in this chapter. Nevertheless, the absolute level of research activity in a country can obviously be assessed only by knowing the absolute magnitude of its research expenditure; and monetary figures are needed if expenditures per researcher are to be compared. Exchange rates must then be used, but is it that simple?

The obvious approach is to employ the 'market' exchange rates used in normal financial transactions across national boundaries. However, in recent years the OECD have used the concept of 'Purchasing Power Parity' (PPP) exchange rates. These are designed to take account of different purchasing powers in different countries, so that the expenditure of a certain sum of money in one country, when converted at the relevant PPP rate, should buy the same goods and services in another. (Tables of PPP exchange rates can be found in publications such as OECD 1990; PPP rates are not, one might add, posted by banks, or used in the real market.)

The PPP rates are calculated on the basis of all the goods and services comprising the GDP. However, as pointed out by Atkinson *et al.* 1990, the costs of R&D activities tend to relate more to international pricing than do the costs of the totality of a country's activities: for example, for scientific equipment, market rates more nearly obtain, and scientists are much more mobile across national boundaries than are workers on average.

A particular situation exists for member countries of the European exchange rate mechanism, which links their currencies. In this case, and certainly with the advent of the Single European Market after 1992, economic pressures should remove any remaining need to use PPP rates within Europe. I note that PPP exchange rates are not used in the USA when comparing the cost of research conducted in California with that, say, in Georgia, although living costs may be lower in the latter state than in the former.

That very different results can result if PPP rather than market exchange rates are used may be judged from the following figures for conversion to pounds sterling, for 1987 (the PPP rates being from OECD, 1988 and the market rates from Irvine *et al.* 1990). Note that for Germany, the PPP rate is 44 per cent higher than the market rate.

at PPP rates £1 = FF12.74 = DM 4.25 (= \$US1.69)
at approximate market rates £1 = FF9.85 = DM 2.95 (= \$US1.64)

There is a special problem in comparing research between countries with very different economies, or with exchange rates not controlled by the market, for example the USSR. At present there is really no option but to use PPP rates. However, Atkinson *et al.* 1990 suggested that a study should be made of the costs of conducting a number of typical research projects in different countries. From such data, special R&D purchasing power parity rates could be calculated, from which more realistic comparisons of research effort in different countries could be made.

Third-party funding

In some countries, at least, the costs of universities' activities – particularly in research – are increasingly covered by grants and contracts for specific work; the proportion of their income from general public sources, which tend not to be earmarked, is falling.

The trend towards increasing levels of third-party funding raises major issues of policy about the nature of universities and the type of work they do – particularly for contracts for applied research.

To what extent, however, do we know the facts in this important area – so that we may follow these trends more intelligently? Some relevant information was shown in Figure 4.3 for HEIs in France, West Germany and the UK. From this it can be seen that in all three countries 'third-party' funding was at least one-third of overall income in 1987. Similar information for other countries must be present in the OECD's databases: it should be published. It would also be useful to be able to separate third-party funding through grants (often 'responsive') from that through contracts (which are usually 'directed'); however, such information is not available from the OECD or, generally, from elsewhere. Figure 4.3 does, however, show the levels of contracts from industry, see above.

National data on third-party funding are sometimes available. For example, such data are published for UK and for West German universities (USR 1989; *Wissenschaftsrat* 1986).

Overheads on research contracts

A major current issue, in a number of countries, is the level of overheads charged by HEIs for their research under contract – and, in some countries, on their research grants. In the UK the rates charged rarely reflect the real costs of the work; thus industrial, and other, customers may well be getting quite a bargain. In the USA different universities charge widely different overheads but, for government agency grants or contracts, the rates used are approved and audited by central federal authorities.

The question of overheads is another important issue in which further studies are needed – particularly when the overheads do not reflect the full costs, so that a small contract (perhaps for applied research) may occupy a disproportionate part of a university's own funds, effectively subsidizing the customer in any area which may not accord with the university's own priorities.

Other issues

There are many other interesting questions and issues on the funding of research in the higher education sector for which space is not available here.

1. How big should be the overall size of a country's basic research activity, and how much of that should be performed in the higher education sector?
2. How may Treasuries be persuaded of the value of basic research?
3. How may the output of basic research best be measured?
4. How effective are the various processes for setting funding priorities, including those of peer (and merit) review?
5. 'Big Science' versus 'Small Science' – which can also be expensive.
6. Directed science versus responsive science.
7. Is basic research best performed by the higher education sector or by government-type research institutes with full-time researchers?
8. Why is science and its funding a matter for intense public debate in some countries (for example France) but not in others?
9. To what extent are statistics manipulated – and funds allocated – for political reasons?

Conclusions

Although I have presented here several graphs and figures, that does not mean that the real resources devoted to research in the higher education sector are known with any precision. All that can be said with certainty is that in most developed countries the universities and other institutions of higher education perform the bulk of the world's basic research – and are therefore a precious resource.

This precious resource is also a very expensive one, occupying many very bright people. Governments need to be better informed about the sector, if the money which they spend is to be sufficient, and is to be spent effectively. And the public deserves to know better how the money from its taxes is used.

With this in mind I have drawn attention to several key problems which call for further study. I hope that someone (if not I) will take them up.

References

Annual Review (1989). *R&D 1989: Annual Review of Government Funded Research and Development*. London: HMSO.

Atkinson, H. H., Rogers, P. A. and Bond, R. (1990). *Research in the United Kingdom, France and West Germany: A Comparison*, vol. 1. Swindon: Science and Engineering Research Council.

—— (1991). *Research in the United Kingdom, France and West Germany: A Comparison*, vol. 2. Swindon: Science and Engineering Research Council.

BMFT (1988). *Bundesbericht Forschung 1988; Bundesminister fur Forschung und Technologie*. Bonn.

Clayton Report (1987). *The Measurement of Research Expenditure in Higher Education*. Research Report Commissioned by the Department of Education and Science. London: HMSO.

CVCP (1972). *Report of an Inquiry into the Use of Academic Staff Time*. London: Committee of Vice-Chancellors and Principals.

Irvine, J., Martin, B. R. and Isard, P. A. (1990). *Investing in the Future: An International Comparison of Government Funding of Academic and Related Research*. Aldershot: Edward Elgar (and Brookfield, Vermont).

Martin, B. R. and Irvine, J. (1986). *An International Comparison of Government Funding of Academic and Academically Related Research*. London: Advisory Board for the Research Councils.

OECD (1981). *The Measurement of Scientific and Technical Activities: Proposed Standard Practice for Surveys of Research and Experimental Development (the 'Frascati' Manual)*. Paris: Organization for Economic Co-operation and Development.

—— (1988). *OECD Main Economic Indicators*, July.

—— (1989). *The Measurement of Scientific and Technical Activities: R&D Statistics and Output Measurement in the Higher Education Sector (supplement to the Frascati Manual)*. Paris: Organization for Economic Co-operation and Development.

—— (1990). *OECD Main Science and Technology Indicators*, no. 2. Paris: Organization for Economic Co-operation and Development.

Rapport Annexe (1989). *Projet de Loi de Finances pour 1990: Rapport Annexe sur l'état de la recherche et du développement technologique*. Paris: Imprimerie Nationale.

USR (1989). *University Statistics 1987–88*, vol. 3 *(Finance)*. Cheltenham: Universities' Statistical Record.

Wissenschaftsrat (1986). *Drittmittel der Hochschulen 1970, 1975, 1980 bei 1985*. Cologne: Wissenschaftsrat.

5

The Impacts of State Technology Programmes on American Research Universities

Irwin Feller

Introduction

'Centers of excellence', 'competitive research grant programmes' and 'manufacturing modernization programmes' are salient features of the new entrepreneurial roles undertaken by American state governments to revitalize their economies.

The effect of these programmes' political aspects on research universities is evident, yet muted. State technology development programmes are direct sources of institutional funds as well as means of leveraging industrial and federal government funds. Thus for any university, participation in a state advanced technology programme, especially in the housing of a centre for excellence, contributes simultaneously to institutional enhancement and state economic development objectives. However, these programmes represent new opportunities for specific universities or groups of institutions to seek changes in the terms under which state governments apportion resources for higher education among different categories of universities – public/private; research universities/comprehensive universities/community colleges. In an opposing manner, they require that universities with established claims on state funding or as the designated assignees of other missions or entitlements conferred by the state, justify their continued entitlement. From the state's perspective, these new programmes raise issues that centre on the relative apportioning of funds between targeted and generic forms of university support, and the relative importance of different classes of higher education institutions to state objectives.

This chapter contains a brief background on the new economic development strategies of American state governments and a typology of the R&D strategies embedded within state advanced technology programmes. Treatments of three aspects of the impact of state technology development strategies on research universities are described:

1. the origins of state strategies
2. budgetary support for higher education
3. technology transfer programmes.

Finally there are some summary observations.

Background

In the early 1980s the economic development strategies of American state governments emphasized technological innovation, including the enhancement of the international competitiveness of existing high-tech firms through a continuing stream of state-of-the-art products and processes, the spawning of new firms through spin-offs from academic research, and the location of firms (or major federal government research and development facilities) through development of high-quality research and graduate education programmes at universities within the state (Roberts and Peters 1987; Rogers 1986). Adoption of a technology-based strategy in any or all of its several forms made research universities 'pivotal institutions in state high-tech policy for economic development' (Eisinger 1988: 275). By the late 1980s many states had added to or broadened their initial strategy to emphasize 'technology transfer', a programmatic concept that encompasses the dissemination of research findings from centres of excellence and the technological modernization of existing firms.

The movement by state governments toward the university sector in search of a partner in economic development was readily met by the increased commitments of American colleges and universities to 'active' roles in national, regional and local economic development (Watkins 1985). These new roles involved bilateral and multilateral partnerships/new alliances/strategic alliances with industry and with federal, state and local governments, and encompassed a range of university activities (basic research, applied research, technology transfer programmes, incubators, small business development centres, commercialization of new technologies), conducted through a range of existing and newly established organizational units (Fairweather 1988).

The joining of university activities with state economic development objectives was not simply a response by universities to state imperatives and incentives. Throughout the 1980s public and private universities adopted entrepreneurial stances to a whole range of activities associated with the promotion and commercialization of faculty research, incubators and research parks that extended well beyond responses to state (or federal government) initiatives (Etzkowitz 1983). These university initiatives reflected searches for revenue streams independent of state appropriations; leap-frogging efforts among competing universities to offer the state more than the state had requested (or desired?); institutional aggrandizement; local economic boosterism; and the work of competitive dynamics wherein once some universities altered their policies on intellectual property rights or conflicts of interest, other institutions were forced to adopt similar policies to retain faculty.

To develop an approximate indicator of the level of university activity, the American Association of State Colleges and Universities (AASCU) gathered information on economic development programmes in public higher education institutions. The AASCU reported finding 382 such programmes at 170 public higher education institutions in 1987, but noted that its compilation was not exhaustive (American Association of State Colleges and Universities 1989). The more recent expansion of university patent and technology licensing activities is indicated by Goldstein and Luger's survey of vice-presidents for business and finance in eighty-nine institutions of higher learning, where 80 per cent of responding institutions (N = 75) reported providing patent and licensing assistance to their faculties and engaging in joint research with private industry (Goldstein and Luger 1990).

The development of these university–industry–government alliances and the concomitant issues have been extensively recounted elsewhere, and act as a backdrop for this chapter (see Fosler 1988; Osborne 1988; Schmandt and Wilson 1987). Of greater interest here is determining what in fact is meant by the proposition that research universities are pivotal to a state's technology-based, economic development strategy. One straightforward, almost reflexive, response to this question is that teaching and research represent both the historical and contemporary contribution of research universities to state and national economic growth.

This view charitably may be said to be a university, not a gubernatorial or legislative, perspective on the task of reinvigorating state economies. It assigns universities a lead role as 'engines of growth'; it implicitly (and politically naively) subordinates a governor's leadership role to that of being a strong supporter of increased appropriations to higher education. By way of contrast, state advanced technology programmes in most cases have been gubernatorial projects that have highlighted innovative, entrepreneurial qualities in executive leadership (Feller 1984).

The defining hallmarks of the state technology development programme are accountability and appropriability (of credit for outcomes). The fact that most of the grant awards made to universities are administered by state science and technology offices (75 per cent) or by departments of commerce or economic development (20 per cent) demonstrates clear intent to target funds toward economic development. Only three states administer these funds through boards responsible for higher education. Most state programmes require that university proposals for state funding include cost-sharing by industrial firms; similarly, state programmes provide for industry representation on the state boards that make awards. These provisions are designed to ensure that the university-based research supported by the programme has a 'commercial' rather than an 'academic' orientation. The provisions reflect state government's wariness of the proclivities of university administrators and research faculty to garner resources under one mission rubric and then to use these funds to get ahead in the race for academic preeminence. As Lambright and Teich (1989) note, placement of S&T programmes within departments of commerce 'naturally predisposes S&T agency priorities in the direction of industrial innovation, rather than fundamental research at universities' (Lambright and Teich 1989: 137).

State technology development programmes have typically been viewed in terms of their organizational and administrative features. For this chapter a more useful analytical perspective can be gained by examining the models of innovation. From these models that link academic research, technological innovation and regional economic growth flow the generic roles assigned to universities and the criteria used to make awards to specific centres of excellence or for specific research projects. Conversely, the role assigned to universities by the state's strategy affects institutional assessments of the compatibility of new responsibilities to foster state economic development with institutional objectives and missions.

Most of the larger state programmes share many common features and are eclectic in design and decentralized in operation. The result is a prolix number of specific programme activities that generate many common comparative features. Still, differences in initial strategy and emphasis that relate to impacts on research universities are manifest in the larger state programmes.

Figure 5.1 arrays a number of the larger state programmes such as those found in Ohio, Pennsylvania, New York, New Jersey and Texas in terms of a conventional basic research/applied research/development continuum.[1] Arrows point to the proximate reach of the programme into other R&D stages.

Reading from the basic to the development band of the spectrum, the Texas Advanced Research Programme and Advanced Technology Programmes have been described by state officials as reflecting the state's belief that its long-term economic growth depends on the quality of its human capital, including the attract of world-class university researchers and the recruitment, training and retention of graduate students.[2] Given this orientation, each Texas programme focuses on individual researchers rather than on centres; is oriented more towards education than technology transfer or job creation (the common

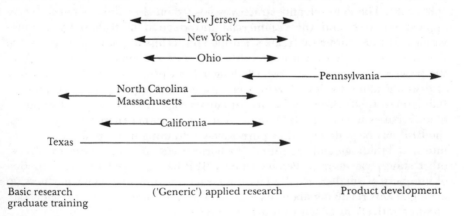

| Basic research | ('Generic') applied research | Product development |
| graduate training | | |

Figure 5.1 R & D strategy underlying state advanced technology programmes.

outcome criteria in other state programmes); and encourages but does not require the contribution of matching funds by industry as a condition of awarding state funds.

Presented as applied R&D programmes with extensive links back to more basic research programmes are New York State's Centers of Excellence and New Jersey's Advanced Technology Centers. The phrase 'applied research and development' appears repeatedly in their programme descriptions. Yet in the choice of scientific and technological fields selected for state support and in the mix of participating universities and firms, these two programmes, in practice, place primary emphasis on developing closer ties between research universities and R&D-intensive firms.

Ohio's Thomas Edison Centers Programme demonstrates the span of R&D activities possible within a single state programme. Ohio's nine Edison Centers perform a range of R&D activities for a diverse set of clients. These include

> Problem solving, training, and transfer of existing technology as services to technologically less sophisticated, usually smaller companies; Development of state-of-the-art knowledge and transfer of that knowledge, usually from universities to larger companies; and, Commercialization of cutting-edge research from universities, medical centers, or the Edison Center itself, sometimes by creating new companies (National Research Council 1990: 6).

Ohio's programme is also an excellent example of how this span of S&T activities accommodates the activities of different academic institutions. The Cleveland Advanced Manufacturing Programme, for example, encompasses 'advanced generic research' on intelligent systems and senior technology performed by Case Western Reserve University, 'engineering problem solving' conducted at Cleveland State University, and technical trouble-shooting and employee training performed by Cuyahoga Community College.

Pennsylvania's Ben Franklin Partnership Program (BFP) has emphasized the 'more rapid commercial application of R&D into the marketplace' (Plosila 1986: 268). The Pennsylvania strategy is posited on close links between (very) applied research and the commercial introduction of technological innovations. It thus implicitly treats scientific and technical knowledge as a stock that may be readily drawn upon, although there are indications of a shift in the programme's priorities towards longer-term projects, which presumably also would allow for less developmentally focused applied research projects (Christman 1988). Also, as if to accentuate its concern over the putative power of universities to convert state funds to academic rather than state objectives, the BFP has been described as purposively refraining from 'pour[ing] money into new buildings and institutes' (Osborne 1988: 48). Far more than most other state programmes, Pennsylvania's BFP has involved the participation of numbers of smaller, locally based colleges and universities in partnership arrangements revolving about its four advanced technology centres, which are administratively attached to research universities.

The North Carolina Microelectronics Center and Massachusetts Microelectronics Center are included in this typology as illustrations of state strategies that seek, through direct support of the construction of physical plant and purchase of equipment followed by support of continuing operations, to enhance locational attractiveness to R&D-intensive firms by enhancing research and graduate education in institutions of higher education, both public and private. An important element in each state's action was the construction of shared research and teaching facilities among a number of institutions. The Massachusetts Microelectronics Center, for example, provides 'sophisticated instruction in microtechnology' which otherwise would not be offered by Massachusetts colleges and universities because the expense for the equipment required for this advanced training 'could not be borne by one institution alone' (Merrigan and Smith 1987:89).

As suggested by this typology, state technology development programmes intersect with the politics of higher education at the juncture of R&D strategies and institutional competencies. The relative roles of research universities and other institutions of higher education, public and private, depend upon the state's strategy. For example, a state strategy to develop, nurture and maintain a world-class industrial sector in emerging technologies, such as superconductivity, is far more likely to support fundamental studies in its research universities related to these technologies than to provide utilitarian technology to local industry. Similarly a state strategy geared to near-term spin-offs from academic research is likely to eschew support of such R&D projects.

Typologies of roles and strategies that nominally provide for rational divisions of labour among universities in terms of relative degrees of expertise to perform specific knowledge-based, economic development tasks indeed float through many treatments of the higher education–economic development connection. For example, Stanford Research Institute (SRI) International's 1986 report, *The Higher Education–Economic Development Connection*, offers a typology of the likely involvement of different types of higher education institutions in economic development that suggests, for example, that flagship universities (e.g. Pennsylvania State University) would engage in basic research as well as other technological activities, while regional universities (e.g. Western Carolina University) would engage in applied research. In several respects, as illustrated by Ohio's Edison Centers, the SRI format and the operations of several state programmes correspond closely.[3]

However useful the framework, the prescriptive force of the assignment of roles on the design or implementation of state technology development/transfer programmes is limited. From the university perspective, initial conditions provide too much practical overlap among types of research, too many overlapping capabilities among institutions, too many special, historical relationships with specific firms or industries that encompass all of the above tasks, and too much real and potential financial and political capital at stake, for any one institution to abdicate a role willingly to others on the grounds that it lacks adequate competency to contribute meaningfully to an important state objective. Four of the five types of universities identified by SRI (regional, urban, technological and flagship) are viewed as likely to be involved in applied research and technical assistance – the core activities of state S&T programmes. No institution can afford not to compete vigorously to be a prominent participant in the state's programmes or to seek to shape the state's programme to encompass what it, the institution, believes to be its strength. Conversely, coupling the centrality of higher education institutions in the new state programmes with the *de facto* requirement for geographically dispersed benefits implies that the state's overall technology development/transfer strategy will encompass activities compatible with the abilities of at least one institution in each politically salient region.

Questions concerning impacts

Differences in strategy and role

What accounts for differences among the states in their technology develop-ment strategies, and thus for differences in the roles projected for research universities? Tacitly, it would seem that differences in the R&D strategies underlying state programmes would reflect different configurations of the intellectual and political influences on state agency officials, university admin-istrators, industry representatives, legislators, scientific and engineering com-munities, and consultants.

In several of the early accounts of state S&T programmes, these pro-grammes were presented either as emerging from the paradigmatic, rational, problem-solving approach or as an entrepreneurial response on the part of the governor to state needs. These accounts have largely focused on single states, and thus have left questions relating to the role of different stakeholders in the formulation of a state's strategy, and to the options considered (and rejected), unanswered and unexamined.

Recent studies by Portz and Eisinger and by Atkinson have adopted com-parative frameworks to address these questions. Each thus offers insights that relate to the role of research universities as actors in the formulation of state programmes as well as to the role assigned to research universities by other parties involved in shaping the state programme. Although sharing several common elements, the two explanations are only partially consistent. More-over, as the number of studies of the origins of state programmes increases, so too do differences in interpretations of events within specific states. Differ-ences are also increasingly apparent in the meaning and (political) conno-tation of terms such as academic, basic and applied research. These differences are carried over into depictions of past events and current perceptions of the responsiveness of universities, particularly research universities, to state objectives.

Examining the increased support provided by state governments to biotech-nology research in the 1980s, Portz and Eisinger offer three models of public policy-making. The first reflects a 'response to public or private interests in the policy community'; the second, decisions evolving 'from a strategic planning process that attempts to capitalize on existing biotechnology resources'; and the third, outcomes that 'may depend upon an initial strategic assessment, followed by an allocation process that responds to interested parties' (Portz and Eisinger 1990: 8–9).

The role of universities is highlighted most prominently in the interest model, where the influence and activities of university administrators and researchers are seen as playing a key role (alongside that of biotechnology firms and federal, state and local officials) in the establishment of the Maryland Biotechnology Institute and the Massachusetts Biotechnology Center of Excellence.

The strategic planning process involved studies by external consultants (Battelle Columbus Laboratories in the case of New York), and internally prepared agency studies (the Department of Commerce in Pennsylvania) both designed to identify selected technologies that if nurtured through additional research and development would spawn increased economic activity in the state. Universities are not directly visible as active participants in the shaping of these plans. This approach emphasizes the identification of key technologies. Modes of support and the role played by universities as performers of R&D constitute the crux of the question on the impact of state S&T programmes on research universities,· and emerge later as implementation issues.

The hybrid model typically involves elements of a strategic planning process, followed by a competitive process in which 'individual and institutional practitioners from all of the targeted technologies vie for funding' (Portz and Eisinger 1990: 16). As related to research universities, Portz and Eisinger note that in this hybrid model, 'scientific merit is an important criterion, but various political factors, typical of an interest model, also play a role' (1990: 17). In particular, geographic considerations play a role in decisions concerning the number of centres created in a state and, relatedly, to the fields of science and/or technology selected for strategic development.

Atkinson offers two distinct patterns of policy-making (Atkinson 1991). 'Business as usual' policy-making is characterized by weak support or even opposition by external groups, including universities; a strong legislative role; little state planning effort; and a 'moderate or minimal commitment to economic development by governors and "policy entrepreneurs".' Such a policy process leads, in Atkinson's view, to low levels of policy effectiveness, as represented by Illinois and Massachusetts. The alternative model, 'active stewardship', involves moderate or strong support from external groups, 'executive, rather than legislative leadership . . . a strong planning effort, and strong commitment to economic development by the governor and policy entrepreneurs' (Atkinson 1991: 34). The outcome of this process is believed to be high levels of policy effectiveness, as represented by Michigan and Pennsylvania.

Atkinson offers several scenarios of the impacts of university pressure on three basic characteristics of state S&T programmes:

1. the total sums spent on university-related S&T programmes
2. the organizational design of the programmes
3. the direction of research.

University pressure is held to have been high in Michigan and New York and to have resulted in the development of several university-related programmes involving large amounts of money on university-based centres of excellence and research grants programmes. In Massachusetts, the pressure exerted by the public universities for new S&T programmes was weak, while the private universities evidenced relative indifference to state support. The result was little concerted pressure on the executive or legislative branches for major new programmes. University pressure in Illinois is viewed as having been dissipated by intense competition among public universities, vitiating efforts to lobby jointly for state support of university-based state technology programmes.

The effect of university pressures on the design of individual state programmes is viewed as being more mixed. Efforts by research universities to channel state support to centres of excellence that addressed sunrise fields of science and technology such as microbiology, robotics, and microelectronics, or to allocate funds through competitive review processes (a strategy that would have led to a concentration of state support in the leading research universities), typically collided with the claims of other universities, public and private, for participation in the new state programmes. In general, the outcome of these deliberations was the incorporation of administrative or procedural provisions that ensured a broader institutional (and geographic) dispersion of funds.

Finally, according to Atkinson, universities have sought to maintain control over the direction of the research being performed by centres or funded through competitive research grant programmes, with the view to 'support basic, rather than more applied research'. New York, for example, is described as a state in which 'the major research universities have consistently and successfully opposed efforts by the state to have the Centers for Advanced Technology pursue a more applied research agenda, which could more easily lead to commercialization' (Atkinson 1991: 37). Pennsylvania's Ben Franklin Partnership Program (as noted above) has been more oriented to applied research and was able to implant this orientation on the programme from its inception. According to Atkinson, 'this difference is due to the fact that policy-makers presented the already designed program to the universities as a *fait accompli*' (1991: 37). Moreover, most universities did not pressure policy-makers to orient the programme to the support of basic research. The exception, according to Atkinson, was the Pennsylvania State University, which unsuccessfully pressured the state to orient the programme to basic research.

I would assert that the interest group approach to state S&T programmes is limited, at least as used to date, because it does not fully identify the sets of interests about which different stakeholders may choose to co-operate or compete (Feller 1990). Similarly, attention to the presence or absence of strategic planning is an incomplete explanation if it does not account for the theories of technological innovation underpinning the state's overall strategy.

As a complementary hypothesis, I would suggest that the more central the involvement of officials from advanced technology firms is in shaping the design of a state's programme, determining awards, and reviewing outcomes, the greater will be the latitude contained in the state's programmes toward support of basic research and graduate education at research universities, the more qualitative will be the standards by which programme success is measured, and the longer will be the period of time over which projected benefits are expected to be realized. Conversely, the greater the involvement of state officials and/or representatives of smaller firms is in the shaping of a state programme, the more likely it is that the programme will emphasize near-term commercializeable outcomes and employment data.

The basis for the hypothesized difference in R&D strategies is simple, if ironic: technology-intensive firms have an interest in having research universities generate a continuing stream of basic/precompetitive research findings. Born from experience, they accept the proposition that R&D is an inherently risky undertaking frequently characterized by unpredictable and delayed benefits. The behaviour of state officials, by way of contrast, is predicated on an emerging school of state development theory that emphasizes entrepreneurial start-ups or spin-offs and the need to demonstrate results within the political tenure of the governor or state official initiating the programme (Allen and Haywar 1990).[4]

Three examples suggest the role of founding coalitions on the shape of state S&T programmes, and thus on the role assigned to research universities.

First, the emphasis on strengthened faculty research and graduate education found in the Massachusetts and Texas programmes, according to state officials, derived from a coalition of representatives from high-tech firms in the microelectronics industry and from universities able to transform the association between basic research and economic growth found in these two states into political and programmatic terms. Merrigan and Smith note that in Massachusetts, 'Unquestionably the most important decisionmaker in science and technology policy is private industry. In Massachusetts, the numerous partnerships among government, industry, and academia have served to link strongly industry leaders and public decisionmakers' (Merrigan and Smith 1987: 75). A prominent feature of the state's strategy to 'encourage the development of the state's science and technology sector' is support of public education: 'University research staffs, faculty, and graduates are a main source of the entrepreneurs who start up the new firms that have played such an important role in the state's economy' (Merrigan and Smith 1987: 75). Most accounts of the origins of the Texas programme trace it to a coalition of legislative leaders, university officials, and industrial leaders (Muller 1987). The prestige of the high-tech industrial leaders and Nobel Prize laureates who actively promoted the need for a state programme, provided a political coalition for the support of a basic research–graduate education orientation to the Texas Advanced Technologies Research Program that has been unacceptable in most other states. The state's successes in attracting the Microelectronics and Computer Technology Corporation, Sematech, and the Superconducting Supercollider – each of which required a demonstration by the state of the research and educational qualities of its universities – reinforced the belief that this strategy was economically productive.

Second, a different intellectual influence is evident in Pennsylvania that may also have been interwoven in other state programmes. David Osborne's (1990) account of new state economic development programmes points to an economic development network of state officials and consultants that influenced the design of programmes in several states. In particular, these individuals sought to shift state economic development activities away from smokestack-chasing toward retention of existing firms and the expansion of new firms. Heavily influenced by David Birch's (1987) findings on the importance of small firms to job creation, they have focused on an entrepreneurial policy and have placed considerable emphasis on the use of commercially oriented academic R&D as the springboard for the formation of new firms. This account is consistent with Atkinson's account of Pennsylvania's Ben Franklin Partnership Program which (as noted above) was presented as a *fait accompli* to university representatives by state officials.

Third, the development of Michigan's extensive array of technology development and technology modernization programmes similarly highlights the difficulties in using the interest group model as a single explanation for a state's programme. Contributing to the formulation of what came to be Michigan's strategy under the Blanchard Administration was a task force headed by the state's Director for Commerce but 'composed primarily of academic researchers rather than corporate, labor and academic leaders' (Jackson 1988: 120). According to Jackson, the academic composition of the task force 'established that the effort would be an objective examination of the state's economy and of how state actions might alter that economy' (1988: 121), rather than as with earlier commissions being comprised of 'prominent corporate, labor and political leaders who arrived with strong, preconceived agendas for altering the state's economy' (ibid.). One consequence of this 'objective' examination by academic researchers was a highlighting of the limited capabilities of research (and other) universities to meet state economic development objectives (despite claims to the contrary by university officials).

The most direct link between research universities and state programmes in Michigan was the Research Excellence Fund. The Blanchard Administration originally proposed a $25 million research excellence fund to be apportioned among the state's four major research institutions (University of Michigan, Michigan State University, Wayne State University and Michigan Technological University) to support projects that would promote economic development. The research fund, however,

was treated as an educational pork barrel by the legislature and about half the funds were redistributed to all state supported colleges and universities, with minimal controls on whether the money was used for research related to economic development. Supplemental appropriations recommended by Blanchard and approved by the legislature subsequently restored some of the money originally intended for the larger research institutions (Jackson 1988: 128).

The Research Excellence Fund has been the cynosure of those who have written about the Michigan experience. In part, it does highlight the tensions inherent in state S&T programmes between state and university objectives and between efficiency and distributive criteria in the allocation of state funds. However, Michigan's economic development strategy, far more so than in other states, has involved the creation of hybrid research institutions, such as the Industrial Technology Institute and the Michigan Modernization Service, that are separate from the university setting. Indeed, Michigan's S&T programmes are most striking because rather than having research universities or other institutions of higher education play pivotal roles in the state's attainment of economic development objectives, the state experiments with new institutions.

Relationship between funding of state S&T programmes and support

What is the relationship between a state's economic development strategy and state financial support of public and private institutions? At the macro-level, a state's capacity to support higher education depends on the vitality of the state's economy; thus public universities have a stake in contributing to the enhancement of state economic growth as a matter of long-term self-interest.

Establishing these programmes often involved the personal endorsement of activist governors, and it is reasonable to assume that state technology programmes meant incremental state funds for universities. However, more specific budgetary relationships are difficult to determine. State funds flow to universities through multiple channels – state expenditures for R&D, academic R&D funded by state and local governments, and state S&T initiatives. Without knowing the extent of the relationship between funding decisions and different programmes, it is not possible to determine the net financial impacts of an S&T programme. At this date, the most that can be said is that decisions are essentially disconnected. For example, based on their survey of S&T programmes in their states, Lambright and Teich write that 'there is little sense of integration among the new "high tech" S&T activities, the old economic development efforts, and broader higher education policy' (Lambright and Teich 1989: 145).

Estimates of expenditures by states for science and technology programmes have been difficult to develop because of the multiple sources of funding for these programmes, the recent origin of many competitive research grant programmes, and the different definitions within states of these programmes (Burton 1989; Minnesota Department of Trade and Economic Development

Table 5.1 Surveys of state S&T-related expenditures

Unit of analysis	Estimates of state expenditures ($1,000)	Financial year
State expenditures for R&D	764,677	1988
Academic R&D funded by state and local governments	1,003,000	1987
State S&T initiatives; 'total state technology budget'	550,000	1988
State technology development programmes; 'annual state government expenditures'	400,000	1987
State S&T agency programme expenditures	203,000	1987
State research grant and contract programmes	143,000	1988

Source: L. Burton (1989). 'Indicators for state science and technology programs'. *Policy Studies Journal* **18**(1): 166.

1988; US Congress, Office of Technology Assessment 1984). Table 5.1, drawn from Laurence Burton's compilation of surveys of state S&T-related expenditures, highlights the fact that, 'in general, the lion's share of state-funded R&D continues to be distributed through the more traditional channel: largely separately-budgeted state appropriations to research universities' (Burton 1989: 167).

The presence of many intervening influences (e.g. per capita income; relationships between absolute levels and growth-rates; election cycles; economic cycles) complicates formal tests between state expenditures for technology development and for higher education. As a first approximation, I used data from the Center for Higher Education at Illinois State University (the 'Chambers–Hines' data) to compute relative rates of growth of state expenditures for higher education. Recognizing the reservations expressed about these series, no relationship can be discerned from 1980 through 1988 concerning total state expenditures for centres of excellence and research grants programmes, on the one hand, and its rank among the states in per capita expenditures for higher education, on the other. Put differently, those states that have been most supportive of technology development programmes (e.g. Michigan, New York, New Jersey, Ohio and Pennsylvania) have not improved their relative position by this measure of state support. (This finding, of course, does not imply that support of higher education in these states is not greater than it would have been if an economic development programme was not present.) Data for 1988–9 pointed to increases in state support for higher education in some of these states (e.g. Pennsylvania, New Jersey – Jaschik 1988), but this appears to be a one-shot occurrence, for by 1989–90 these states' relative levels of support had slipped. Reduced budgets for some of the larger state programmes (e.g. Pennsylvania) are evident in 1990, with intimations that further reductions or threats to programme viability are increasingly likely as most states face austerity in 1991 (New Jersey Commission on Science and Technology 1990).

The bifurcated claim on state budgets that universities now make through separately funded appropriations and S&T programmes is likely to be subjected to increasingly critical scrutiny by budget offices or legislative appropriations committees as state budgetary straits in the early 1990s begin to affect appropriations to higher education (Blumenstyk and Cage 1991). To the extent that state officials look at the total resources flowing into higher education, increases in state dollars that go to universities for activities related to economic development objectives can serve as constraints on the dollars allocated for general institutional purposes. Where such a total constraint is imposed, *de facto* trade-offs will occur between a university's ability to secure increases for its general operations – which include instructional, research and outreach programmes related to economic development – and increases for targeted economic development programmes.

Other sources of tension between the mainstream activities of research universities and state S&T programmes are increasingly evident. These include the relative role of academic and commercial priorities in the setting of R&D agendas in the state programme, the use of state technology development programme support for academic infrastructure, and trade-offs between the funding of academic research through targeted technology development programmes that emphasize economic development, and core appropriations. As Lambright and Teich note in their survey of state science and technology (S&T) programmes:

> The respective roles of the state university and the S&T agency are an issue in most states. Neither state universities nor even private universities are eager to go through a special S&T agency for research funds. They prefer funds appropriated directly (Lambright and Teich 1989: 140).

These strains are already evident. State technology development practitioners have criticized the industry–university research centre model that received nearly 40 per cent (of the estimated $550 million in 1987) of state support of technology development. Echoing this criticism, Osborne has contended that this model 'appears to be seriously flawed'. He says that

> In most such programs, academia is clearly in the driver's seat, and business is not intimately involved in defining the research agenda. As a result, little technology transfer takes place. States watch sizable portions of their investments disappear into new academic research facilities and a stream of academic papers, with little impact on local business and, hence, little impact on economic development (Osborne 1990: 57).

The critique rests on questionable propositions about processes of technology transfer and on the economic interests of the firms that participate in the centres. It is nevertheless indicative of growing pressures upon centres of excellence to identify specific economic outcomes – products, firms and jobs

– that have resulted from prior state investments, which in a select number of states have now entailed expenditures in excess of $100 million. Moreover, the critique suggests that academic and basic have become politically opprobrious adjectives, with research universities likely to suffer most from this development. If acquiesced to, these pressures point state programmes to an ever more developmental orientation, and raise new prospects, particularly at research universities, for dissonance among the interests of state officials, university administrators and faculty.

Also raised in Osborne's critique is the issue of state support of the physical infrastructure for academic research, and implicitly the use of state S&T programme dollars to either directly finance these facilities or serve as leveraging funds to permit the university to seek funds for facilities through another state agency or a federal agency. Several issues are commingled here: the generic need of American universities to modernize physical plant and equipment; the distributive criteria evident in the manner in which 'centres of excellence' programmes were implemented in several states; and the efficiency and political consequences of decentralization.

From the perspective of university officials seeking funds to rebuild and re-equip research and instructional facilities, any state dollar for capital facilities is a good dollar. If state support can be obtained more readily by institutional assertions that a laboratory can contribute to economic development than by hearing generic statements about a research university's need to have state-of-the-art equipment to maintain its ability to train students and attract top rank faculty, then so be it.

The interactions among distributive politics, modernized academic research infrastructure, and the effectiveness of state S&T research support are obvious, but the characteristics of the outcomes have yet to be systematically assessed. Osborne has argued that legislative politics have guided the location of new research centres in a spread-the-wealth-evenly pattern, diluting each centre's impact: 'Because of such lapses, significant state funding has at times gone into the construction of new laboratories and buildings, rather than new relationships with business' (Osborne 1990: 16). Similarly, Lambright and Teich, calling attention to the placement of state-funded centres in each of New York's major universities so that 'all parts of the state are represented', observed that 'Few state governments can resist distributive pressures indefinitely' (Lambright and Teich 1989: 138).

The issue of the optimal number of centres to fund, as well indeed of the optimal number of research awards to make, has yet to be openly addressed in many state programmes. Moreover, state-funded centres have already begun to gain standing as revered local institutions, with strong grass-roots political ties. Dispersion of funds for state S&T programmes among many institutions when such budgets are static may simply add to the number of institutions doing battle within capital corridors.

Adding to the possibility of increased competition between conduits for state appropriations is that the distance between the objectives, interests, and activities of S&T programmes and research universities may be widening.

State technology programmes have their own missions, budgets, personnel and clientele to protect. As they approach eight to ten years of operation, it is increasingly apparent that these programmes have lost their novelty. All have lost the protection of their founding governors: Thornburgh (Pennsylvania), Celeste (Ohio), Kean (New Jersey) and Blanchard (Michigan) have left office. Most have also lost the policy entrepreneur who first headed the programme; several have gone through many rounds of administrative direction. Increasing pressure for demonstrated economic benefits may be expected.

Maturation thus dilutes the special status and treatment accorded these programmes, and highlights the degree to which they appear to be a supplemental channel for state funding of higher education. As states confront budget reductions as part of overall budget retrenchments, state S&T programmes must rebuild their base of political support. Whether this base exists in public research universities is not readily evident. Which appropriations item does the president of a public research university that receives awards from a state technology programme emphasize in presentations before the governor or the legislature's appropriations committee – the state technology programme or the institution's own need for core support? What internal mechanisms of co-ordination and control does a university president use (or need) to assert the institution's priorities for direct general appropriations over other units in the institution more directly tied to targeted economic development programme?

Complicating any assessment of the impact of these several budget battles on research universities are the different interests of public and private research universities. State technology development programmes typically include both sets of institutions in their targeted technology development programmes. As a matter of historical mission as well as contemporary territoriality, public research universities have asserted their comparative advantage as agents of state governments. The high-tech/applied R&D focus of most state initiatives, however, has provided a singular opportunity for private universities, particularly those with strong engineering programmes, to make a strong case for state funds; indeed, officials from universities such as Rensselaer Polytechnic Institute in New York, Lehigh, Drexel, and Carnegie Mellon Universities in Pennsylvania, and Case Western Reserve University in Ohio have been among the most vocal supporters of the state programmes. By way of contrast, universities with an orientation toward discipline-oriented, basic research, in Atkinson's view, 'experienced more conflict'. Falling into this category, according to Atkinson's interpretation, were several premier public research universities: Pennsylvania State University, University of Illinois, University of Indiana and University of Massachusetts.

Research universities and technology transfer

What comparative advantage do research universities have in operating technology transfer programmes, if any? An answer to this question depends on differentiating between 'technology transfer' and 'technical assistance' as these terms are generally used in discussions of state S&T programmes, and on the operational implications of these differences for research universities. In the context of centres of excellence and competitive research grant programmes, technology transfer relates to provisions for the transfer of research findings from university researchers to industrial firms that result in the commercial use of the new knowledge. Implicit in this process is the assumption that the firms contributing to the support of the research have the in-house capability needed to transform academic findings, even if classified as applied research, into commercial products (Mowery 1980).

A thrust toward increased emphasis on technology transfer activities in established centres of excellence programmes is emerging. This emphasis, however, does not obscure the central mission of the centres, which is to generate new knowledge, again most typically under the appellation of either applied research or generic research, that can be absorbed and assimilated by the adopter firms.

A second conceptualization of technology transfer, termed here technical assistance, relates to the upgrading of the technological base of manufacturing firms. Increased attention by states to technical assistance reflects a mixture of strategic and political considerations. Strategically, it is part of a growing national move in the United States toward 'base modernization', that is toward narrowing the gap between 'best-practice' and 'average-practice' techniques in manufacturing (US Congress, Office of Technology Assessment 1990). At the national level this thrust may be seen in the provisions of the Omnibus Trade and Competitiveness Act 1988, particularly the establishment of Manufacturing Technology Centers. The newer state programmes precede this federal government initiative, but derive from a common diagnosis of the obsolescence of the USA's technological base in the face of existing, more efficient technologies, and a common prescription that industrial extension services provide a demonstrated means of modernizing industrial technologies.

Politically, attention by states to manufacturing modernization through technology transfer is a response to criticisms that the centres of excellence and competitive research grant programmes discussed above have produced benefits for a select number of (large) industries (and universities) and urban/suburban areas, and have largely ignored the needs of small- and medium-sized firms, particularly those in non-metropolitan areas.

Technical assistance differs from technology transfer in the type of knowledge supplied and type of firm served. In general, state-supported technology extension services serve small- (150 employees or less) and medium-sized (500 employees or less) businesses. Approximately two-thirds of the firms served by these extension services report that their primary need is to gain access to existing off-the-shelf technology; only one-third report requiring access to new technologies (National Governors Association 1989: 2).

The needs of these firms do not accord well with the activities and incentives of research universities. Indeed, Shapira has characterized the role of universities as a source of technical assistance as follows:

> universities place their highest priorities on research and teaching; with some exceptions, universities have generally allocated few resources to assist technology upgrading in manufacturing. Most university faculty have little industrial experience. Moreover, faculty are generally more interested in working on advancing research frontiers than applying what is already known. . . . When universities work collaboratively with industry, it is usually with larger firms who have both technical and financial resources to share with faculty researchers (Shapira 1990b: 19).

Academic administrators also have called attention to the difficulties experienced by research universities in transferring technologies to small firms within the state (Williams 1986).

The states' current emphasis on technical assistance has thus resulted in a mix of approaches. These approaches in part build upon and expand industrial extension programmes based in land-grant universities, while at the same time experimenting with a myriad of new approaches. For purposes of this inquiry, they share the distinctive common trait of being based either in other academic institutions or in non-academic organizations.

The oldest and best known of the university-based technology assistance programmes are Georgia Tech's Industrial Extension Service (IES), established in 1960, and Pennsylvania's Pennsylvania Technology Assistance Program (PennTAP), established in 1965. Georgia Tech's programme involves a network of regional offices and field staff that provide technical and management information to small- and medium-sized manufacturers. PennTAP is a joint programme of Pennsylvania State University and Pennsylvania's Department of Commerce. Like the Georgia Tech programme, PennTAP employs full-time, professionally trained technical specialists who provide direct assistance to firms. These specialists draw upon their own experience, technical libraries and other sources of information. A more recent example of this approach is the Maryland Technology Extension Service, established in 1983.

The underlying logic of placing industrial extension service programmes within research universities is the putative capability of field staff to draw upon the research or specialized expertise of faculty to augment their own technical knowledge, and to use real world problems as pedagogical exercises for students. The cogency of this logic depends on two overlapping empirical questions: first, do the problems for which firms seek answers require knowledge beyond the capacities of field staff? Second, when they require assistance, when do field staff turn to and receive assistance from faculty? Links indeed do exist between field staff and faculty. Maryland's Technology Extension Service field agents report that about 45 per cent of its cases require them to call upon faculty to provide specialized assistance (Shapira 1990a: 36). Maryland also operates 'a challenge grant program, which matches private and university resources to solve particular firm problems' (Shapira 1990b: 197).

However, the case made for locating state-supported technology transfer programmes within research universities is inconclusive. In part, this conclusion reflects the paucity of systematic evaluations of the cost-effectiveness of industrial extension programmes. More importantly, it reflects increasing recognition that manufacturing modernization requires more than technology alone; instead, it requires a 'broad view of technology needs, including the improvement of work force training, quality control, shopfloor organization, management systems, and inventory control, as well as the use of the machines' (Shapira 1990a: 38–9). Faculty at research universities have little specialized knowledge of these needed skills.

Indeed, recent state initiatives in technology transfer strategies suggest that states are beginning to explore service delivery modes other than those organized about higher education institutions. The major example of a state-based technology modernization programme is Michigan's Modernization Service (MMS). First established in 1985, the MMS is now operated within the Industrial Technology Institute (an independent non-profit organization funded through a combination of state and industrial funding). MMS employs its technical staff and consultants to provide consultation to small- and medium-sized manufacturers. This service includes assessments of a firm's manufacturing, training and market needs.

Other examples of variegated organizational forms of state technical assistance programmes may be seen in Ohio's Technology Transfer Program (OTTO), which employs technology transfer agents based at two-year colleges; New York's Industrial Innovation Extension Service, which works through regional organizations operating under contract to the New York Science and Technology Foundation, with services provided by the staff of these organizations; and Pennsylvania's Industrial Resource Centers Programs, which fund centres organized about discrete technologies intended to transfer existing and new technology to small- and medium-sized manufacturing firms.

Rather than focusing on the existence of alternative models to a university-based technology transfer system, the question to be answered is whether it is in the interest of research universities to endeavour to become actively involved in these programmes if, or as, state economic development programmes place greater emphasis on this role. Land-grant universities, in particular, would appear to be facing choices among comparative advantage, tradition and market share. As shown by surveys of users of technology transfer programmes and the above descriptive vignettes, the configuration of knowledge required by the clientele of these services has only glancing contact with the research activities of research universities. Ties to instructional programmes (e.g. classroom projects, master's essays) are likewise episodic rather than systemic occurrences. In practice, most of the technical assistance is provided by full-time staff whose interaction with academic programmes is limited. Less evident, but likely, is that housing an industrial extension service may be a loss-leading honour for a research university, involving the subsidization through internal university funds of visible, public-service activities at the expense of the less visible foregone opportunities to increase support for academic programmes. Land-grant (research) universities may thus find themselves in competition for leadership with other public institutions, especially state college systems and/or community colleges who see themselves as equally qualified to service the needs of small, locally situated firms and/or state agencies seeking to formulate and administer their own programmes.

On the other hand, land-grant university officials continue to operate in the penumbra of their distinctive historical achievement – the co-operative extension service – and to speak as though technology transfer to manufacturing firms was a (simple) matter of transfer of a tried-and-true model to a new clientele. There are multiple rents in this rhetorical cloak. Links between research performed by university faculty or extension specialists and the knowledge transferred by county extension agents – the functional rather than traditional justification for basing extension within the university – is in fact tenuous in many states. Also, fundamental differences rooted in the character of competitive markets exist between the transfer of technology in agriculture and in manufacturing (Feller 1989).

However, not all land-grant universities are the states' research universities; not all states are committed to a technology development strategy; the historic imagery of the land-grant university role in co-operative extension may readily overshadow more careful inquiry. Thus, for one reason or another, technology transfer may be the role best played by some land-grant universities within a state economic development programme. They may champion such a thrust, particularly if the state is considering its initial strategy or seeking to broaden its existing technology development focus.

Conclusions

For the most part, public research universities were not (visibly) present at the creation of the major state programmes. Where they were, the universities offered programmes that jarred with conventional political pressures for widespread institutional and geographic dispersal of funds, and for short-term state demands for tangible economic benefits. For much of the 1980s, public research universities have hurried to be responsive to the explicit agendas of state governors to promote economic growth. Whether these activities have simultaneously satisfied the dual criteria of relevance to a region's economic needs and to areas of academic excellence is a question yet to be systematically answered.

All research universities confront the fact that their instinctively offered proposition that support of 'generic basic research' and graduate education is an effective way of stimulating technology-based economies, even if valid, is politically unpersuasive. However, the categorization of research – e.g. basic, fundamental, generic, precompetitive, applied, etc. – that permeates discussions of university–state government relationships has been as much a symbolic and political as a scientific matter. Projects are defined and classified in terms of programme eligibility criteria and the time horizons for politically important outcomes rather than in terms of their intrinsic content, or for that matter, whether they were accompanied by industrial funding. Thus, accounts noting that some research universities emphasized basic research in opposition to the orientation of the state's programme, position without co-ordinates, which are the product of the state's technology development strategy. The pronounced near-term, product development orientation of the Ben Franklin Partnership Program, for example, has characterized projects as basic that might have qualified as applied in other states.

To date, private engineering universities have probably gained most from state technology development programmes. These programmes permit private research universities to secure state funds for programmatic development that would otherwise have been difficult to obtain through conventional appropriation processes, and to highlight the public sector's stake in the vitality of private institutions.

The situation for public research universities has been more complex. The same benefits available to private research universities, especially the opportunity to garner incremental state funds and to highlight the contribution they make to key state objectives, of course exist for public universities. Public research universities act in a different political realm than do other state-supported colleges and universities or private universities, however. For public research universities, the gains from technology development programme funds are at stake, and there is a potential for losses in the rate at which general state appropriations are increased. Public research universities must play alongside the state in its game of entrepreneurial economic development because they are less able to gainsay participation in economic development activities that have little to do with academic excellence, and indeed may impair their ability to maintain research and instructional programmes by diverting internal institutional resources and administrative energies.

State S&T programmes offer new risks to public research universities in the context of economic recession and fiscal tightening. State technology development programmes have the potential to serve as politically attractive ways for a state to squeeze short-term technology and economic development gains from relatively small sums by substituting support of these programmes for general appropriations to its universities.

Compounding these political risks is the baneful consequence of the statements by research universities of their accomplishments, capabilities and commitments to serve as engines of state economic growth. These statements reinforce propensities among state officials to allocate funds for targeted programmes rather than for the general operations of public universities. Allusions by state officials to the fact that future levels of support for universities will depend on the relative contribution made by institutions to the state's economic development objectives, have already surfaced (Evangelauf 1986).

Economic development may be a risky face for research universities to feature in their efforts to secure state appropriations because state governments may conclude (with good reason) that investment in other aspects of economic modernization, such as improving labour-force skills, is a more cost-effective approach. A modification in strategy could result in their turning to educational institutions that are viewed as better able to conduct the related programmes. Data on state support of higher education in the two-year 1988–89 period indeed suggest a shift in emphasis that gives an increased role (and financial support) to community colleges in state economic development programmes (Jaschik 1988: A28).

Within the fluid policy created as incoming administrations seek to place their own stamp on state activities, research universities may yet have opportunities to secure a closer match between state technology development strategies and their capabilities. To capitalize on these opportunities, however, requires recognition that excellence in research and instructional programmes and technology development are only partly compatible activities, and that the research university may lose some of itself in its self-depiction as an engine of economic growth.

Notes

1. The linear R&D model is used here as an expository concept; it is not meant to be an analytical depiction of the innovation process. Indeed, contemporary theories of technological innovation emphasize the 'messy' non-linear, multidirectional flow of causation among stages (Kline and Rosenberg 1986).
2. Two of the critical assumptions of the Texas programme are that, first, 'Universities best serve the economic development needs of their state by achieving excellence in their primary missions of teaching, research and public service', and that, second, 'The most important way that universities transfer technology from their laboratories is by educating young scientists and engineers' (Texas Higher Education Coordinating Board 1988).
3. SRI advances this typology in part to point out to universities and colleges the risks of entering into activities they are ill equipped to perform:

   > Some universities may add new functions that are inappropriate for them because of careless initiation of models from different institutions. . . . Others may develop roles that conflict with their missions. . . . Even state sponsorship of research in particular areas of economic importance to the state may conflict with faculty research interests and lead to the politicization of research awards. Increased funding in technical areas may lead to decreased support in more traditional fields (SRI International 1986: 7).

4. As Rees and Lewington have observed, 'the economic gains from such programs can be judged only in the long run, while the short-term concerns of political decision makers may prove to be the death knell of many creative endeavors' (Rees and Lewington 1990: 209).

References

Allen, D. and Hayward, D. (1990). The role of new venture formation/entrepreneurship in regional economic development. *Economic Development Quarterly* 4: 55–63.

American Association of State Colleges and Universities (1989). *Directory of Economic Development Programs at State Colleges and Universities.* Washington, DC: AASCU.

Atkinson, R. (1991). Some states take the lead: explaining the formation of state technology policies. *Economic Development Quarterly* 5: 33–44.

Birch, D. (1987). *Job Creation in America.* New York: Free Press.

Blumenstyk, G. and Cage, M. (1991). Public colleges expect financial hardship in 1991, as budget crises imperil state appropriations. *Chronicle of Higher Education* 9 January: 1ff.

Burton, L. (1989). Indicators for state science and technology programs. *Policy Studies Journal* 18(1): 164–75.

Christman, R. (1988). Testimony before the Senate Committee on Community and Economic Development Concerning the Sunset Audit of the Ben Franklin Partnership Program, 12 July, Pennsylvania General Assembly.

Clarke, M. (1986). *Revitalizing State Economies.* Washington, DC: National Governors Association.

Eisinger, P. (1988). *The Rise of the Entrepreneurial State.* Madison, Wis: University of Wisconsin Press.

Etzkowitz, H. (1983). Entrepreneurial scientists and entrepreneurial universities in American academic science. *Minerva* 21: 198–233.

Evangelauf, J. (1986). Higher education gets $32 billion in state funds. *Chronicle of Higher Education* 33(9): 1, 23.

Fairweather, J. (1988). *Entrepreneurship and Higher Education.* ASHE-ERIC Higher Education Report no. 6, Washington, DC: Association for the Study of Higher Education.

Feller, I. (1984). Political and administrative aspects of state high technology programs. *Policy Studies Review* 3: 460–6.

—— (1988). The transferability of the agricultural extension model. Paper presented at the Appalachian Regional Commission Conference, *Taking Technology Home to Appalachia.* Greenville, South Carolina, 28–29 September.

—— (1989). R&D strategies and state economic growth. Paper presented to the American Association for the Advancement of Science Annual Meeting (January).

—— (1990). University–industry research and development relationships. In Schmandt, J. and Wilson, R. (eds) *Growth Policy in an Age of High-Technology.* Boston: Unwin Hyman.

Ferguson, R. F. and Ladd, H. F. (1988). Massachusetts. In Fosler, R. S. (ed.) *The New Economic Role of American States.* New York: Oxford University Press.

Fosler, R. S. (ed.) (1988). *The New Economic Role of American States.* New York: Oxford University Press.

Geiger, R. (ed.) (1989). *Research Perspectives on Research Universities.* A Report to the National Science Foundation on the Workshop held at The Pennsylvania State University, 14 and 15 April.

Gibbons, M. and Wittrock, B. (eds) (1987). *Science as a Commodity.* Harlow, Essex: Longman.

Goldstein, H. and Luger, M. (1990). Universities as instruments of technology-based economic development policy. Paper presented at the 1990 Research Conference of the Association for Public Policy Analysis and Management, San Francisco, Calif.

Gray, D., Johnson, E. and Gridley, T. (1986). University–industry projects and centers. *Evaluation Review* **10**(6): 776–93.

Jackson, J. (1988). Michigan. In Fosler, R. S. (ed.) *The New Economic Role of American States*. New York: Oxford University Press.

Jaschik, S. (1987). States trying to assess the effectiveness of highly touted economic programs. *Chronicle of Higher Education* 3 June: 19ff.

—— (1988). Spending by states on higher education totals $36.2 billion. *Chronicle of Higher Education* 19 October: A-1, A-28.

John, DeW. (1987). *Shifting Responsibilities: Federalism in Economic Development*. Washington, DC: National Governors Association.

Johnson, L. (1984). *The High-Technology Connection: Academic/Industrial Cooperation for Economic Growth*. ASHE-ERIC Higher Education Research Report no. 6, Washington, DC: Association for the Study of Higher Education.

Kline, S. and Rosenberg, N. (1986). An overview of innovation. In Landa, R. and Rosenberg, N. (eds) *The Positive Sum Strategy*. Washington, DC: National Academy Press.

Lambright, W. H. and Teich, A. (1989). Science, technology and state economic development. *Policy Studies Journal* **18**: 134–47.

Merrigan, K. and Smith, S. (1987). Massachusetts. In Schmandt, J. and Wilson, R. (eds) *Promoting High-Technology Industry*. Boulder, Col: Westview Press.

Minnesota Department of Trade and Economic Development (1988). *State Technology Programs in the United States*. Minnesota: DTED.

Mowery, D. (1980). The relationship between intra and contractual forms of research in American manufacturing, 1900–1940. *Explorations in Economic History* **20** (October): 351–75.

Muller, B. (1987). Texas. In Schmandt, J., and Wilson, R., (eds) *Promoting High-Technology Industry*. Boulder, Col: Westview Press.

National Governors Association (1986). *Promoting Technological Development: The Role of State and Federal Extension Activities*. Washington, DC: National Governors Association.

—— (1987). *The Role of Science and Technology in Economic Competitiveness*. Washington, DC: National Governors Association and the Conference Board.

—— (1989). *Promoting Technological Development: The Role of State and Federal Extension Activities*. Washington, DC: National Governors Association.

National Research Council (1990). *Ohio's Thomas Edison Centers: A 1990 Review*. Washington, DC: National Academy Press.

New Jersey Commission on Science and Technology (1988). *Commission on Science and Technology Quarterly Report*. Trenton, NJ: NJCST.

—— (1990). *Quarterly Report, November 1990*.

New York State Science and Technology Foundation (1986). *The New York State Centers for Advanced Technology*. Albany, NY: NYSSTF.

Osborne, D. (1988). *Laboratories of Democracy*. Boston, Mass: Harvard Business School Press.

—— (1990). Refining state technology programs. *Issues in Science and Technology* **6**: 55–61.

Plosilla, W. (1986). A comprehensive and integrated model: Pennsylvania's Ben Franklin Partnership Program. In Gray, D., Solomon, T. and Hetzner, W. (eds) *Technological Innovation*. Amsterdam: North-Holland.

Portz, J. and Eisinger, P. (1990). Biotechnology and economic development: the role of the states. Madison, Wis: University of Wisconsin-Madison, Robert LaFollette Institute of Public Affairs Working Paper Series, Working paper no. 1.

Randall, E. (1987). CIT's short, turbulent history. *Ronanoke Times & World-News*, 12 April: F 1ff.

Rees, J. and Lewington, T. (1990). An assessment of state technology development programs. In Schmandt, J., and Wilson R., (eds) *Growth Policy in the Age of High Technology*. Boston: Unwin Hyman.

Roberts, E. and Peters, D. (1987). Commercial innovation from faculty research. *Research Policy* **10**: 100–26.

Rogers, E. (1986). The role of the research university in the spin-off of high technology companies. *Technovation* **4**: 169–81.

Schmandt, J. and Wilson, R. (eds) (1987). *Promoting High-Technology Industry*. Boulder, Col: Westview Press.

Shapira, P. (1990a). *Modernizing Manufacturing*. Washington, DC: Economic Policy Institute.

—— (1990b). Learning from state initiatives in industrial extension. *Economic Development Quarterly* **4**: 186–202.

SRI International (1986). *The Higher Education–Economic Development Connection*. Washington, DC: American Association of State Colleges and Universities.

Texas Higher Education Coordinating Board (1988). *Advanced Research Program*, Preliminary Report (June).

Teich, A., Nelson, S., Sauer, S. and Gramp, K. (1990). *Congressional Action on Research and Development in the FY 1991 Budget*. Washington, DC: American Association for the Advancement of Science.

US Congress, Office of Technology Assessment (1984). *Technology, Innovation, and Regional Economic Development*. Washington, DC: US Government Printing Office.

—— (1990). *Making Things Better*. Washington, DC: US Government Printing Office.

Watkins, C. (1985). Technology transfer from university research in regional development strategies. *Journal of Technology Transfer* **10**(1): 51–63.

Williams, J. (1986). University–industry interactions: finding the balance. *Engineering Education* **86** (March): 320–5.

6

The Industrial–Academic Research Agenda

Michael Gibbons

The question of industrial involvement in the academic–industrial research agenda is indeed of primary importance not only for firms and universities but also for national economies. It is clear that the industrialized economies, particularly the advanced ones, are passing through a time of transition which amounts to a major structural change. It would be surprising if, in a change of this magnitude, the relationships between universities and industry were left unchallenged. Changes in these relationships are being driven by the imperatives of international competitiveness on the one hand and by the dynamics of knowledge production on the other.

Industry: the challenge of international competitiveness

The agenda for the developed economies is once again changing and unless one grasps the dynamic which is currently driving industry it will not be possible to appreciate how the industrial–academic research agenda is likely to be modified. Although the new dynamic may take many years to effect its transformation, the result will be, in all probability, to render obsolete much of the institutional structure which currently supports scientific and techno-logical research within nations. The universities in particular will need to adopt novel approaches to both teaching and research if they aim to avoid obsolescence. To grasp the pressures facing industry it will be necessary to look, briefly, at the context of international competitiveness; at the changing nature of manufacturing; at the role of knowledge in the innovation process; and at the changing nature of the entrepreneurial function.

Industry in each of the advanced industrial economies now operates under increasing pressure of international competition. So much so, in fact, that international competitiveness now puts a severe constraint on the ability of national economies to grow. The US economy is perhaps the clearest example of this constraint.[1] Despite investment and the availability of perhaps the world's most highly trained work-force, productivity growth has remained sluggish. The 'productivity paradox' (as it is sometimes called) has been subjected to an intensive analysis by economists and others but there seems no unequivocal explanation of why it is that American industry is unable to commercialize its investments in science and technology and produce high value added products at competitive prices. Governments in many other countries are experiencing the same difficulty as previously solid market positions begin to crumble. There is a huge adjustment taking place in world trade. Not only is the volume increasing but also the number of nations who are now significant actors has increased.[2] What we are experiencing is the (perhaps not entirely unexpected) result of the world-wide diffusion of the industrial mode of production.

To survive under the exigences of international competitiveness requires that firms become involved with and committed to an ongoing process of technological innovation. Those firms prosper who are not merely able to bring products quickly to the market but who can continually develop their technologies in response to evolving needs. Governments also realize that if their own nationally based firms are to be able to perform at this level they must be underpinned by a good infrastructure and a steadily improving level of 'average best practice' throughout industry as a whole.

This much, it seems, is well known if not well understood. The pressure of continuous technological innovation is bringing some unusual features in its train. In particular, managers now realize that sustained profit growth involves moving away from investment in routine manufacturing operations.[3] Value-added comes increasingly from the ability to configure knowledge and competence to meet specialists' requirements. In fact some analysts now agree that competitive advantage lies in being able to assemble specialist knowledge round the production of relatively small batches of high-performance products for increasingly sophisticated markets. In this context the innovation (and hence the profit growth) lies in the insight that connects technological opportunity and market needs. If the insight is going to be more than a bright idea it will involve intensive knowledge of technology and markets as well as their propensities to develop. Innovation, in brief, is becoming more and more about the commercial exploitation of knowledge.

There is involved in this shift in the loans of value-added a major change in behaviour among industrial leaders. Since at least the 1930s, innovation has been conceived within a framework of mass production of more or less standard commodities. Profits were made primarily using the technologies of mass production and Taylorist work organization to drive down unit costs while at the same time increasing throughput. Initially, customers seemed willing to be satisfied with products which were differentiated in rather superficial ways but this has ceased to be so in a wide variety of goods and services. Customers are willing to pay high prices for uniqueness, quality and high performance. Increasingly business opportunities lie in niche markets and niche markets are profitable to the extent that the technologies of batch production can compete with mass production technologies. It remains to be seen if the technologies of flexible manufacturing are capable of providing the stream of productivity gains that mass production ones have supplied over the past several decades.

The point to highlight is the fact that small quantities of highly sophisticated products, whether it be in steel, chemicals or designer jeans is largely about configuring knowledge from highly specialist sources; materials science for steel coatings, nuclear magnetic resonance techniques for fine chemicals, computer-assisted design and manufacturing (CAD/CAM) technologies for jeans. The configuration of knowledge is itself now becoming a specialist skill which extends far beyond that which is conventionally referred to as R&D. Although knowledge generation is not unimportant in this regime the high value is added by those individuals or groups that are able to develop technologies, who can spot a market opportunity and who have the skill and resources to marry the two. Robert Reich refers in this context to the rise of the 'symbolic analyst'.[4] We are not suggesting, as is sometimes done, that mass production industries are doomed; automobiles and videotape recorders (among other things) may always be mass-produced commodities. What we are saying is that the stream of profit-opportunities from these activities is not growing rapidly and that the benefits stemming from them may well lie with the low wage economies. Low wages are not a realistic option for most developed economies. They are constrained to look for innovations that can yield productivity gains in the context of rising wage levels because rising wage levels have always been associated with an increasing standard of living.

Two other points need to be made. First, the method of discovery, whether in science or technology, is now well known. It has been diffused world-wide and the relevant expertise resides currently in hundreds of government research establishments, universities and corporate laboratories. Further, it would appear that in terms of job satisfaction, experts are excited by the prospects of working on challenging projects and exhibit no particular organizational or, more worryingly, national loyalties. Expertise is now a commodity and it trades in international markets in a not very different way from that which characterizes the flows of investment. Second, management in this regime is about how to generate, acquire and manage these 'intangible assets', in much the same way as successful management used to be about managing tangible assets, that is plant, machinery and a large articulated work-force. Firms – even those engaged in routine operations – know that they no longer need to set up R&D facilities to extend their knowledge bases. In fact they can no longer afford to do so, pharmaceuticals being an important exception. Rather, they seek opportunities to share a risk and to spread the burden of costs; they form consortia and joint networks.

In sum, the pressures of international competitiveness, particularly in the advanced industrial economies, has undermined the linear mode of innovation with its *sequence* of operations; research, development, production, marketing and sales. In the new regime these formalized functions are being replaced by transient constellations of skills in the service of linking a technological opportunity and a market need. In this context, what roles are left for universities and government research establishments whose missions were originally conceived as the 'front end' of the innovation process? In particular, what relationship can be established between universities and those firms which compete internationally in the most advanced technological sectors? What would a joint research agenda look like?

Universities: aspects of contemporary knowledge production

Before we go on to answer these questions, we need to examine the knowledge production process as it takes place in the contemporary university setting. Universities themselves have changed significantly since the 1940s. In fact, contrary to popular perception, the better universities have proved to be more flexible in adapting to new modes of knowledge production than many firms and most government bureaucracies. The reason for this lies less in the dynamism of university administrators and more in the fact that the fundamental loyalties of academics lie outside the institutions which pay their salaries and with the peer groups from whom they seek recognition for their ideas, theories, general scientific competence. Since science and technology are themselves dynamic processes, the best academics, if they are to maintain their reputations, must constantly strive to open up new areas; to set the trends in research rather than to tidy up some corners of it. This dynamic is now well established in the university system. Not only does it bring unremitting pressure on the system for resources (money, equipment and space) but also it continually undermines its own mode of organization. Thus, there is little understanding of contemporary science to be gained by thinking in terms of traditional disciplinary labels – physics, chemistry, biology or engineering. In fact, it is not very useful, any longer, to separate scientific and technological activities as if one had priority over the other. We must realize that both scientific and technological ideas make genuine, authentic and significant contributions to the growth of knowledge. We must become more aware that

> knowledge is a matter of knowing how as well as of knowing what, and that accumulation of know-how represents an advance of knowledge just as much as the accumulation of observation and items of information. When we think of the frontiers of knowledge today and the most challenging and significant fields of research, we no longer think of the most basic scientific fields, and of disinterested investigations. We think also of fields like genetic engineering and biotechnology, information theory and information technology, artificial intelligence research, micro-electronics, the science and technology of materials. These and many other important recent fields of work concern themselves not only with general aspects of the world but with specific ordered structures within it. They seek to understand the special features of these structures with a view to predict-

ing and controlling their operations in specific conditions and circumstances. They are concerned to produce knowledge which will guide and inform specific human actions, rather than knowledge generally valid as the basic nature of things. A stock image of knowledge as cosmology or world view, which is of questionable adequacy of course, even when applied to traditional basic sciences, is simply out of the question as a representation of knowledge in these more recent fields: an image of research producing universally valid truths, and technological developments finding uses for these truths, falls apart completely when confronted with the way in which these fields operate. In these fields research produces knowledge in a way directly conditioned by possible applications (just as indeed it has long been produced in fields such as metallurgy and medicine). Clearly, therefore, there is a need for a stereotype of knowledge which stresses its instrumental character; its manifestation as technique, competence, practice; its intimate connections not so much with perception as action. And indeed such a stereotype does seem slowly to be emerging.[5]

In particular, the traditional disciplinary organization of science and technology is breaking down, though for the purposes of teaching it may retain a vestigial usefulness. The organization of scientific and technological activities is being taken over by the dynamics of the subspecialty and the grouping of these subspecialties for relatively limited periods of time around a particular problem – for example the human genome project. As a consequence it is becoming increasingly difficult to separate scientists and technologists by type of activity or to identify them with a particular disciplinary structure. It is often said that scientists are more loyal to their peers than to their institutions. Could it be that they are becoming more loyal to 'the project' than either their peers in their original specialism or their institutions?

Thus contemporary universities, particularly the better ones, are – at least in terms of knowledge production – fairly dynamic entities. This dynamism frequently involves collaboration across specialisms, with research institutions dotted around the world as well as with industry. As long as one believed that scientific discovery constituted the wellspring of technological innovation it was possible to uphold the pretence that all the bright people were in universities, 'doing the fundamental work'. The contemporary organization of knowledge production will no longer sustain this fable. Scientists and technologists collaborate independently of institutional affiliation.

None the less, the idea of the priority of scientific discovery in the innovation process has been difficult to dislodge. It provides, after all, a very simple image of knowledge generation which gives out easily into a number of policy recommendations. The image still enjoys substantial public and political support. In particular, it has been used to develop policies which urge universities to undertake more research relevant to social and economic needs. Universities have responded to these pressures by adding new functions to their traditional one of teaching. Immediately after the Second World War, research in its contemporary sense was institutionalized in universities together with the teaching function and so it remained for a number of years. But latterly new functions have been added: industrial liaison, technology transfer, patenting and licensing, equity participation with industry, continuous education and training. Each of these functions has modified the nature of each university in more or less subtle ways but none so dramatically as in the research function itself. The research portfolio of a contemporary university is a complex animal, fed from many sources and fulfilling a variety of functions from the politically expedient (it is important to be in this area) to the downright utilitarian (we need the money). In this portfolio still lie a more or less small number of grants driven entirely by the curiosity of the investigator.

But the bulk of research carried out in universities is not of these types. It is neither political, nor trivial, nor purely curiosity oriented. Research nowadays is oriented to socio-economic need. And the process of orientation has not been imposed by industry alone but by government with the support of industry. In this sphere, lie the vast number of projects, programmes, clubs, consortia, interdisciplinary research centres, and so on, which carry out research purported to be of social but usually of industrial relevance. Many, but not all of these, are government sponsored programmes that receive funds from industry as a *quid pro quo* for being able to have a say in the formation of the original research objectives. But the basic thrust of these objectives has changed over the years. Originally, the rationale for government-funded research turned on the fact that research was a social good; an investment from which the investor (usually industry) could not capture *all* the benefits and as a result tended to under-invest in it. Governments were persuaded to fill the gaps. Latterly, however, the emphasis has turned much more on providing research support for strategic industries (aircraft, computing, and so on) or for developing generic technologies (microelectronics, molecular biology, information technologies), which underpin a large number of firms or even a whole industry. There is little to be gained from even a summary listing of these 'joint ventures'. The point is that the majority of the programmes are supported in some way or other by industry and they are expected to promote social, economic but especially industrial objectives.

Over the past fifteen years a new category of research – 'strategic research' – has emerged. Strategic research differs from curiosity-oriented research in that problems do not arise entirely from within a discipline; and from mission-oriented research in that the projects are not selected to achieve some specific technical goal. Strategic research is research of whatever kind – long-term, short-term; academic or industrial; scientific or technological – carried out under the framework of a broad technological objective; say, for example, developing the architecture for the fifth-generation computer. Now, strategic research is an interesting entity because it presupposes a framework at the level of national needs which can act as a filter – a programme selector; that filter in most cases is industrial need. The argument for government support for strategic research is not, however, based upon the externalities argument; these industries don't under-invest because they can't capture all the benefits.

It is rather that they could not possibly invest enough to keep pace with international investments in specific areas. In other words, if one government is targeting specific technologies and industries, so too, must all the others if one's competitive position is to be maintained. Strategic areas, then, are intended to shore up or protect a country's competitive position. Inevitably, of course, since everybody is watching everybody else, a policy *ricochet* emerges. Thus, every nation carries out strategic research in new materials, biotechnology and information technologies and one is bound to ask whether the overlap of effort in these areas eliminates any possibility of strategic advantage.

Within the universities of the developed economies there has been since the early 1970s a proliferation of joint university–industry research initiatives. While some of these initiatives aim to solve specific problems, the majority operate at one remove, so to speak, by developing fundamental technologies which it is believed underpin a nation's industrial performance and which will make its firms more competitive in the international market-place. There is, however, a systematic bias in the objectives of the majority of these programmes. For the most part these objectives are devoted to generating knowledge, the presumption being that knowledge, once generated, will find its way into productive use. Alas, this is seldom the case and consequently in most countries but particularly so in the United States, the knowledge generated has not led to improved economic performance. Productivity growth, it seems, is still stagnant. Why? Put simply, knowledge generation is a necessary but not sufficient condition for improved economic performance and the fact is not altered by trying to tailor the knowledge produced more clearly to the needs of the final users. Before knowledge can have any economic impact it has to be diffused into society and for an industrial society this means commercializing the results of scientific and technological research. Thus, universities are relatively good at knowledge generation but relatively poor at diffusing the results of research beyond the region of its immediate peers. Industry, on the other hand, is relatively good at wringing productivity gains in a systematic fashion from its existing knowledge base but relatively poor in adding in a significant way to or replacing its knowledge base. It appears, then, that much of the knowledge generated through strategic programmes is either not commercialized at all or, because the information is relatively freely available, is commercialized by scientists and engineers in other countries that have developed systems for translating information into improved technological performance. The Japanese, it would seem, have developed this latter process into an art form. Diffusion of the results of research is neither an easy nor automatic process. But as long as the linear model of innovation continues to dominate popular thinking and policy-making, the results of research programmes will fall short of expectations. The problem is not a lack of new knowledge but the lack of understanding of what to do with it; how to make the most productive use of knowledge that is already available. There is a systematic deficiency of insight in how to exploit knowledge resources.

The acquisition and management of knowledge resources for the purpose of commercialization is the subject and substance of the notion of technology transfer. Using the linear model of innovation, technology transfer can be interpreted to refer to the transfer of an idea or a prototype from the laboratory to a firm for commercialization. In this model, the universities remain the knowledge generators while industry exploits (or applies) that knowledge to commercial advantage. This rather primitive view is responsible for much of the legalistic writing about ownership of intellectual property; about defining background and foreground knowledge in research contracts; about the balance of royalties that will flow to the inventor from the exploiter. Protection of intellectual property has long been a routine activity for industry but lately it has become a developed function for most universities. For many universities the need to define and defend their intellectual property is not a very high priority. It has rather been forced upon them by the increase in the numbers of research contracts involving one or more industrial partners. A comparatively few universities have moved into the intellectual property business which involves not only protecting intellectual property rights via patents but also vigorously looking for interested clients who might be prepared to purchase this knowledge through licensing agreements. Even fewer institutions have taken the step of becoming actively involved in the commercialization process either by establishing their own companies to exploit technology or by taking equity participation in joint ventures with industry.[6] The benefits to universities of these forms of collaboration are clear enough; an increase in income to both university and the academic inventor as well as the development of a collaborative relationship which offers the possibility of ongoing research contracts. Of course, there are costs of collaboration as well; principally those concerned with industry having an undue or inappropriate influence on academic development within the university. At present, each university is developing its own unique agenda *vis-à-vis* collaboration with industry which reflects its nature, its financial position, and its regional and national ambitions. Apart from any flows of funds consequent upon exploitation of technology, the entrance of universities into the technology transfer business also enhances the diffusion process generally by increasing the likelihood that knowledge generated within its research programmes will be made much more generally available whether it is embodied in patents or licences or more tangibly in new products and processes. It is precisely because of this that industry, from its point of view, would prefer to control the rate and direction of diffusion as long as it can. Yet it is difficult to see how industry can do this effectively and within reasonable cost constraints. As we have been trying to point out, knowledge producers whether they work in universities or industry do communicate with each other. In fact each probably belongs to more than one network of experts which are engaged in trading knowledge in order to be sure that they are kept informed of the latest developments in particular areas. It is hard to envisage how this process can be controlled. Who, after all, is the owner of the intellectual property rights to knowledge and information that is circulating within networks? What are the boundaries of the network; are they geographical or cognitive? Do different networks interact, overlap? Intellectual property considerations are clearly important to the extent that protection of a position conveys some sort of competitive advantage but the flows of information around networks are probably not identifiable in such terms. In fact, to try to control it would reduce much of the necessary variety upon which eventually successful commercialization depends. The extension of the universities into the commercial world through the process of technology transfer is having its main impact less in the proto-products it might generate and more in the fusion of academic and industrial knowledge networks; less in the generation of new knowledge than in the diffusion of what is already known if not necessarily published.

The point we are trying to make is that the processes which organize knowledge production in universities and industry have begun to converge, and the vehicle of convergence is the academic/industrial (professional) network. These networks are relatively transient affairs in which interesting problems and projects do for a time occupy centre stage but then eventually dissolve only to reappear in another configuration. Membership of networks is determined largely by dint of competence. Lack of competence can break the bond of exchange holding a network together by introducing noise into what is in fact a fragile communication system.

We have now come full circle. In the first section, we attempted to indicate that the pressure of international competition on the advanced industrial nations is having the effect of shifting the focus of innovation away from routine production and services. High value added – high profit growth opportunities – lie in the brokering of advanced technological capabilities with sophisticated markets to produce products and services which may never be required in sufficient quantities to take advantage of what has been traditionally called 'economies of scale'. The knowledge/information which will enter into innovations of this type will draw on numerous networks of scientific and technological expertise but will be managed by individuals whose particular skill lies in being able to see the potentialities of this knowledge in the particular market situation. The effectiveness of the knowledge brokers will, to a large extent, be determined by the quality of the infrastructure within which it operates, and this in turn will be influenced by the diffusion processes which enhance average best practice. These diffusion processes are being influenced by the entry of universities into the commercialization process; where increasingly 'commercialization' means transient involvement in projects in which the collective expertise constitutes a 'unique' knowledge resource to be deployed in joining a technological capability to a market need. Because of the mutual interdependence of scientific and technological advance, academics who remain aloof from technological innovation will find themselves excluded from important peer groups to their individual and institutional disadvantage while firms that refuse to broker knowledge will find themselves fighting to gain productivity growth from routine operations that can be easily imitated anywhere in the world.

Policy: the academic–industrial research agenda

There are a number of important implications for policy-makers who will be concerned with the question of industrial involvement in the academic–industrial research agenda. Policy will have to be formulated in the light of an understanding of the environment in which industry now has to operate. That environment is formed by the growth of international competition and involves being able to maintain (or increase) one's international markets through a vigorous process of technological innovation. It is probably not true to say that under internationally competitive conditions prices do not matter, they do. None the less, prices cannot be the single determinate in markets whose characteristics are developing rapidly and where the technology is required to meet those characteristics may themselves be in an experimental stage. It is the uncertain, hence experimental, nature of the innovation process that puts a premium for industry on learning by doing and on the customer for learning by using. To meet the costs of this premium requires industry to generate, acquire and process large amounts of knowledge and information; information which by and large they do not possess and which would be too costly for them to generate internally. It is the growing dominance of the experimental mode of behaviour in most advanced industrial sectors together with the speed of imitation of routine operations that puts a premium on insight and the need to generate high value added products from those configurations of knowledge which can demonstrate a competitive advantage in the international market-place.

Industry's involvement in the academic–industrial research agenda in the future will depend upon the extent to which academics – through their expertise – can make a contribution to the production of high value added goods and services. As explained above, this contribution will be made primarily from the skills and abilities of academics to interact with others in 'challenging projects'. In these projects academics bring knowledge, much of it tacit, that is circulating in various networks to which they belong in virtue of their competence. In these networks there is no longer a significant distinction between science and technology because science is guided not only in part by theory but also in part by the actions upon nature made possible by new technological devices. The 'challenge' in the challenging projects will lie in the ability of academics to work creatively with others who possess distinct competences to weld knowledge into new configurations to meet commercial needs. Now, this will not happen on its own, automatically, as it were. That is why a new generation of knowledge brokers is emerging. Their job is largely heuristic; to see in outline where opportunities might lie and how in general the requisite conditions might be met. However, the conditions will actually be met by experts wielding highly specialized knowledge.

A further policy conclusion to be drawn from this, as far as it affects the academic–industry research agenda, is the need for a new kind of competence.

In brief, we could say that to the traditional academic competence based upon excellence in their specialisms the universities need to add a competence related to the creative use of distinct bodies of knowledge, technical competences and databases. Industry will be seeking not only specialist competence, which, of course, it will always need but also communicational skills of an extremely high order. There is much research to be done, for example, in constructing experiments the data of which can be processed by computers and the results distributed via telecommunication links around networks. The ability to 'handle' these data – that is to interpret them, to fit them into new configurations producing fresh insights and research questions as well as identifying blind spots and blockages – is a creative skill of a high order; some would say of a higher order than generating the results themselves.[7] Industry will be demanding these skills and will support the research programmes where they are likely to be developed.

The dynamics of international competition, then, with their emphasis on management of knowledge resources may call into question the nature and effectiveness of programmes aimed at promoting generic technologies to underpin the manufacturing activities of firms in a wide variety of industries. It is sometimes argued that these programmes are ineffective because they lack sufficient suppleness to meet the needs of specific firms. Much more likely is the fact alluded to above that these programmes are aimed primarily at knowledge generation rather than diffusion. Industry will want to become involved in broad-based generic programmes only if there is some prospect of the generic work being translated into their specific context. Although this is a sensible idea it carries with it the risk that strategic programmes will collapse into a series of development projects for specific industries.

There is also, with the new pattern of innovation, a number of deep-seated problems concerned with the management and protection of intellectual property. These problems are deep seated because they are structural. As we have seen, industry, in the future, will be seeking to involve academics in challenging projects in which the key problems will be concerned with configuring knowledge in novel ways. In such projects it is far from clear what the product is and who owns which particular aspect of it. Eventually, in any case, the knowledge will circulate through a variety of networks substantively but this knowledge or 'experience' will also constitute a real currency – an indicator of competence which will allow continuance in existing networks or perhaps even the ability to join others. The transient nature of each 'challenging project' and the fact that the skills employed on it will eventually be configured in other ways with different competences creates a real problem for industry because they know that to constrain the academics too tightly will prevent their full participation in the networks and hence in delivering the knowledge that might be required. On the other hand, free circulation of knowledge and expertise poses a constant threat in that others may find configurations of knowledge inputs that will undermine their current market position.

The thrust of this argument is that in future the academic–industrial research agenda will be organized around the notion of 'the challenging projects' and that these projects will involve diverse competences. Some of these competences, but only some, will be within the universities. A number of questions remain. 'How will the academic competences be generated in the first place?' 'In what areas?' On challenging projects of a multidisciplinary nature or within traditional specialisms and subspecialisms? These questions pertain more to the *academic* involvement in the developing academic–industry research agenda and will have to wait for another day.

Notes

1. This problem is fully discussed in S. S. Cohen, and J. Zysman, (1987). *Manufacturing Matters: The Myth of the Post-Industrial Economy*. New York: Basic Books.
2. S. Ostry, (1990). *Governments and Corporations in a Shrinking World: Trade and Innovation in the United States, Europe and Japan*. New York: Council on Foreign Relations Press.
3. See, for example, R. B. Reich, (1991). The real economy. *Atlantic Monthly* February: 35.
4. R. B. Reich, (1990). *The Work of Nations: Capitalism in the 21st Century*. New York: Alfred A. Knopf, esp. chs 18 and 19.
5. B. Barnes, (1985). *About Science*. Oxford: Basil Blackwell.
6. I. Feller, (1990), Universities as engines of R&D-based economic growth: they think they can. *Research Policy* **19**: 335–48.
7. J.-F. Lyotard, (1979). *The Post-Modern Condition: A Report on Knowledge*. Manchester University Press, pp. 47–53.

Part 2

The Institutions

7

Research Productivity and the Environmental Context

Mary Frank Fox

Research productivity and publication productivity are not strictly equivalent. Rather, the one (publication) is an indicator of the other (research) – with time lags between the two. It is outcomes of research that are observed; the research is not directly observable. No guarantee exists that a big producer of publications makes significant contributions (or that a given non-publisher makes no contribution), but in the aggregate, the correlation is high between quantity of publications and scientific impact,[1] assessed through awards and citations (see Cole and Cole 1973 on physicists; Blume and Sinclair 1973 on British chemists; Gaston 1978 on British high-energy physicists).

Yet focus upon outcomes (publications) of research is not just a matter of observability or measurability. Indeed, publication is a central social process of science because it is through publication that research findings and results are communicated and exchanged, and that priority of work is established. Unpublished work and informal exchange are also important to the development and communication of knowledge. But informal communication is haphazard, unpublished work cannot be widely assessed, and neither qualify as the *public knowledge* (Ziman 1968) central to science (Fox 1985a). Research becomes certified knowledge (Mulkay 1977: 111) after it is communicated, published and endorsed.[2]

Understandably, then, publication is critical to recognition in science. Scientists sometimes say that the process of research is its own reward, and that they require no further compensation (Hagstrom 1965). One problem with this claim is that the 'significance' and 'importance' of research depend upon the response of the collegial group, that is the recognition of colleagues (Mulkay 1977). The link between research, recognition and rewards is highlighted also in the priority disputes that have raged throughout the history of science (Merton 1973). Being the first, or the second, or the simultaneous party to a discovery does not necessarily diminish the quality of the work process or the satisfaction of the research. But it does determine recognition derived.

Yet relative to the centrality of publication to science, rates of publishing are low. In my national sample of social scientists,[3] the mean number of journal articles published or accepted for publication in a three-year period is 2.4. The number varies by degree granting level of faculty's department, with the mean being 1.1, 1.9 and 3.6 for faculty in BA, MA and PhD departments, respectively. In another national US sample of scientists who received their PhD in 1969–70, the median number of publications per scientist over the entire (1969–79) decade was 10 (10.33) in biochemistry, 5 (4.81) in physics, and 8 (8.14) in zoology (Porter *et al.* 1982). These levels of publication are corroborated by other investigations both within and between fields (see Cole and Cole 1973; Ladd and Lipset 1977; Reskin 1977).

However, while overall levels of publication are low, the variation in publication among scientists (and scholars in other fields) is very high (see Allison and Stewart 1974; Cole 1979; Cole and Cole 1973; Gaston 1978; Reskin 1977). Whether one looks at publication over a year, a five-year span, or a professional lifetime, productivity varies enormously. What the distribution looks like is this: low, even null, performance is most frequent, and high, or even moderate, performance is rare. To put it another way: the distribution of publication productivity is strongly, positively skewed, with a few producing most of the work and the majority publishing little or nothing.

Thus in my sample, 40 per cent did not publish a journal article in a three-year period; if we include articles published or accepted for publication, 36 per cent published nary an article. In another sample of social and natural scientists, 53 per cent failed to publish a single paper one or two years after the doctorate – which are traditionally prolific years for scientists (Cole 1979). In most years, 70 per cent of the scientists published nothing. Likewise, following the careers of chemists throughout the first decade after the PhD, Reskin (1977) found that (except in one year) more than 60 per cent did not publish in a given year, and 15 per cent of the chemists contributed one-half of the total (2,000) papers published over the decade.

Documenting publication productivity is one thing, and explaining it quite another. The differences in rates and variation may be clear; the explanations are not. The variation in publication productivity is one of the most perplexing problems in the sociology of science.

In explaining publication productivity, personal traits and dispositions such as motivation, stamina, or perceptual and intellectual style play a part (Fox 1983). But these characteristics do not exist in a vacuum; and such factors alone do not account for published productivity. No direct relationship exists between productivity and measured creative ability (Andrews 1976) or intelligence (Cole and Cole 1973), for example. Rather, these individual characteristics are strongly influenced by the social and organizational setting in which they exist. Thus, creativity does not result in scientific productivity, unless scientists are able to exercise power and influence over decisions in their units (Andrews 1976). Since scientists (as well as scholars in other fields) are a highly select group to begin with, it is understandable that their personal characteristics – ability, intelligence – are not nearly as unequally distributed as productivity and thus that traits and talents are an insufficient explanation for performance.

Fundamentally, it is difficult to separate the performance of individual scientists (or scholars) from their social and organizational context (Fox 1991). Work is done within organizational policies and procedures. It relies upon the co-operation of others. It requires human and material resources. Further, the scope and complexity of research and the use of advanced technology in science, in particular, have heightened reliance upon facilities, funds, apparatus and teamwork. In this way, science is essentially more 'social' than the humanities. Compared to sciences, the humanities are more likely to be performed solo rather than as teamwork; to be carried out in the absence of equipment and instrumentation; to require modest funding; in short, to be more self-sufficient enterprises.

Institutions do not do research; individuals do. But institutional conditions affect productivity. Productivity is tied to the organizational environment of work – the signals, priorities, human and material resources that provide the ways and means of research (Fox 1991). The notion of academics in spontaneous intellectual creation outside of administrative or organizational frameworks is simply illusory (Blau 1973). Research is a social process. And so is research productivity.

In the association of institutional environment and productivity, it is true of course that selectivity factors can operate so that more productive persons are recruited to more resourceful and prestigious settings. However, longitudinal studies, which have monitored publication histories over time and between locations, indicate a stronger causal effect of location upon productivity (rather than vice versa).[4]

Long (1978) reports that while the effect of publication upon prestige of location is weak, the effect of location upon productivity is strong. For academics moving into first position, publication is not immediately affected by location; rather, it is affected by early, predoctoral location. However, after the third year on the job, productivity is more strongly related to prestige of department than to previous predoctoral publication. Specifically, those in prestigious departments increase their publication and those in less prestigious settings publish less.

In a subsequent study, Long and McGinnis (1981) extend these analyses beyond prestige of academic department to the effects of larger organizational contexts – the research university, non-research university or four-year college, and non-academic or industrial sectors. The chance of obtaining employment in a context is unrelated initially to publication level. Once in the job, however, publication comes to conform to the context – but only after three years in the location. The fact that it takes some time for the new location to take effect suggests that productivity levels are not simply a result of changes in the individual's goals or global barriers to publication in some settings.

However, while establishing a relationship between context and productivity, this does not tell us how environment operates, how some settings (particularly prestigious ones) facilitate and others obstruct productivity. We need to look more closely at social and organizational processes. First, we must consider how factors such as collegial interaction, collaborative opportunities, work climate, diversity of activities, and resources affect productivity. Second, and this is more subtle, the same institutional setting (major research university, minor research university, or liberal arts college, for example) may, in fact, offer different constraints and opportunities for one group compared to another – gender, racial or age groups, for example. A bias in previous work lies in the presumption of uniform effects, the presumption that a given type of environment presents the same conditions across various groupings of faculty. I argue that environment does not necessarily operate neutrally or uniformly.

How, more specifically, does environment mediate productivity?

First and fundamentally, productivity is influenced by the orientations and activities of one's colleagues as well as one's own. It is not a matter of collegiality influencing productivity, but rather of *research-based* collegiality, the company of persons who inhabit a shared 'normative world' (to use Salaman's phrase – 1974: 26). Collegial exchange on research problems and discoveries stimulates involvement by testing ideas, activating interests, and reinforcing the work. To be a participant in such a collegial group, one must have an active research programme and be able to share in discussions about research (Blau 1973: 113). Under these conditions, social rewards (membership, recognition, respect) hinge upon research involvement – and the scientist is deprived of the one without the other.

The more prestigious departments presumed to provide a context favouring productivity do have stronger patterns of such collegiality. In my survey, a big dividing point is between BA and MA compared to PhD granting departments. In the latter, faculty are more likely to speak with colleagues about research, to report a primacy of work (compared to leisure or other facets of life), and to cite the importance for themselves of obtaining (or maintaining) national recognition.

Collegiality is important because scientific work, more so than that of other fields, relates to, builds upon, and extends existing knowledge (Garvey 1979). The productive scientist must continually shape his or her work, assess its significance, and update its potential contribution. This takes place informally and interactively – both in and out of the local setting. But ongoing, face-to-face contact within the work-place serves a special function: It helps provide ideas, catch errors and stimulate development (see Pelz and Andrews 1976). It provides room for speculation, retraction and immediate feed-back on failures as well as successes. Thus, factors such as size of department, number of active researchers, and numbers within subareas become important as they influence possibilities for communication and exchange.

Related to collegiality and in turn, to productivity, is the matter of collaboration. Collaboration is important because independent research is difficult to initiate, sustain and fund, and because solo authors are handicapped in their rates of publication and probably their rewards. Thus for those in my sample who published at all in the previous three years, the correlation is high (0.79) between the total number of articles published in refereed journals and the number published in collaboration.

In scientific fields, co-authored papers are more likely to be accepted by journals than are single-authored papers (Gordon 1980). This may be due to a number of factors, including the greater tendency for co-authored papers to result from funded compared to non-funded projects (Heffner 1981) and to be experimental rather than theoretical pieces, which are, in turn, easier to review and presumably accept (Meadows 1974; O'Connor 1969).

Beyond this, co-authorship can provide a means of checking and monitoring. Thus an examination (Presser 1980) of papers submitted to a major social psychology journal showed that while co-authorship may do little to produce superior papers, it helps avoid very bad ones with outright errors. Accordingly, co-authored papers are more likely to be cited and to be more visible – at least in the sciences.

At the same time, numbers of factors about collaboration and productive alliances are not well understood (Fox and Faver 1984; Fox 1985b). For example, are parallel or divergent approaches, skills and perspectives of colleagues more effective for research productivity? How do factors of colleagues' rank affect collaboration – that is what are the costs and benefits of peer compared to more junior–senior alliances? Is it better to have a few significant collaborators working on a problem or a more diverse but diffuse team? And how do each of these factors vary by discipline? Furthermore, since collaboration is both a means to and an indication of involvement in the scientific community, a causal problem remains: to what extent is collaboration prior to or a consequence of productivity?

A more diffuse environmental issue as it relates to productivity is that of work climate. Climate of a work-place is something like personality for a person. It refers to the perceived and experienced qualities of the environment, along such dimensions as organizational competence, responsibility, practicality, impulse and freedom. Organizational climate can activate interests, convey standards and arouse (or deflate) needs for achievement.

Most of what we know about work climate and scientific productivity derives from industrial, governmental and agency (rather than academic) settings. In these settings, productivity is higher where scientists are free to select, initiate and terminate their own research (see Box and Cotgrove 1968; Pelz and Andrews 1976; Vollmer 1970). Further, in scientists' own subjective impressions about conditions that support productivity they stress freedom and autonomy (see Parmerter and Garber 1971). And creative researchers, especially, emphasize the importance of 'loose rein' and 'loose structure' in their work-place (Gantz *et al.* 1969).

The academic work-place differs from other organizational settings, in that members tend to have greater autonomy, as well as greater diversity of activities and frequently, conflict of demands (teaching, administration, research). Yet academic settings are not constant, and it is important to understand how factors such as organizational freedom, degree of group co-ordination, and style of administrative leadership both vary and affect productivity in academia.

Interestingly, productive outcomes may not necessarily be situated in comfortable climates. In my sample of social scientists, mean levels of productivity rise with degree granting level of the department – BA, MA, PhD. Yet faculty in higher (particularly PhD) compared to lower degree granting departments are significantly more likely to characterize their departments in ways tense rather than comfortable: as cold, unjust, intolerant, unfriendly, unhelpful, competitive and even as irresponsible. At the same time, faculty in higher compared to lower degree granting departments also characterize their settings as significantly more strong, scientific and creative.

Along with these aspects of collegiality, collaboration and climate, environment influences productivity through the availability (or unavailability) of material resources. In science, particularly, instrumentation, space, computing facilities, stipends for assistants, journal holdings, budgets for phone, and money for travel are basics, not frills. Yet across academia, faculty express strong misgivings about their work environment with complaints of 'too little office and laboratory space, woefully obsolete equipment, inadequate supplies, far too little clerical support. . . . and travel funds preposterously low' (Bowen and Schuster 1985: 156).

These misgivings represent, of course, faculty *perceptions* about resources. Perceptions about the availability of resources and objective (department, unit or institutional) availability of resources do not necessarily go hand in hand. I find in my sample that correlations are positive, but only moderate, between faculty's subjective appraisal of the quality of resources and the objective indicators of resources within their institutions. Specifically, the correlations between faculty's subjective ratings of quality of resources and the objective institutional resources indicated by levels of endowment, revenues, research expenditures, and library volumes are, respectively, 0.13, 0.22, 0.24 and 0.23. Given my argument that environments do not operate uniformly across categories of faculty, the modest correlations become understandable; the same environment can provide differential opportunities and resources.

All of this – both the human and material resources of the environment – has consequences for equity as well as performance. Productivity differences increase with career age: as scientists age, the productivity differences between them get greater and greater. But the mechanisms that generate the pattern are poorly understood. The perspective of cumulative advantage has it that scientists who experience early success are able to command increased time, facilities, and support for continued research. Once these rewards are established, they have an independent effect upon the acquisition of further rewards, so that the rich get richer and the poor get poorer. Although this perspective is appealing, tests of it are difficult. They require data on scientists' productivity and resources – assistance, funding, collegial and collaborative networks – over time. These data have been largely missing and their utility depends upon understanding of the environmental mechanisms that mediate productivity.

In summary then, research productivity and publication productivity are not strictly equivalent, but the one is an indicator of the other. Moreover, because publication (an outcome of research) is a central social process of science, it is worth the attention. Yet what we know conclusively about publication productivity is precious little: the rate is low and the variation is high. Individual factors (abilities, motivations, etc.) play a part, but these characteristics do not exist in a social vacuum and such factors alone do not account for publication productivity. Fundamentally, it is difficult to separate the performance of an individual scientist from his or her social and organizational context – the work-place as well as the larger collegial community that is or is not accessible.

The argument that more prestigious settings facilitate and less prestigious obstruct productivity is valid to the extent that the correlation is positive between scientists' productivity and prestige of location. But this tells us little about mechanisms that might account for the relationship, and it tends to carry a presumption about uniform effects of given types of locations. Thus, I look more closely at social and organizational factors such as collegial interaction, collaboration, work climate, and resources (as well as type of research, departmental reward structure, teaching load and type, work interests and work habits – not addressed in this chapter). Understanding performance – and the distribution of equity – depend upon increased clarity about the environmental mechanisms that mediate productivity in research.

Notes

1. Throughout, the focus is upon sciences and social sciences in academia, these being both the subject of my work (supported by the National Science Foundation, SES-850851) as well as most of the data in sociology of science. In this chapter I do not address arts, humanities and other fields in higher education, unless so indicated.
2. This is not to overlook alternative (less manifest) functions of publication (Fox 1985b). By reinforcing standards of success, the reward structure of publication can perpetuate intellectual hegemony. It can also function to control junior members of the academy, disguise power struggles, and justify decisions that are non-merit based. And perhaps most significantly, publication helps support faculty control of the university. Because research originates with faculty and is evaluated by peers, the faculty gain an authority over each other that outsiders cannot exercise.
3. The data come from a survey based upon a national random sample of US faculty, stratified by social science department (economics, political science, psychology, sociology), degree granting level of department (BA, MA, PhD) and gender. This sample of faculty was surveyed by mail in up to four repeated mailings in 1986–7. The survey resulted in a response rate (excluding ineligibles) of 69 per cent – 2,560 people.
4. Studies of other groups and settings (non-academic and non-scientific) also show that structure is logically prior to individual attainment (see Baron and Bielby 1980). Yet attainment research and theory have treated individual performance and

careers as relatively independent of the organizational structure in which individuals are employed, that is the size of the firm, the sector of the labour market, and the organization of the work (relations among people, places and objects).

References

Allison, P. and Stewart, J. (1974). Productivity differences among scientists. *American Sociological Review* **39**: 597–606.

Andrews, F. (1976). Creative process. In Pelz, D. and Andrews, F. (eds) *Scientists in Organizations*. Ann Arbor, Mich: Institute for Social Research (revised edition).

Baron, J. and Bielby, W. (1980). Bringing the firms back in: stratification, segmentation, and the organization of work. *American Sociological Review* **45**: 737–65.

Blau, P. (1973). *The Organization of Academic Work*. New York: John Wiley.

Blume, S. S. and Sinclair, R. (1973). Chemists in British universities: a study of the reward system in science. *American Sociological Review* **38**: 126–38.

Bowen, H. and Schuster, J. (1986). *American Professors*. New York: Oxford University Press.

Box, S. and Cotgrove, S. (1968). The productivity of scientists in modern industrial research laboratories. *Sociology* **2**: 163–72.

Cole, J. (1979). *Fair Science: Women in the Scientific Community*. New York: Free Press.

Cole, J. and Cole, S. (1973). *Social Stratification in Science*. Chicago: University of Chicago Press.

Fox, M. F. (1983). Publication productivity among scientists. *Social Studies of Science* **13**: 285–305.

—— (1985a). Introduction. In Fox, M. F. (ed.) *Scholarly Writing and Publishing: Issues, Problems, and Solutions*. Boulder, Col: Westview Press.

—— (1985b). Publication, performance, and reward in science and scholarship. In Smart, J. (ed.) *Higher Education: Handbook of Theory and Research*. New York: Agathon.

—— (1991). Gender, environmental milieu, and productivity in science. In Zuckerman, H., Cole, J. and Bruer, J. (eds) *The Outer Circle: Women in the Scientific Community*. New York: W. W. Norton.

Fox, M. F. and Faver, C. (1984). Independence and cooperation in research. *Journal of Higher Education* **55** (May/June): 347–59.

Gantz, B., Stephenson, R. and Erickson, C. (1969). Ideal research and development climate as seen by more and less creative research scientists. *American Psychological Association Proceedings 1969*: 605–6.

Garvey, W. (1979). *Communication: The Essence of Science*. Oxford: Pergamon Press.

Gaston, J. (1978). *The Reward System in British and American Science*. New York: John Wiley.

Gordon, M. D. (1980). A critical reassessment of inferred relations between multiple authorship, scientific collaboration, and the production of papers and their acceptance for publication. *Scientometrics* **2**: 193–201.

Hagstrom, W. (1965). *The Scientific Community*. New York: Basic Books.

Heffner, A. (1981). Funded research, multiple authorship, and subauthorship collaboration in four disciplines. *Scientometrics* **3**: 5–12.

Ladd, E. C. and Lipset, S. (1977). Survey of 4,400 faculty members at 161 colleges and universities. *Chronicle of Higher Education* 21 November: 12; 28 November: 2.

Long, J. S. (1978). Productivity and academic position in the scientific career. *American Sociological Review* **43**: 899–908.

Long, J. S. and McGinnis, R. (1981). Organizational context and scientific productivity. *American Sociological Review* **46**: 422–42.

Meadows, A. J. (1974). *Communication in Science*. London: Butterworths.

Merton, R. (1973). Priorities in scientific discovery. In *Sociology of Science*. Chicago: University of Chicago Press.

Mulkay, M. (1977). Sociology of the scientific research community. In Spiegel-Rosing, T. and Price, D. (eds) *Science, Technology, and Society*. London: Sage.

O'Connor, J. G. (1969). Growth of multiple authorship. *DRTC Seminar* **7**: 463–83.

Parmerter, S. M. and Garber, J. D. (1971). Creative scientists rate creativity factors. *Research Management* **14**: 65–70.

Pelz, D. and Andrews, F. (eds) (1976). *Scientists in Organizations*. Ann Arbor, Mich: Institute for Social Research.

Porter, A., Chubin, D., Rossini, F., Boeckman, M. E. and Connolly, T. (1982). The role of the dissertation in scientific careers. *American Scientist* **70**: 475–81.

Presser, S. (1980). Collaboration and the quality of research. *Social Studies of Science* **10**: 95–101.

Reskin, B. (1977). Scientific productivity and the reward structure of science. *American Sociological Review* **42**: 491–504.

Salaman, G. (1974). *Community and Occupation*. Cambridge: Cambridge University Press.

Vollmer, H. M. (1970). Evaluating two aspects of quality in research program effectiveness. In Cetron, M. J. and Goldhar, J. D. (eds) *The Science of Managing Organized Technology*, vol. IV. New York: Gordon & Breach.

Ziman, J. (1968). *Public Knowledge*. Cambridge: Cambridge University Press.

8

Constraints on the Individual Researcher

Maurice Kogan and Mary Henkel

There are classic statements, usually autobiographical, of the triumphs and trials of the individual academic researcher; the self-advertising account of Arnold Toynbee in his book-lined study, James Watson's *Double Helix* saga (1968), C. P. Snow's *The Search* (1958). But all are cast within the traditional frame of academic work in which deference to Academic Plans, performance measurement and cost centres had no place. Researchers were admitted to the academic freehold in order to move to their own rhythms. This was of course a beau ideal saying nothing about the deference expected of juniors in some tightly autocratic departments or research teams. In the present environment we have to move forward to ask whether the freedom from constraint in the ideal model is essential to good research work.

In this note we set down two sets of linking considerations. First, what are the arguments for individual freedom from constraints for the researcher? Second, what in fact are the constraints that operate and to what effect?

The first set of considerations can be organized again under two heads. First, there is the principled argument that the disinterested pursuit of knowledge – the highest achievement of the academic and that which differentiates him or her from the other knowledge mongers – must be unconstrained in the choice of subject, in the methods used and in the use of results, if the academy is to be fearless and politically untrammelled in what it seeks to investigate.

The second argument in favour of freedom from constraint is that it is essential to high-quality work, that as a matter of work organization research cannot make its singular contribution of testing and improving on old concepts and knowledge if it is restricted by other groups setting its purposes and modes of working. This is the argument for deficiency as opposed to contract-based grants, and for security of tenure.

What are the constraints? They might first result from the setting of objectives. Whereas previously objectives were a matter for the researchers, who might be required to justify them when seeking grants, but who might have never needed to seek grants anyway, statements of overarching objectives arranged in priority order, forming part of academic plans, are required now by the two British funding councils. The defining characteristic of the new arrangements is that objectives will be set outside the researcher level itself, no doubt partly through a process of negotiations, but with deference to recent government prescriptions in favour of research that forms part of a strategy and is geared to economic objectives. It is right to recall that in the immediate post-war period the British UGC expressed strong doubts (UGC 1953) about money reaching universities from government rather than from private benefactors or the UGC itself, presumably to ensure that researchers would continue to be in command of their own objectives.

But the slide into dependency must not be laid wholly at the door of the most recent cohort of heroic ministers and the co-opted academics who implement their policies. The intrusion of exogenous objectives came earlier and as part of a largely negotiated process. It was in the 1960s and 1970s that higher education became thoroughly habituated to undertaking mission oriented or sectorally determined research. Social science academics began to catch some of the positivistic fervour that, following in the wake of the Johnsonian Great Society in the USA, reached Britain as belief in research on community development, the cycle of deprivation, and many other programmes in the areas of public policy. So too there were massive increases in medical and scientific–technological research that government or private industry was prepared to finance. In fact the MRC successfully saw off the DHSS when they attempted, following the Rothschild Report (1971), to assert the objectives for research in some of the clinical areas covered by the policy of transferring research council monies back to government departments. But the trend generally was for negotiated accommodation between academia and sponsors.

Intrusion in the setting of research objectives by outside agencies must be taken case by case. In economics for example there is some evidence (Boys *et al.* 1988) that even leading applied research groups feel they must undertake research that is conceptualized as acceptable to policy-makers whose views are anticipated carefully by research councils. So labour economics might shift attention from trade unions' interests to personnel management. It is very unlikely, however, that in the most traditional disciplines work on theory or pure scholarship is affected except by the increased burdens caused by stop stills in staff recruitment, by the extra students who must now be taken and by some shortages of money. It is the laboratory subjects which have complained loudest and their complaints have been well certificated by the usually deeply loyal Advisory Board for Research Councils. In physics appointments have been made in deference to areas likely to be favoured in the market-place of sponsorship rather than by a strict ordering of the academic merits of those applying for jobs, as used to be the case in our most esteemed institutions.

Nor have such influences been merely percolative. The government-led research advisory system, increasingly responding to steers from machinery located in the Cabinet Office rather than in the Department of Education and Science, has promulgated support for 'strategic research', that is research which is still fundamental but also discernibly likely to have an economic pay-off. This is a concept not familiar to the world of science; a defining characteristic of fundamental research is that its objectives are set by researchers whose whole motivation is towards the development of theory that is required by the demands for conceptualization put up by their disciplines. Strategic research demands, it would seem, a placing of the instrumental horse before the academic cart.

Yet, there are areas where degrees of contamination by outside reference groups might be beneficial or unavoidable, even to the individual seeking freedom. A great deal can be made of the difficulties encountered in social science contract research. Certainly some public sponsors are becoming cheekier in demanding quite mechanistic pieces of operational or survey research for which tiny financial and virtually no academic rewards are visible. But judging from our direct experience of a great deal of work for government, departments may be far less prescriptive about objectives than are research councils. Moreover, policy-makers can often present a problem which throws up taxing conceptual issues. They may also give access to a world unavailable to researchers working alone. And often they want researchers to help them define the objectives of the research which will help them assay their policy problem. At their best they can serve as a living laboratory and supportive reference group. So far from being obtrusive, the common experience is that having commissioned the research they then feel they have done their bit for culture and science and ignore it; the DES, the British Ministry for Science, is the lead example here, possibly because it can rely so heavily on the incomparable wisdom of HMIs.

A further set of constraints, well observed by Jennifer Platt (1976), is more indigenous to certain forms of research. Researchers working in teams most usually divide between the grant-holders, usually tenured teaching staff, and research workers on a contract of anything between six months and five years. Multiple constraints might then be evident. The whole group can be forfeit to the judgement of the funders if continuation is sought and that pressure compels all concerned to look to visible productivity, within the prestructured terms of reference of the contract. The relationship of untenured temporary staff to their tenured directors will vary from what some regard as unalloyed peonage, to ethical concern for junior staff's academic future and for their adequate training.

In cases of team work depending on grants and contracts, managerial dependency might derive from the exogenous pressures. In some major departments in the 'hard sciences' or technologies, however, team research is nearer business as usual so that the justification for controlling the individual free spirit would have to rest on the functional need for shared objectives and work programmes. Splitting particles is unlikely to be an individualistic business. But that need not be the end of the argument. Even when external sponsorship or the nature of the research demands strong deference to collective norms the seniors can involve the juniors in decision-making, and encourage them to work out their individual schemes of publication. This is all the more important at a time when many able researchers cannot get established academic jobs.

Other constraints on the researcher might result from the expectations of institutions whose priorities are certainly being affected by the need to present both plans and outcomes for funding body review. At the extreme an institution could deem individual researchers' plans unlikely to yield benefit in its dealings with a funding council and discount their research activities by increasing their teaching and administrative load and decreasing their research resources. We can quote no such cases but such practices would be within the new planning logic. Universities are explicitly enjoined to be selective in handing out resources for research. What else can such an injunction mean? The researcher is in any event constrained by the kind of outcome accountability induced by performance indicators. In one institution (and maybe others too) departments lose money if even a single member of staff has failed to publish research over the last three years. As a result the modes of production could change; historians might produce many articles instead of a few long books. Articles could be broken up.

The training of individual researchers is relevant to our theme. The tendency is towards a more discernible and uniform structure for research training in place of the near anarchy that has ruled until recently. There are pressures to reduce the length of doctoral training to a maximum of four years. There are less contestable attempts to make the training sequence more systematic and reliable. There have been fluctuating fortunes for the notion that doctorates should be awarded on a combination of systematic courses and a dissertation. For the most part these attempts can be seen as moves towards the stronger professionalization of research and thus likely to strengthen the capacity of individuals to hold their own in an environment which has become tougher, both in terms of employment and opportunity and in terms of the standards demanded.

Finally an associated area is whether the knowledge rules, epistemologies, are altered if the constraints referred to here are felt. Elzinga (1985) has elegantly depicted the dangers of 'epistemic drift'; we feel, however, that he is mainly referring to external intrusions on objectives and the use made of the outcomes. His particular point was that the criteria for assessment will be set up by the sponsors. This might affect the inner knowledge rules – of logic, quality of evidence and the like – but could be restricted to objectives and outcomes rather than methods or epistemologies as such.

In part, we have already discussed the point from the perspective of certain areas of social science. In those areas where problems important to society are set, and where the testing is pragmatic rather than rigorously scientific, e.g. conceptualizing delivery systems in health or education or social services, the academic will collect the evidence and cases and apply logical tests to them, perhaps to discover the logical consistency of different objectives and their relationship to the actions mounted and systems established. But parallel reference lines will be drawn inasmuch as reference groups from practitioners and policy-makers will test the findings in terms of feasibility and the exercise of power. This process must not disturb the knowledge rules of the researcher but a dual epistemology, a second set of truth criteria, may then be introduced.

That these might be constraining for the researcher need hardly be doubted. It will cause epistemic drift if the researcher allows the social pragmatism to outweigh the research logic. Evaluation can involve the exercise of authority. The location of that authority, peer group or sponsor, is critical to the individual researcher.

We have based this note on personal observation and surmise but we hope that a challenging field of study is opened up by it. How far will the new patterns of funding and planning affect researchers' ability to select their own objectives; how far will the balance of subjects studied be changed as a result; will the basic knowledge rules, of evidence, logic and relevance change, as Elzinga has implied? And, finally, who will care if they do?

References

Boys, C. J., Brennan, J., Henkel, M., Kirkland, J., Kogan, M., and Youll, P. (1988). *Higher Education and the Preparation for Work*. London: Jessica Kingsley.

Elzinga, A. (1985). Research, bureaucracy and the drift of epistemic criteria. In Wittrock, B. and Elzinga, A. (eds) *The University Research System: The Public Policies of the Home of Scientists*. Lund, Sweden: Alnqvist and Wicksell International.

Platt, J. (1976). *Realities of Social Research: An Empirical Study of British Sociologists*. London: Chatto & Windus for Sussex University Press.

Rothschild Report (1971). *The Organisation and Management of Government Research and Development*, Cmnd 4814. London: HMSO.

Snow, C. P. (1958). *The Search*. London: Macmillan.

University Grants Committee (1953). *Report on the Years 1947 to 1952*. Cmnd 8875. London: HMSO.

Watson, J. D. (1968). *The Double Helix: A Personal Account of the Discovery of the Structure of DNA*. London: Weidenfeld & Nicolson.

9

Toward a Broader Conception of Scholarship: The American Context

R. Eugene Rice

The old teaching versus research debate has drawn faculty in American colleges and universities into a hopeless quagmire. We have heard all the arguments and find them tiring – minds are closed, not opened. The language and polarities used to frame the present discussion of the relationship of teaching and research need to be set aside. The time is ripe for a basic reassessment. To move beyond the current impasse we need to be willing to take a fresh approach and think more creatively about what it means to be a scholar in the contemporary context.

The present conception of scholarship is much too narrow. During the expansionist period in American higher education, what Jencks and Riesman (1968) called 'the academic revolution' (c.1957–74), scholarship was equated with research on the cutting edge of a discipline. Further, it took on significance only when it was publishable in a refereed journal – one narrow facet of the scholarly enterprise, one way of knowing.

To meet the growing demands of a knowledge-based society and to attract the best of a new generation into the academic profession, we need an enlarged view of scholarship: one congruent with the rich diversity that is the hallmark of American higher education; one that is more appropriate, more authentic, and more adaptive for both our institutions and the day-to-day working lives of faculty.

Scholarship in context

In trying to make sense of what has happened to American faculty in recent years, I find myself being driven back to my own discipline (sociology) and particularly the sociology of religion. I am convinced that much about life is defined and shaped by socially constructed fictions, patterns of meaning that cohere in a particular time and place. The American poet Wallace Stevens said it best:

The final belief is to believe in a fiction, which you know to be a fiction, there being nothing else. The exquisite truth is to know that it is a fiction and that you believe in it willingly (Stevens 1957: 163).

Nowhere in the contemporary world do socially constructed fictions have more power than in the professions. And no profession – with the possible exception of medicine – takes its own professional imagery more seriously than the academic. Reference needs only to be made to the years of graduate school socialization and to the power that academic mentors have in the lives of their protégés to make the argument.

The image that dominated the academic profession prior to the Second World War, particularly in the liberal arts colleges that then played a larger role in higher education, was that of the teacher-scholar. After a two-year study of faculty development programmes in twenty of the nation's selective liberal arts colleges, William Nelson (in 1981) published a book calling for the renewal of the 'teacher-scholar'. The call for renewal is itself testimony to the demise of the occupational ideal. During the earlier decades of the twentieth century, however, the teacher-scholar was an image widely shared. Nelson finds the teacher-scholar ideal articulated best in the faculty handbook of Davidson College:

> Ideally the college professor would be a widely respected scholar excited about learning and capable of communicating this excitement to others, a teacher deeply concerned with the welfare of students and eager to have them learn and grow, one who teaches imaginatively both by books and by personal example, a demanding yet compassionate person who respects the moral worth of students and their potential for growth (Nelson 1981: 7).

Sometime after the mid-1950s, following the impact of the GI Bill of Rights and the launching of Sputnik, a major shift took place in the image of what it meant to be an academic professional. Scholarship became research; teaching and research became activities that competed for the faculty member's time. The term scholarship, if it was used at all, referred to research, not teaching. Teaching became a derivative activity. In the consciousness of the faculty, as they thought about their working lives, the teacher-scholar as a model to be emulated had migrated from the core of the profession to the margins.

This expansionist period in higher education brought with it a new conception of the academic professional. The constituent parts of this new professional image existed in nascent form throughout the early history of American higher education, with roots going back to England, Scotland and Germany. But it was only in the heady days of what seemed to be limitless growth, affluence and societal influence that the component elements fused to form a powerful and dominant conception.

In an essay on the professions, Talcott Parsons (1968) described the 'educational revolution' that he saw coming to full fruition in American society after the Second World War. Fundamental to this revolution was the process of professionalization, a process he regarded as 'the most important single component in the structure of modern societies'. According to Parsons' elaborate theory, the keystone in the arch of the professionally oriented society is the modern university, and 'the profession *par excellence* is the academic'. He also described the impact of professionalization on the role of the typical faculty member:

> The typical professor now resembles the scientist more than the gentleman-scholar of an earlier time. As a result of the process of professionalization, achievement criteria are now given the highest priority, reputations are established in national and international forums rather than locally defined, and the center of gravity has shifted to the graduate faculties and their newly professionalized large-scale research function (Parsons 1968).

What is most striking about this statement is that what he describes is not the typical professor. What he articulates is the dominant fiction by which typical American professors measure themselves and their colleagues as professionals. The image of the academic professional that emerged during the expansionist days of higher education not only shaped the self-conceptions of faculty but also informed institutional policies and determined, in large part, who received promotion, tenure and such amenities as leaves of absence and funding for travel and research.

Clustering around this dominant professional image were the following basic assumptions:

1. Research is the central professional endeavour and the focus of academic life.
2. Quality in the profession is maintained by peer review and professional autonomy.
3. Knowledge is pursued for its own sake.
4. The pursuit of knowledge is best organized according to discipline (i.e. according to discipline-based departments).
5. Reputations are established through national and international professional associations.
6. The distinctive task of the academic professional is the pursuit of cognitive truth.
7. Professional rewards and mobility accrue to those who persistently accentuate their specializations.

This professional vision and the interrelated complex of assumptions on which it was built contributed to an extraordinary advancement of knowledge. The increased specialization, the new levels of funding for research, and the rigorous exchange and critique of ideas produced undeniable benefits.

Each of the assumptions listed above has, however, a shadow side, and it is the other side that is at present receiving attention – and funding – in the majority of our colleges and universities. This cluster of assumptions is being questioned here, not because it is inappropriate in itself; in fact, most of the elements have been fully institutionalized in the research university. This view of the academic profession is being questioned because it continues to be normative for the majority of faculty and dominates faculty thinking about themselves professionally in institutional contexts where it is counterproductive and causes faculty to begin to see themselves as less than professionally adequate.

In institutions facing retrenchment or when tenure and promotion decisions are made, the older academic conception is being used to rationalize very difficult and often arbitrary judgements. In some institutions in distress, it is being invoked as an anaesthesia in the management of pain. Junior faculty are having a particularly difficult time, caught between the older image and new institutional expectations. Bowen and Schuster, in their fine book, *American Professors* (1986), characterize the recent career of the junior faculty member as 'an admixture of terror and resignation'.

One of the places where we see the older professional model having its most pernicious influence is when institutions are launching a renewed drive toward academic excellence – frequently this comes with inauguration of a new president. Excellence – increased quality – is defined in terms of the improved productivity of faculty, increased national visibility and more research (usually without the increase in resources needed to make this possible without detracting from undergraduate instruction). When pressed for a definition of academic quality we return to the older conception. What we need now is a broader, more appropriate, view.

Toward a broader view

This is a particularly propitious time for the re-evaluation of what is meant by scholarship. The structural diversity of higher education has created a press for change and the recent research on the American professoriate and the undergraduate experience have demonstrated the need. In the Carnegie Foundation's report *College*, Ernest Boyer (1987) drew national attention to the widespread confusion about the role of faculty and the narrow conception of scholarship dominating the profession:

> Scholarship is not an esoteric appendage; it is at the heart of what the profession is all about. All faculty, throughout their careers, should themselves, remain students. As scholars they must continue to learn and be seriously and continuously engaged in the expanding intellectual world. This is essential to the vitality and vigor of the undergraduate college (Boyer 1987).

Ernest Lynton and Sandra Elman (1987), in their recent call for *New Priorities for the University*, press the argument further urging that special attention must be given to the scholar's role in and the university's responsibility for the application and the utilization of knowledge. It is now time to reframe our thinking about scholarship, challenge the faculty evaluation procedures and reward systems that are presently in place, and replace the current vertical arrangement that devalues the work of the majority of this nation's faculty with a broader view.

Different ways of knowing

If we build on the recent inquiry into the structure of knowledge and alternative approaches to learning, a different configuration, a more constructive way of framing the discussion emerges. A review of the literature on the various dimensions of learning reveals two fundamental polarities: concrete–abstract and reflective–active.

The concrete–abstract polarity

The first polarity deals with how knowledge is perceived. At one pole is the abstract, analytical approach usually associated with traditional academic research. This learning orientation strives for objectivity, requires high levels of specialization, and takes pride in its claim to being 'value-free'. At the other end of this first continuum is an orientation that begins with concrete experience and what is learned from contexts, relationships, valuing communities. This is a very different approach to knowing, one that builds on connection and relationships, where values reveal rather than mask what is worth knowing. Recent literary studies that attempt to understand literature in terms of time and place would be found here. Ethnic studies and women's studies, in their struggle for legitimacy, have helped us recognize the power of context, relationships and community in our approach to knowing and learning. Certainly, knowledge comprehended through objective reasoning and analytical theory-building must be acknowledged and honoured, but knowledge apprehended through connections grounded in human community – relational knowing – must also be seen as legitimate.

The reflective–active polarity

The second basic dimension of learning has to do with how knowledge is processed. Do we learn best through detached reflection and observation or through active engagement? The liberal arts tend to be more reflective, with an emphasis on learning for its own sake. In contrast, so many of the more recent developments in American colleges and universities and, particularly, the comprehensive institutes have moved toward the more active pole, towards active engagement with the world, making a difference. The new programmes in business, computer sciences and communications are found here. The emphasis is on learning that is instrumental, a means to a more practical end.

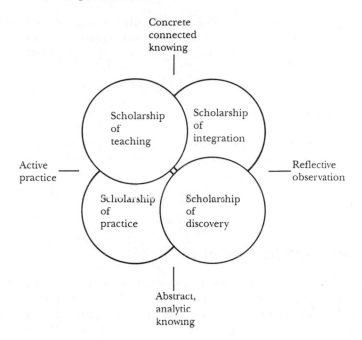

Figure 9.1   An enlarged view of scholarly work.

Again, we want the approaches to learning represented at both poles of the continuum to be recognized and honoured. Certainly, knowledge rooted in scholarly reflection and observation has its place, but so does knowledge generated out of active practice.

David A. Kolb (1984) and others have taken these two basic dimensions of learning, how knowledge is perceived (concrete–abstract) and how it is processed (reflective–active), and constructed a learning model that is particularly helpful in our effort to define scholarship more broadly. Just as learning can be characterized as a multidimensional process involving different styles and approaches to learning, so our broader conception of scholarship can be depicted as an interrelated whole with distinctive components and different approaches to knowing. (See Figure 9.1.)

The forms of scholarship

Enlarging our understanding of scholarship became a central concern of the Carnegie Foundation for the Advancement of Teaching during the two-year period between 1988 and 1990. Drawing heavily on the previous work of Ernest Boyer, Ernest Lynton, Lee Shulman and others, four forms of scholarship were identified:

1. the scholarship of discovery
2. the scholarship of integration
3. the scholarship of practice
4. the scholarship of teaching.

The scholarship of discovery

The first element in this broader conception of scholarship – still a key element – is the discovery of knowledge. On this facet, everyone agrees; in no way do we want to be perceived as detracting from the significance of specialized research. If that were the result of this effort we would have been seriously misunderstood. The place of pure research, the pursuit of knowledge for its own sake, needs to be assiduously defended, particularly in a society primarily committed to the pragmatic and too often concerned more with whether something works over the short term than with whether it is of lasting value.

In 1919, in his famous address on 'Science as a vocation', Max Weber acknowledged that the western world had entered into a phase of specialization previously unknown and that in his words:

> Only by strict specialization can the scientific worker become fully conscious, for once and perhaps never again in his lifetime, that he has achieved something that will endure. A really definitive and good accomplishment is today always a specialized accomplishment (Weber 1958: 135).

The contention of this noted German scholar is persuasive. There is no disputing that, if scholarship is to be sustained in our day, the specialized advancement of knowledge is required. In fact, we should urgently insist that scholarship have as one of its anchor points the discovery of new knowledge – what has traditionally been known as original research.

The scholarship of integration

The extension of the frontiers of knowledge is, however, not enough. The second element of scholarship is the integration of knowledge, an undertaking as critical to the understanding of our world as the discovery of knowledge that is new. In fact, the extension of specialization itself requires new forms of integration. Without the continual effort at reintegration, we have fragmentation. It was also Weber who warned of the possibility of a modern world filled with 'specialists without spirit, and sensualists without heart'.

The integration of knowledge requires a divergent approach to knowing – a different kind of scholarship – one that reaches across disciplinary boundaries, and pulls disparate views and information together in creative ways. Scholars are needed with a capacity to synthesize, to look for new relationships between the parts and the whole, to relate the past and future to the present, and to filter out patterns of meaning that cannot be seen through traditional disciplinary lenses.

It is through integrative inquiry that ethical questions will be raised in a natural and systematic way. We will not have to suffer through the ethics spasms that now grip higher education about every decade, triggered either by a Watergate or a scandal on Wall Street. This is not a call for the 'gentleman scholar' of an earlier time, or the dilettante who dabbles here and there, but broadly educated men and women who are serious about making the kinds of scholarly connections so much needed in our time.

Clifford Geertz (1980), the anthropologist, writes about shifts in the world of scholarship as fundamental changes in 'the way we think about the way we think'. The older disciplinary boundaries are being challenged on every hand, knowledge constantly spills over. The strength of our disciplines is often more political than intellectual.

The scholarship of practice

The third form of scholarship is the most distinctively American. The great land-grant institutions were established during the nineteenth century precisely for the purpose of applying knowledge to the enormous agricultural and technical problems confronting society. These schools and their utilitarian missions matched the mood and needs of an emerging nation. In the academic profession today, however, there is a disturbing gap between what is valued as scholarship and the pragmatic needs of the larger world.

This ironic development in American higher education has multiple roots, but one important strand can be traced back to the emergence of professional education and, specifically, to the impact of the Flexner Report (1910) on medical education (incidentally, one of the first of Carnegie commissioned studies). The major effect of the Flexner Report was to move medical education into the research university and greatly increase its scientific component. The other professions followed medicine's lead. Practical competence became professional when grounded in systematic, preferably scientific knowledge. The application of knowledge took on value – rigour and prestige – when derived from original research. In the most pragmatic society in the world, scholarship was conceptualized as independent of, and prior to, practice.

Professional schools are now beginning to challenge this hierarchical conception of scholarship that makes the application of knowledge derivative, and consequently, second best. Donald Schon's (1983) work on 'the reflective practitioner' calls for a reassessment of the relationship between scholarship and practice – a new 'epistemology of practice'. His work is especially influential in the field of architecture where the relationship with the research university and its established definition of scholarship has been one of perpetual tension.

Even in medicine, the connection between basic research and practice is being realigned. Harvard Medical School has instituted a 'New Pathways Program' that attempts to build clinical practice into medical education from the very beginning. Ernest Lynton, Sandra Elman and others are raising a whole range of important questions about the relationship between scholarship and professional service. Should not the application of knowledge to the problems of society be acknowledged as a scholarly endeavour of the first order?

The scholarship of teaching

This brings us to the fourth dimension of scholarship – the relationship of teaching and scholarship. This is the most difficult form of scholarship to discuss because we do not have the appropriate language. In the working lives of individual faculty, scholarship and teaching are often seen as antithetical – competing for one's time and attention. This is a reflection of the way in which we conceptualize both tasks. We want to challenge this understanding and argue that quality teaching requires substantive scholarship that builds on, but is distinct from original research, and that this scholarly effort needs to be recognized and rewarded. This is a special kind of scholarship that has for too long been implicit, unacknowledged, and virtually unnamed. Some are now willing to talk about 'a missing paradigm'.

This fourth dimension of scholarship has an integrity of its own, but is deeply embedded in the other three forms – discovery, integration and practice. In addition, the scholarship of teaching has at least three distinct elements: first, the *synoptic capacity*, the ability to draw the strands of a field together in a way that provides both coherence and meaning, to place what is known in context and open the way for connection to be made between the knower and the known; second, what Lee Shulman calls *pedagogical content knowledge* (Shulman and Sykes 1983), the capacity to represent a subject in ways that transcend the split between intellectual substance and teaching process, usually having to do with the metaphors, analogies and experiments used; and third, *what we know about learning*, scholarly inquiry into how students 'make meaning' – to use William Perry's (1970) phrase – out of what the teacher says and does.

While we want to treat the four forms of scholarship as individually distinctive, we also want them to be understood as interrelated and often overlapping – an interdependent whole, with each distinctive form encompassing each of the other three. For example, scholarship that is primarily integrative can also lead to important discoveries and provide the intellectual undergirding for the best sort of undergraduate teaching.

The view of scholarship being proposed here is more inclusive, reaching out to encompass a wider array of scholarly activities than does the present conception. While being more inclusive, however, this enlarged view has its own boundaries; the four aspects of scholarship are discrete types but form a conceptual whole that is every bit as important as the parts.

Implied here are assumptions about the kind of scholarship appropriate for the academy – colleges and universities. For instance, teaching that is *not* grounded in the most recent research in the field and is oblivious to the interconnections with other disciplines is not appropriate for a college or university setting. Instruction of this sort might better be found in the corporate classroom or the military. On the other hand, it is important that narrow, specialized research take place in a broader scholarly context – a university – where critical questions are raised and scholars are made mindful by students and colleagues that academic freedom carries with it special responsibilities. The recent debate over genetic engineering underscores the point. As Alfred North Whitehead (1929), in his essay on 'Universities and their function', observes:

> At no time have universities been restricted to pure abstract learning. . . . The justification for a university is that it preserves the connection between knowledge and the zest for life, by uniting the young and the old in the imaginative consideration of learning (Whitehead 1929: 137).

We know that what is being proposed challenges a hierarchical arrangement of monumental proportions – a status system that is firmly fixed in the consciousness of the present faculty and the academy's organizational policies and practices. What is being called for is a broader, more open field where these different forms of scholarship can interact, inform, and enrich one another, and faculty can follow their interests, build on their strengths, and be rewarded for what they spend most of their scholarly energy doing. All faculty ought to be scholars in this broader sense, deepening their preferred approaches to knowing but constantly pressing, and being pressed by peers, to enlarge their scholarly capacities and encompass other – often contrary ways – of knowing.

Faculty scholarship and institutional mission

Institutionally, we have a crisis of purpose in our colleges and universities. Our comprehensive institutions, particularly, are trying to be what they are not, and falling short of what they could be.

Awareness that the dominant notion of scholarship is inappropriate and counterproductive for the majority of our faculty, as well as our institutions, is widespread. The concern runs deep, yet when individual faculty are regarded and 'emerging' institutions launch drives toward higher standards of academic excellence, the older, narrow definition of scholarship as research is reasserted and given priority. As Everett Ladd (1979) points out: 'When a particular norm is ascendant within a group and institutionalized in various ways, it is very hard for a member of a group to deny its claim, even if intellectually he is fully convinced of its serious deficiency.'

What is especially needed is greater congruence between individual faculty scholarship and institutional mission. It is this congruence that gives special meaning to academic work, sustains morale, cultivates commitment, and makes possible a more direct relationship between performance, evaluation and reward.

An enlarged conception of scholarship would address a number of critical problems currently plaguing both individual faculty and colleges and universities across the several sectors of higher education. It would free us to celebrate individual strengths – the rich variety of scholarly talents represented in the faculty – and make it possible for colleges and universities, not committed primarily to specialized research (the majority) to feel pride in their distinctive scholarly missions.

Scholarship and democratic community

In 1837 Ralph Waldo Emerson presented to the 'president and gentlemen' of Harvard's Phi Beta Kappa Society his famous address 'The American Scholar'. In that provocative statement, described by Oliver Wendell Holmes (1952) as America's 'intellectual Declaration of Independence', Emerson (1971) articulated a vision of the role of the scholar in the new democracy. He called for the rejection of a past that was alien and debilitating and for the adoption of a new approach to scholarship and the role of the scholar in society – a role that would be vital and self-confident, in his words, 'blood warm'.

Emerson's address was not so much an assertion of intellectual nationalism as a statement of his own struggle with the problem of vocation, with the nature and meaning of scholarly work in a changing society. It is this same issue – what it means to be a scholar in an evolving democracy – that confronts faculty in American higher education today.

Just as Emerson's American scholar was struggling to break away from the dominance of 'the learning of other lands', from patterns of deference that engendered self-doubt and the depreciation of new, adaptive roles, so the majority of faculty in the USA's colleges and universities are wrestling with a conception of scholarship that is much too narrow and singularly inappropriate for the rich diversity – the educational mosaic – that has become the hallmark of American higher education. That 1837 speech of Emerson's called for a new approach to scholarship and the role of the scholar, one that would be fully engaged with the needs, realities of, a vibrant, developing democracy.

One hundred and twenty-six years later – scarcely a block from where Emerson spoke – Clark Kerr addressed the future of the American university and identified four challenges that would transform higher education in this country. He told his Harvard audience: 'The university is being called upon to educate previously unimagined numbers of students; to respond to the expanding claims of national service; to merge its activities with industry as never before; to adapt to and rechannel new intellectual currents' (Kerr 1972). Kerr then predicted that only when this transformation had taken place would we have 'a truly American university, an institution unique in world history, an institution not looking to other models but serving, itself, as a model for universities in other parts of the globe.'

American higher education stands now on the threshold of that transformation. Over the past thirty years, colleges and universities have taken on the diverse challenges articulated by Kerr and much has been accomplished. Other nations – Asian, European, African – are looking to the United States as a model, a decentralized but coherent model, meeting diverse societal needs and responding to the call for both equity and excellence. Looming especially large in our immediate future are the challenges posed by the immense demographic changes in our society. The rich racial, ethnic and cultural diversity marking the USA from its beginning has taken on new significance as the minorities in our cities, and even states, such as California, become majorities. Diversity, which US higher education sees as one of its primary strengths, has taken on new meaning

What it means to be a scholar in US colleges and universities must be seen within this larger frame. Not only do our institutions have diverse missions – commitments to serving a wide range of scholarly needs within region, states and nation – but also there is the special commitment to the education of an increasingly diverse population, to the intellectual preparation of the educated citizenry necessary for making a genuinely democratic society possible. Scholarship in this context takes on broader meaning.

An enlarged view would nurture inclusion, draw together rather than separate, and embrace students and their learning as well as faculty and their research. This understanding of scholarly activity would also acknowledge and build on the relational nature of knowledge as well as more abstract, objective ways of knowing. The narrower view no longer suffices. For American colleges and universities to contribute fully to the vibrant pluralistic democracy the nation is becoming, a vision of the distinctively new American scholar is needed.

References

Bowen, H. and Schuster, J. H. (1986). *American Professors: A National Resource Imperiled.* New York: Oxford University Press.

Boyer, E. L. (1987). *College: The Undergraduate Experience in America.* New York: Harper & Row.

—— (1990). *Scholarship Reconsidered: Priorities of the Professoriate.* Princeton, NJ: Carnegie Foundation for the Advancement of Teaching.

Emerson, R. W. (1971). *The Collected Works of Ralph Waldo Emerson, Volume 1: Nature, Addresses, and Lectures.* Introductions and notes by R. E. Spiller, text established by A. R. Ferguson. Cambridge, Mass: Belknap Press of Harvard University Press.

Flexner, A. (1910). *Medical Education in the United States and Canada: A Report to the Carnegie Foundation for the Advancement of Teaching.* Princeton, NJ: Carnegie Foundation for the Advancement of Teaching.

Geertz, C. (1980). Blurred genres: the refiguration of social thought. *American Scholar,* Spring.

Holmes, O. W. (1952). In Jones, H. M., Leisy, E. E. and Ludwig, R. M. (eds) *Major American Writers* 3rd edition. New York: Harcourt Brace.

Jencks, C. and Riesman, D. (1968). *The Academic Revolution*. New York: Doubleday.

Kerr, C. (1972). *The Uses of the University, with a 'Postscript 1972'*. Cambridge, Mass: Harvard University Press.

Kolb, D. A. (1984). *Experiential Learning: Experiences as a Source of Learning and Development*. Englewood Cliffs, NJ: Prentice-Hall.

Ladd, E. C. (1979). The work experience of American college professors: some data and an argument. *Current Issues in Higher Education* **22**: 135–54.

Lynton, E. A. and Elman, S. E. (1987). *New Priorities for the University*. San Francisco: Jossey-Bass.

Nelson, W. C. (1981). *Renewal of the Teacher Scholar*. Washington, DC: Association of American Colleges.

Parsons, T. (1968). Professions. In Sills, D. L. (ed.) *International Encyclopedia of the Social Sciences*. New York: Macmillan.

Perry, W. G. Jr. (1970). *Forms of Intellectual and Ethical Development in the College*. New York: Holt, Rinehart & Winston.

Schon, D. A. (1983). *The Reflective Practitioner: How Professionals Think in Action*. New York: Basic Books.

Shulman, L. and Sykes, G. (eds) (1983). *Handbook of Teaching and Policy*. New York: Longman.

Stevens, W. (1957). *Opus Posthumous*. New York: Knopf.

Weber, M. (1958). Science as a vocation. In H. Gerth and C. W. Mills *From Max Weber*. New York: Oxford University Press.

—— (1974). *On Universities: The Power of the State and the Dignity of the Academic Calling of Imperial Germany*. Translated, edited with an introductory note by E. Shills. Chicago: University of Chicago Press.

Whitehead, A. N. (1929). *The Aims of Education and Other Essays*. New York: Macmillan.

10

Teaching and Research

Sir Christopher Ball

Context

'More Means Different', the title of the recent Royal Society of Arts (RSA) report on widening access to higher education, provides a useful introduction to, and summary of, the challenges facing those who teach or undertake research in higher education today – and those who lead, direct or manage it.[1] Whether in the UK or other countries the key issues are the nature, scale and funding of higher education and research. Each of these is undergoing change, but what is happening to the teaching function of higher education is different from what is happening to research.

Concern about education is a world-wide phenomenon. In the UK the great national debate was inaugurated by Jim Callaghan's Ruskin Speech of 1976 and is by no means ended yet. Although a Conservative government has been in power since 1979, this sense of general unease is not confined to one political party. Nor is it merely a local problem. Many nations, rich or poor, in each of the three worlds and all of the five continents, exemplify the interesting modern paradox of dissatisfaction with their systems of education and desire to increase educational opportunities. They seek both 'more' and 'different'.

This creative dissatisfaction is the result of social, political and economic pressures. The most important of these are the issues of wealth-creation, equity and cost. The claim that 'learning pays', while difficult to demonstrate conclusively, is probably true; it is certainly widely believed to be true. Of course, the benefits of learning are long term rather than short term, and are distributed between the individual learners, their employers and society at large. But, with all these qualifications, it is now commonly agreed that learning (education and training – and particularly higher education) plays a significant role in wealth-creation and contributes in no small way to national economic success. In developed nations and redeveloping countries like the UK, it is becoming clear that the quality of the education and training of the work-force is the single most important factor in determining economic competitiveness.

The issue of equity is no less important. The benefits of graduation are obvious and well-recognized. They are both real and positional; that is a degree has both an intrinsic and a scarcity value. The Department of Education and Science has argued that 'the personal rate of return in higher education is a great deal higher than the rate of return to society in general. It is also well above that available on almost all other forms of investment'.[2] If that is so, the principle of social equity would suggest that higher education should be available to all those who seek it and are able to benefit from it. Since the 1987 White Paper this has been national policy in the UK.[3]

But such a policy of widening access, if taken seriously, must challenge not only the capacity of the existing system of higher education, but also traditional definitions of quality and excellence. In other countries equity and excellence are not necessarily seen as alternatives. For example,

> without such a commitment to excellence and equity, as the core of California's agenda for higher education from now until the year 2000, California cannot build the society it will need in the new century. The failure to achieve these goals in an interdependent, highly competitive international environment will diminish its standard of living, enfeeble its economy, and impoverish the lives of all Californians.[4]

All this will cost money. The expansion of higher education and the growth of scientific research in the twentieth century has created a new and significant demand on public resources. The number of teachers in higher education in the UK today exceeds the number of students at the beginning of the century. In 1963 Derek de Solla Price calculated that personnel and publications in science were doubling every ten to fifteen years.[5] In Australia, which is not untypical of other developed countries, higher education has doubled in size three times since 1950. This exponential growth (in both students and science) cannot be sustained. Indeed, the levelling-off in scientific research is already evident and painful. In Australia expansion slowed to a trickle after the oil-price shocks of the 1970s. Understandably, governments of the left or the right in the UK and other countries have been forced to give attention to what is in effect a major growth industry dependent substantially on public funding. They look for increased efficiency of operation, greater cost-effectiveness, and opportunities for economies of scale as expansion takes place. They are right to do so.

The tension between the arguments for expansion to improve wealth-creation and equity, and the need to control public expenditure, is unresolved. One widely canvassed solution is to shift part of the burden of funding higher education from public to private resources. While fund-raising and specific grants from business and industry make a most welcome contribution to reducing deficits and enabling innovation, sometimes at the expense of some distortion to the strategic plan of universities or polytechnics, their role in the overall funding of higher education and research is unlikely ever to be more than marginal.

The alternative is to require the student to pay. The success of the Australian graduate tax scheme demonstrates both the willingness of individuals to contribute to the costs of their own higher education and one effective method for channelling private funds towards the universities and polytechnics. Other methods, such as the use of the National Insurance system or the imposition of (means-tested) supplementary fees, have also been considered. But the delivery mechanism, though undoubtedly important, is a second-order issue. The question of principle is prior; are students to be required to contribute to the cost of their own higher education, as well as their maintenance? If not, how can the system expand to satisfy the national needs for wealth-creation and equity? As far as research is concerned, since it is unlikely that business and industry will be prepared to take the major responsibility for funding basic (as opposed to applied) research, there seems to be no alternative to creating and managing a steady-state system governed by the cash-limited sum available from public resources.

Teaching

In every generation the same three questions recur in education: how many? What and how shall they learn? What is the best solution to the cost-effectiveness equation? They are questions that require principled answers, but rarely receive them. The tyranny of the status quo is usually too powerful to permit a radical analysis. But the practice of the past, at least in education, is not often the best guide for the future. For example, the exclusion of women from the ancient universities until the latter part of the nineteenth century, the resistance to the development of subjects like engineering, or business and management, the slow response to the possibilities of distance learning (in spite of the success of the Open University), and the stubborn defence of a student–staff ratio on no better grounds than custom, have done little to help develop a system of higher education appropriate to today's needs, let alone the challenges of tomorrow.

The idea that higher education should be available for all who wish, and who can benefit from it, is a radical departure from the past. It offers no obvious limit to the widening of access and implies a gradual development of a mass (or 'popular') system of higher education to replace the inherited elite model which provides a participation rate of not much more than 15 per cent at present.

But the appropriate scale of higher education is not only a function of the participation rate. The growing recognition that lifelong learning must replace the outdated concept of a 'sufficient initial education' has major implications for the size and nature of the system. A 'continuing education' model would provide not only for the basic higher education of 18 year olds (and mature students) but also for the regular updating, extension, broadening and supplementation of their skills and knowledge throughout life. Planning and provision for systematic continuing education defined in this way is still in its infancy.

If the future task of higher education is to provide for a majority, rather than a minority, of the population and to offer them a coherent combination of basic and continuing learning, then many existing practices must be questioned. These include the full-time residential model, the three-term year, the domination of the specialized three-year (full-time) honours degree, and the doctrine of the inseparable nature of teaching and research. Good courses will no longer be recognized primarily by their success in providing a sound basis for postgraduate study and research. Instead, they will need to link more closely with the needs, capabilities and wishes of a broad range of 18 year olds and mature adults and prepare them for continued learning in a wide range of employment. This will lead to changes in the content, process, duration, assessment and outcomes of courses. Quality and excellence will need to be redefined in terms of added values and fitness for purpose.

There are two key issues in the welter of change confronting those who teach in higher education. They are the student–staff ratio and the question of research. During the last ten years student–staff ratios have almost doubled, from about 8:1 to about 16:1, in the Polytechnics and Colleges of Higher Education. They have also increased in the universities, but not to the same extent. Although they must logically stabilize in due course there is as yet no sign of the increase coming to an end. Nor is there any coherent analysis of where the optimum point might lie in terms of cost-effectiveness. My own view is that the figure will ultimately prove to be not less than 20. In saying this, I am not advocating the 'continental' model of over-crowded lecture halls and high drop-out rates, merely more effective use of our most valuable and scarce resource – good teaching.

At first glance, the question of research offers an awkward dilemma. The 'university-model' of higher education is built on the principle that teaching and research are as inseparable as wool and mutton on a sheep-farm, that they mutually reinforce one another, and, in particular, that it is one of the non-negotiable defining features of what is meant by *Higher Education* that the teaching is provided by those who are themselves active in research. A useful restatement of this traditional claim has recently been made by John Horlock, building on his own experience as Vice-Chancellor of the Open University.[6]

If that view is correct, then we well might ask ourselves why we are prepared to allow more than half the students in UK higher education to earn their degrees and diplomas in Polytechnics and Colleges of Higher Education excluded from the dual-support arrangements for research; or why the London external degree was an acceptable form of higher education for so many in the past; or why we are prepared to tolerate the teaching of higher diploma courses, and the 'franchising' of part of degree courses, in Colleges of Further Education, where there is no tradition or ethos of research.

Students on such courses achieve success, gain employment and in appropriate cases proceed to postgraduate study without difficulty. The strong form of the doctrine of the inseparability of teaching and research is contradicted (as far as teaching is concerned) by the facts of contemporary UK higher education, and by the practice of higher education in many other countries.

The best solution to the 'research-dilemma' defined above seems to be found in distinguishing different kinds of research. For present purposes three will suffice: fundamental research, contract research and scholarship. Scholarship (and advanced study) are the duty of all who teach in higher education, whether in a college, polytechnic or university. The purpose of scholarship is to enhance the quality of teaching; consequently, its costs form part of the costs of the teaching function. Neither fundamental nor contract research necessarily enhance the quality of teaching – though they may do so – and it therefore follows that they are not a necessary condition for, or accompaniment to, higher education.

Research

The previous paragraphs have considered the doctrine of the inseparability of teaching and research from the point of view of the teaching function of higher education. It also needs to be looked at from the vantage-point of research. The case for a 'fundamental link' (as John Horlock defines it) between the two is even more difficult to sustain from this point of view than when the underlying issue is how best to sustain high-quality teaching. The existence of free-standing research laboratories such as the Rutherford-Appleton or the Mill Hill MRC research centre demonstrates that high-quality research can, and does, flourish independently of teaching. In some other countries the research function is partly or largely disassociated from the universities, which are seen as primarily teaching-institutions. The Max-Planck Institutes in Germany are an interesting case in point. But I am not aware of conclusive evidence that research (or teaching) suffers thereby.

The issues of the nature, scale and funding of research are particularly awkward at present. I have written on them recently in two papers published in the *Higher Education Quarterly*.[7] Those who fail to distinguish the (three) different kinds of research set out above, and who insist on the 'fundamental link' between research and teaching create an insoluble problem for themselves. Such a position is tantamount to arguing that the scale of research and the size of higher education must be interrelated, and that as one grows (or reduces) so must the other. Such an argument has only to be stated clearly to be seen as unpersuasive. In particular, it is hard to see why the scale of national research should increase merely because a nation wishes to provide wider access to higher education.

In fact, the appropriate scale of fundamental research is one of the unsolved problems of our time. While the arguments for global research (in the world as a whole) are powerful and persuasive, the case for investment by any particular nation is less secure. Since some south Asian countries seem to have achieved impressive economic success without major investment in fundamental research, research is in the odd position of not being able to rely on arguments drawn from either wealth-creation or equity. In this respect, research is the poor relation of teaching. Until a clearer link can be established between the fundamental research of a nation and its long-term economic success, defenders of the research-budget have to fall back on the 'good citizenship' argument and tradition. While it is no doubt true that all developed countries should play their part in the world's overall research effort, and it would certainly be a waste of resources to abandon the UK's considerable investment of money and talent in fundamental research, arguments from citizenship and tradition are not nearly as persuasive as ones related to wealth-creation and economic competitiveness.

Difficulties such as these have led to the idea that for the present the best we can do is to secure an appropriate proportion of the national budget for fundamental research. No one has yet proposed a better definition of 'appropriate' than 'broadly comparable to the allocation made by other similar nations to research'. Such a formula is unsatisfactory, first, because it is unprincipled; and second, because it tends to confuse the ideas of 'comparable per cent of GDP' with 'comparable cash allocations'. In any event the funding of fundamental research is thereby firmly linked to the performance of the national economy, and where (as in the UK) this is not progressing as satisfactorily as elsewhere, research inevitably suffers relative decline.

Others have written of the challenge of managing a 'steady-state' system while taking account of the 'sophistication' factor. In brief, this refers to the fact that as each year passes scientific research and experimental equipment become more and more sophisticated and increasingly expensive. The same effect is beginning to be seen in the humanities and social science as the information technology revolution penetrates non-science research. The result is that the 'same amount' of research costs more in real terms each year. A 'steady-state' system in practice requires the management of decline.

As a result, most small nations (and some large ones) have had to establish priorities for fundamental research. Specialization is not easy; for example, should the UK abandon its research commitment to space technology, tropical medicine and oriental languages? The continued growth of knowledge, coupled with a 'steady-state' provision for research, will inevitably and eventually force all nations to make some hard choices.

Considerations such as these have led to the idea of concentrating the funding of fundamental research on a limited number of 'research universities', selected research departments, or outstanding individuals. Whether concentration is confined to the individual level, extended to the departmental level, or allowed to embrace whole institutions, the dual support system for research is called in question. It no longer makes sense to devote substantial sums of money to attempting to provide an infrastructure for fundamental research across the board in as many as forty-five universities in the UK. In my view, the process of concentration and selectivity in fundamental research has hardly started. Before it is finished we shall probably have to identify a small subset of some twelve to fifteen research universities and recognize that the remainder of the existing university system, like the Polytechnics and Colleges of Higher Education, is not primarily concerned with fundamental research (or postgraduate research degrees), but constitutes the 'teaching sector'. (It will, of course, still be the case that teachers in such institutions will be expected to practise scholarship and advanced study, as set out above.)

What is at issue is the challenge of finally breaking 'the fundamental link' between teaching and research. Unless the challenge is faced, we shall neither be able to widen access to higher education nor ensure that the limited national budget available for fundamental research is deployed to the best effect. But facing it will be neither easy nor painless.

Models

Finally, I consider briefly the question of institutional models. The traditional model of the UK university, devoted equally to fundamental research and higher education (and funded accordingly), does not offer a pattern upon which a mass-access system of higher education can be built. The 'research-premium' deriving from the dual-support system adds between 30 per cent and 40 per cent to the costs of educating students. It is now a quarter of a century since the publication of the Crosland White Paper of 1966 which brought the polytechnics into existence.[8] With hindsight it is easy to see how the polytechnics and colleges (so-called 'public sector higher education') have been able to respond more effectively to local and national needs than the traditional university model. They were encouraged to respect eight key principles:

1. local and regional responsibility
2. mixed provision of further and higher education
3. mixture of full-time, part-time and sandwich work
4. primacy of teaching
5. cost-effectiveness
6. responsiveness to student demand, employment need, and the policies of local and national government
7. concern for externally monitored quality
8. co-operation with national planning and funding bodies.

These have stood them in good stead, although the Education Reform Act 1988 reduced the effect of the first two of these principles. The polytechnic model is already proving itself superior to the traditional university model (but not to the Open University), and in the twenty-first century is likely to prevail as access increases and a 'popular' system replaces the old elite idea of Higher Education. Fewer than half of all the students in UK higher education are today in the university sector. And the proportion is reducing each year.

But, although it is more cost-effective than the university model, the polytechnic model is still relatively expensive. It is to be considered whether in the next phase of development we may not see the emergence of a third model. The further education colleges stand ready to be transformed into local community colleges, offering open access to a wide range of courses of both further and higher education up to the level of National Vocational Qualification (NVQ) 4 (i.e. the standard of the Higher National Diploma or Diploma in Higher Education, and roughly equivalent to the first two years of a (full-time) honours degree). It is possible that the definition of higher education in the UK may be changed from one depending on *level* (courses above A level) to one relying on *age* (courses of study undertaken by those over 18), to bring our arrangements into line with those of the USA and a number of other countries. If this happened, the distinction between further and higher education would disappear and the FE Colleges would automatically become part of, and the largest sector within, UK higher education. It is likely that this 'community college' model would operate at student–staff ratios somewhat above 20:1 (though currently the figure is distinctly lower, nearer to the DES norm of 11:1), and make no claims at all on the national research budget. It would be able to adhere to the eight principles outlined above and offer higher education at a markedly lower cost to the student or the nation than either the polytechnics or university models. It has much to commend it.

The important point, however, is not to speculate on the survival of the fittest, but to recognize that as a result of the changes taking place in teaching and research the appropriate institutional model for higher education is bound to be called into question. In this respect, as in so many others, more means different.

Notes

1. C. Ball (1990). *More Means Different*. London: Royal Society of Arts.
2. DES (1989). *Shifting the Balance of Public Funding of Higher Education to Fees*. London: DES.
3. DES (1987). *Meeting the Challenge*, Cm 114. London: HMSO.
4. California's Postsecondary Education Commission (1988). *Preparing for the Twenty-First Century*, a report on Higher Education in California, California's Postsecondary Education Commission. Sacramento: The Commission.
5. D. de Solla Price (1986) [1963]. *Little Science, Big Science . . . and Beyond*. New York: Columbia University Press.
6. J. Horlock (1991). The link between teaching and research in universities. *Science and Public Affairs* **6**(1): 77–83.
7. C. Ball (1989). The problem of research. *Higher Education Quarterly* **43**(3): 207–15; C. Ball (1991). The merging of the PCFC and UFC: probable, desirable or inevitable. *Higher Education Quarterly*. In press.
8. DES (1966). *A Plan for Polytechnics and Other Colleges: Higher Education in the Further Education System*, Cmnd 3006. London: HMSO.

11

Graduate Education and Research Training

Burton R. Clark

What is most interesting about graduate education and research training is how much and in what way they are related to each other. We can certainly have graduate education without research training. Numerous master's level institutions in the USA exhibit this option. They offer a set of taught courses, much as in undergraduate programmes, in a context of very little research. The nearest the student comes to research training is one or two courses in methodology, the degree is generally taken by examination, and if the degree involves a thesis there is little time or resources for sustained inquiry. This first option emphasizes knowledge and distribution while downplaying the present and future production of knowledge.

We can certainly have research training without formal advanced education. Such training is found increasingly in private corporations, public agencies and research laboratories, non-profit or state sponsored, organized outside the university framework. Japanese industry is much involved in such research training, to the point of a virtual displacement of this activity from higher education to industry. The location of much research in France in the framework of the National Centre for Scientific Research (CNRS) places much research training at the job site of the full-time researcher, away from whatever the universities are doing at post first degree level. In the UK formal graduate education is understated. As remarked by Wendy Hirsh in the 1982 Leverhulme Report on the future of research, British officials and academics assume that 'the need for researchers is best met by selecting some of our academically most able graduates and giving them three years in which to carry out one major research project and write a thesis' (Hirsh 1982: 190). This second option emphasizes immediate involvement in research and a related production of knowledge, and downplays the transmission of the existing knowledge that is found in the broad cognitive structure of an entire discipline and in the perspectives of its specialties. It is not surprising that British reform attends to the possibilities of 'taught courses' and a broader form of PhD training.

The third option is the unity option, namely that we can have graduate education and research training in the same place and at the same time or in a defined sequence of courses and research, the two so closely interrelated that one informs the other. As an ideal, this option has had a strong run historically in German, British and American higher education, and in all other systems, or parts thereof, influenced by these major international models. In the purest expression of this ideal, that is the Humboldtian principle of the unity of research and study, first voiced in early-nineteenth-century Germany, research and teaching were completely blended. Professors should teach by setting research problems for students to work on and by training them in how to do research. Professorial research became teaching; student participation in research became a mode of study. As they engaged in research, students joined their teachers in a common quest for the truth.

Humboldt offered a striking formulation: the teacher 'does not exist for the sake of the [student]. They are both at the university for the sake of science and scholarship' (quoted in Gellert 1988). Here was the formulation for all time that put research in the classroom and the classroom in research. It was knowledge production *and* distribution, not student processing, that should be front and centre. And near the end of the twentieth century, one may add, a knowledge-processing analytical perspective tells us more than a student-development approach about the dynamics of systems of higher education. It does so precisely because it insists that we pay attention to the production and reformulation of knowledge as well as its transmission and diffusion (Clark 1983).

Serving as an important part of the cultural legacy of Higher Education internationally, the Humboldtian ideal has been variously expressed during many decades of changing circumstances in Germany itself as well as elsewhere. The ideal was always somewhat fanciful, likely to serve as a blanket of legitimacy thrown over diverse and contradictory practices. But we can still observe its presence in modern dress, under modern supportive conditions, in one system or another, especially where research takes the driver's seat. Witness the description offered by UCLA's Nobel Laureate chemist, Donald Cram, of how within his sphere in his department over some four decades of provision and effort graduate education and research training have become virtually the same thing. Toward later comparisons in this paper, note the size of the research group, which is just one part of a large chemistry department, and the blend of student coursework and student teaching around the primary activity of research (Council of Graduate Schools 1989).

My research group has, for about 40 years, been composed of 17 people, plus or minus three at any given time. Three of the group on average are postdocs and the rest graduate students working for their Ph.D.s. The postdocs stay about a year and a half, and already are independent investigators, but work in my field of specialization. The graduate students spend an average of four years doing their research, the first two years of effort being blended with their teaching duties and the courses they take. The last two years, they work up to 70 hours a week on their research problems (Council of Graduate Schools 1989: 1).

Around their simultaneous involvement in several research studies, the students are much involved with one another and especially with the faculty mentor:

> Each investigator has two or three problems he or she is working on. Usually one of these turns into thesis material. I act as their consultant, critic, judge, advisor, and scientific father. . . . When a project is finished, these students write a detailed report or a thesis describing it. These reports serve as the basis of research papers. I usually write these from parts of reports or theses, which the co-workers then criticize. The better graduate students and co-workers write the first drafts of research papers, which I then rewrite. In this way, our group has published about 370 research papers over the years. . . . Although professors and postdoctoral fellows are important to a research group, the graduate students are the heart of the research effort. If they are talented and motivated, they make excellent teaching assistants and research assistants. They stay long enough to provide continuity and leadership and group memory. They form, during their graduate student days, friendships and contacts that last throughout their lives (Council of Graduate Schools 1989: 8).

Finally there is the output of trained researchers, large but differentiated.

> If the papers constitute the research group's legacy, our immediate products are our freshly-minted Ph.D.s and postdocs. Of the two hundred-plus of them from my lab, about 60 are now professors in academic work, about 12 work for government, about 5 left chemistry to become dentists, doctors, mothers, or businessmen, and the rest do research or research administration in the chemical, pharmaceutical, or oil industries. Of these, about half keep in touch with me at least on a yearly basis. Of the first 80 or so Ph.D.s in my group, about 10 were female. Currently there are more females in my group than males. . . . I would judge almost all of these students to be operationally creative; that is, they can solve problems. Only about 5 to 10 percent, however, are conceptually creative. They are the ones that formulate research objectives. It is this small, latter percentage that will shape the changes in our society. They are the elite of the elite. They not only know how to get things done, but they know what should be done (Council of Graduate Schools 1989: 8)

Delivered this past year to the University of California Regents, the Cram description has been taken up by the American Council of Graduate Schools as 'a very cogent statement of graduate education at its best'. At the same time, 'it describes a particular situation in a large, doctoral-granting institution', and the staff of the Council 'wondered to what extent it represents the activities that are actually going on in graduate departments throughout the country' (Council of Graduate Schools 1989: 1).

The Council's staff have ample reason to wonder, since they are aware of the extreme variety of disciplinary and institutional contexts within which graduate education and research training take place in a national system in which at least eight hundred institutions are involved in the granting of master's degrees alone, or master's and doctoral degrees together. Joseph Ben-David (1977) raised a similar concern in a broader, more universal fashion in his comparative study of higher education in the UK, France, Germany and the United States when he stated that 'far from being a natural match, research and teaching can be organized within a single framework only under specific conditions' (Ben-David 1977: 94). Our task is to identify those conditions that unify and the conditions that fragment and, further, the structures that implement a marriage and those that effect a divorce. The connection between graduate education and research training cannot be analysed independently of their institutional bases.

The conditions and structures that significantly shape this relationship can be pursued as country-specific or as generic in the modern organization of science and higher education. From research now underway with colleagues in the Federal Republic of Germany, France, the UK, Japan and the United States, I hope in time to do both. Since results are still incomplete and highly tentative, I shall limit my comments here to some contrasting observations on Britain and the United States.

The American pattern

In international comparisons as well as in US-centred research, the American education structure appears weak, even highly defective, at lower levels, and strong, even highly functional at higher levels, with post-bachelor's education appearing as a great strength. This is the level that makes American higher education the world's leading magnet system during the last half of the twentieth century, drawing to itself student talent from around the world for advanced training and, notably, faculty and researchers seeking attractive conditions for their work and personal advancement. The top level is highly productive, dynamic and self-amplifying. Underlying its strength are conditions and structures that have evolved over a century of development, from the time that 'the age of the university' took over from 'the age of the college' in the last quarter of the nineteenth century (Hofstadter and Metzger 1955; Veysey 1965; Geiger 1986). The systemic supports can be quickly set forth:

1. largeness
2. decentralized control
3. extensive institutional differentiation
4. dual tiers
5. intense institutional competition
6. diversified finance.

Largeness

Generous admission in a large country has produced a system that is no less than colossal, with many large universities that in turn have large departments for supporting research and graduate education as well as undergraduate instruction. The 100 so-called 'research universities', some as large as 50,000 students on one campus, had 2.2 million students in 1987, offering up an average of over 20,000. Another 100 so-called 'doctoral-granting universities' (less involved in research) had 1.2 million students, over 10,000 on the average. Another 600 'comprehensive colleges and universities', offering master's level work as well as bachelor's degrees, had 3.3 million students, with 5,500 on average (Carnegie Foundation 1987). All along the line in these 800 institutions, modal faculty size in departments will be above twenty, with many departments in the range of forty to a hundred, especially in the major research universities. Department faculty typically teach at both undergraduate and graduate levels, with senior ranks in the universities tilting strongly upward. In numerical size, 'critical mass' is widespread.

Decentralized control

The American pattern of private control and fifty-state public control is so well known that little comment is required. Privateness loomed large historically and plays an important role today, especially among the pace-setting institutions. In the top 10 universities, 7 are private; among the 104 research universities, 33; among 109 doctoral-granting, 46; among 595 master's level institutions, 264 (Carnegie Foundation 1987). Thus we find private institutions along the line, in all university-relevant categories, interacting in the general market of reputation with state institutions as well as with private peers. In turn, the public institutions all fall under the individual states. None is nationalized in its core institutional support. The national government is not the primary patron, hence it is not the primary shaper of institutional character. In the latest reckoning, 'Funds from the federal government – appropriations, grants, and contracts – provided 13 percent of college and university revenue' (American Council on Education 1989: 145).

Extensive institutional differentiation

A long unplanned evolution that has only been seriously dented by some state co-ordination during the last quarter of a century (by state 'master plans') has led to enormous differentiation of types of institutions, ranging from research universities to community colleges, with extensive differences appearing within the types. The evolved ecology contains a plethora of self-determined niches (Clark 1987). The great differentiation has promoted high access to the system at large and the development of low cost segments that have high student–

staff ratios. It also has allowed for extreme selectivity in some institutions, with high costs and low student–staff ratios. And the primordial differentiation has permitted vast differences in the support of graduate education and in the support of research activity, making possible within an extended range of institutions a large number of centres of excellence in graduate education and research training, as judged by international standards.

Dual tiers

For university organization, the most distinctive American contribution has been the evolution of the graduate school as a formal higher tier of operations on top of the undergraduate college (Clark 1983). In the graduate school, everyone understands, research can be, ought to be, and often is in the driver's seat. While the undergraduate level is variously engaged in general education, liberal education, early work in a discipline, the maturation of the young – and is the right place for 250-pound 'kids' to play football – the graduate school is a separate place in commitment and spirit. Department by department, a new search for students is made, on as wide a geographic basis as reputation permits. Once admitted by the graduate school, students face numerous required taught courses and seminars, comprehensive examinations, faculty committee approval of dissertation topic and successful completion. The graduate school and the constituent departments possess teaching assistantships and some institution-funding fellowships. Much formal machinery exists to help faculty bring in research grants that total over $200 million in leading institutions in the late 1980s, a part of which goes for research assistantships for graduate students.

The graduate school is a strong organizational foundation for an organic development of research and research training in a formal educational setting. Faculty members have their heart in it, maintaining a steady pressure for more graduate students and fewer undergraduates. And here is where leading private universities set the pace by offering attractive conditions of far fewer undergraduate students per faculty member and a higher proportion of carefully selected graduate students. The graduate school (leaving aside the graduate-level professional schools) at such private universities as Chicago, Columbia and Stanford, approximates the size of the undergraduate college.

At the same time, decentralized control and extensive sector differentiation in a large system have led to a great variety of graduate programmes. Some are virtually research think tanks with a few very bright graduate students and post-docs involved in many departments and research clusters, such as at Cal Tech, MIT and Stanford. At the other extreme, we find institutions not long out of their teacher college days, offering many different master's degrees, and doctoral degrees in a few fields, while struggling to create a research environment. The variability in quality and quantity of research output and in research-trained PhDs, is very great.

Intense institutional competition

Primary in the intense institutional competition of American higher education is competition for prestigious faculty. For faculty, in turn, what counts most beyond funds for research is the attraction of able graduate students, and often, as in the humanities, the students are the most important resource. Thus, without doubt, institutional competition in the American setting favours the building of the graduate level. Would-be universities are caught up in this dynamic. To advance, institutions have to concern themselves about the conditions for research, the recruitment of graduate students, and the funding and organizational support of each. To fall asleep for a decade in such matters is to fall behind. And labour mobility is promoted, not among 'teachers', but among 'distinguished scholars', 'leading researchers', and 'promising young talent'.

Diversified finance

American universities, whether nominally public or ostensibly private, operate with a diversified financial base: student tuition and fees; funds from multiple federal and state agencies; institutional endowment; non-endowment contributions from private individuals, corporations and foundations; income from hospital services and 'auxiliary enterprises' (American Council on Education 1989: 145–53). And since in the late twentieth century such diversification is the fiscal foundation for institutional autonomy, institutions steadily seek to increase their funding lines. That they do so is especially important for graduate education and research activities. Without it, the votes of constituencies would overwhelmingly favour undergraduate education. State universities receive their core support largely on the basis of undergraduate student numbers. Legislators and the general public centre their attention on undergraduate admission. Private universities find that many alumni, remembering their college days, want to see the college kept strong. They are willing to send money to remodel the old residence halls and the old gym, for the benefit of undergraduates. The graduate level plays to different paymasters; to multiply federal and state lines of research support; to private parties – individuals, foundations, corporations – interested in backing research and research training, who are willing to finance a shiny new lab, a research chair, a set of graduate student scholarships.

Most of all, the graduate level receives internal subsidies. As a product of the upward drift in faculty interest noted earlier, the graduate level receives a steady subsidy of expensive faculty time beyond what is officially conceded in allocations. Additionally, aided by such central officials as a Graduate Dean and a Vice-Chancellor for research, the research-minded faculty press for institutional support of graduate students. Such support (for *some* graduate students) then gradually gets built into the ongoing base budgets. As early as the 1920s and 1930s, graduate fellowships 'were a minor but consistent priority in private universities' fund-raising and a legitimate budget item in appropriations for state universities' (Geiger 1986: 221).

In the aggregate, the many money lines increase organizational slack and the opportunities for commingling funds, opening up operating space for local initiative. And the competition for prestige insures that administrators and faculty alike will seek initiatives that favour the research-based advanced tier. In local, state and national settings where there are so many incentives to promote mass higher education, diversified financing is crucial in the support of the inherently more 'elite functions' housed in the graduate school.

These six features of the American institutional context define a system that is large, sloppy, wastefully redundant, contradictory and confusing, and one in which consumers badly need a Buyer's Guide. It is also – by international standards – a system that is generous and populace-friendly; one that is possessed by a dynamic of competitive excellence, in the top half or more of the institutional hierarchy, in which to the victor goes the spoils of money and talent; and one that is replete with universities that are motivated to build the graduate level of education and to strengthen research training within it. Major problems and serious strains abound, from weak quality control to the militarization of federal R&D, but, as a product of history, the institutional base is both resilient in its capacity for self-determination and biased in its university sectors toward support of the most advanced tier. There is a capacity to retain research within that tier, even as the need and opportunity for research blossoms in non-university settings. Training for research is the hook, to the point where in the mind of Professor Cram and so many others it is assumed to be what graduate education is all about. In as many as a hundred universities, the marriage holds. After so many years together, the two often-quarrelsome partners even come to resemble each other.

The British pattern

With the American pattern as backdrop, I shall be brief and extremely simplistic about some core features of British higher education that seem strongly to condition graduate education and research. I shall slight similarities and emphasize contrasting conditions. The British system's features are:

1. smallness
2. nationalized control
3. minimal institutional differentiation
4. single tier university organization
5. slight institutional competition
6. unified finance.

Smallness

In the UK smallness is a reigning characteristic for institutions and the higher education system as a whole. Modal size universities in the late 1930s were under 1,000 full-time students; in the early 1960s, 1,000 to 2,000; in the early 1980s, 3,000 to 6,000 (Stewart 1989: 275). When ten new universities were established in the 1950s and 1960s, all were in the range of 2,000 to 8,000 students. The most noted one, the University of Sussex, was planned to have a faculty of 350 to 400 for a student body of 3,000, based on the traditional staff–student ratio of 1:8 (Heyck 1987: 215).

If small universities are to be at all comprehensive, they will have small departments for supporting graduate education and research training. At the same time, as disciplines expand and differentiate internally, the thresholds of 'critical mass' rise. These thresholds are increasingly defined internationally in many disciplines by large departments in large universities. At the undergraduate level, the advantages of smallness loom large, since it generally means residential life and intimate faculty–student relations. At the graduate level, disadvantages more quickly outweigh the advantages. When for every three or four undergraduates there is no more than one graduate student, an already small enrolment base shrinks by three quarters or more. Even with a generous staffing ratio, the twin small enrolment bases means small department faculties.

Nationalized control

The change in British higher education from ruggedly independent nineteenth-century universities, to a slowly evolving crypto-*dirigisme* in mid-twentieth century, to a full-throated *dirigisme* in the 1970s and 1980s has been so widely remarked and intensely written about that there is little to add other than to suggest that graduate studies are particularly affected when 'system' is elevated and 'institution' is depressed. Historically, British universities have shown considerable devotion to common standards (in the combination of the undergraduate honours degree and the inter-institutional scrutiny of external examiners), and to a relatively common level of minimal achievement for entry (in the A level passes). Formal nationalization has increasingly stressed such uniformities as a common 'unit of resource', a common salary schedule for faculty, a centrally controlled formula for proportion of staff in different ranks, and, above all, a formula by which central bodies distribute institutional support to the universities (Maclure 1987; Farrant 1987; Trow 1987; Trow 1988). An official system now focuses on the distribution of subjects nationally and assesses the contribution of individual departments. As put by John H. Farrant (1987):

> the UGC adopted thoroughgoing formula funding for its distribution to the universities in 1986. . . . For 1986–90, the framework of allocation

was provided by formulae that differentiated research from teaching, and that allocated a uniform sum to each university for teaching a unit of 'student load' in a given group of disciplines. Judgment was applied to the planned distribution of home student numbers by twenty categories, and three levels of subject studied, and to the relative research standing of universities in at least thirty-seven fields (Farrant 1987: 42).

The 'top-down, hands on' policy style, poorly positioned to consider local variation and need, bypasses the holistic character of individual institutions.

In a nationalized system, the always short supply of tacit knowledge in central bodies is a particular constraint on the provision of graduate education and research training. It is one thing to understand in high councils what goes on in undergraduate education, although that is difficult enough. It is much harder to be aware of the subtleties of what goes on in the many arcane specialties of the most advanced level and in the shifting array of research programmes in all their many institutional combinations. It is particularly in the domains of graduate education and research training, where operational diversity most strongly inheres, that organic development runs counter to the norms of unified system.

Minimal institutional differentiation

Informally as well as officially, academic drift in Britain has been heavily toward institutional similarity within the university sector, the public sector, and between the two. All are expected to hold to high standards that are explicitly defined and pursued across the board. The USA–Britain contrast on this dimension is startling, particularly when we recall the catch-as-catch-can interaction of 1,800 private institutions seeking niches in the emergent ecology of the US system on top of fifty public systems as different as Mississippi and California. Minimal differentiation, especially under nationalization, means similar costs and financial underpinnings as well as similar programmes and general educational ethos. Low cost–high cost differentials are then hard to come by. The promotion of expensive centres of excellence in graduate education and research, and a simultaneous low-cost promotion of undergraduate-only institutions, runs upstream against the flow of common standards, necessitating official debate and action.

Single tier university organization

Structurally and normatively, British higher education has an undergraduate fixation: 'pride of place [is] always accorded to first-degree programmes: it is conventional wisdom that those who practice and supervise research should have a strong base in undergraduate teaching' (Becher and Youll 1988). There is little or no incentive to 'escape' from undergraduates, an inclination widely found in the US system even if exaggerated in critical stereotypes. In Britain, 'university' still means primarily 'college': the honours degree is the centre-piece; the university is organized around the undergraduate level.

The twin commitment to undergraduate education and smallness makes it difficult to promote the graduate level. Large student numbers that would justify a formally organized 'graduate school' are hard to come by. The gradu-ate level is the home of the specialist, in a university system in which 'the generalist type' of individual, destined for public service after a first degree, has been a preferred product. As a result, graduate-level activities face a problem of marginality: 'In most British universities, postgraduates are gener-ally "marginal people", and lack the social integration of either undergradu-ates or academic staff' (Becher and Youll 1988; Kogan and Henkel 1989). At the same time, we may note that the British undergraduate operation is the base for high-quality input to graduate education. It selects carefully twice over, in its own intake and in its classifying of graduates, thereby importantly determining who will be part of a 'pure, thin stream of excellence' in post-graduate studies.

Slight institutional competition

Whatever institutional competition once existed in British higher education has been largely squeezed out by the commonalities of the evolved nationaliz-ation. 'State dependencies', operating under common formula, are not entre-preneurial universities. The job mobility of academics is dampened, the leverage of reputational authority is diminished. Then when expansion stops and/or funding decreases, academics are virtually frozen in place. The 'exit' decision is not available within the system for personal improvement and for a market-type leveraging of system improvement. More weight is put on 'voice', seeking personal and group improvement through political bargaining. And for those determined to leave a particular institution, or made redundant within it, brain-drain channels are the main recourse.

Unified finance

Central in the nationalization of British higher education, of course, has been the gathering and tightening of the purse strings by the national government. And within the government there has been a concentration of the power of the purse in one department formally responsible for all of education and the support of sciences. The combination of centralization and concentration has been carried a long way in the last two decades, to the point where it may be judged to be more single-sourced, more unified, than the counterpart structure of support in France, where there is more structural differentiation among major state-supported sectors and where *grandes écoles* are supported by various ministries, with some of the schools in this elite sector either privately funded or financed by local chambers of commerce (Friedberg and Musselin 1987: 93–100).

When finance is both centralized and concentrated, as the past decade has clearly shown, institutions not only lose much of their autonomy but also become exceedingly vulnerable to downsizing. When the single source reduces its financial contribution, local initiatives cannot play among multiple accounts. As suggested in earlier comments, graduate education is likely then to be particularly constrained, especially given its secondary, even marginal, status.

Conclusions

If there ever was an 'Anglo-Saxon' pattern of higher education, in contrast to a Continental model, it surely no longer exists. This inclusive term always obscured some large differences between the British and American systems; in the 1990s it clearly obscures much more than it reveals. And nowhere is this more true than in the institutional bases of graduate education, research training, and the existing and potential unity of research and study.

There seems little doubt that the unity ideal is well and alive in both countries, looming large in the preferences of academics, as it does in Germany and most other countries on the European Continent. But conditions and structures have long diverged in country-specific patterns, particularly between the USA and other countries, including Britain. The US and British systems *qua* systems have trod different pathways, thereby shaping graduate education and research training in different ways and setting different arrays of strengths and weaknesses, constraints and opportunities. The contrasting conditions to which I have pointed in grossly simplified form outline fundamentally different institutional bases. The American largeness, the British smallness; the American extreme decentralization and deconcentration, the British full nationalization and concentration; the American high degree of institutional competition, the British avoidance thereof; and then finally within the university itself, the American tendency toward graduate-school dominance and the British devotion to the undergraduate realm.

In setting the underlying problems of reform in graduate education and research, and how we go about confronting them, opposites predominate. Whatever happens to the American effort to hold together education and research, the main drift will be largely emergent, born out of the interaction of institutional and state and other 'local' initiatives, with national steerage attempting to get some purchase on a largely unplanned evolution. Any British pursuit of the unity option will be inherently more planned, more explicitly shaped by central deliberation, with local initiatives attempting to find room for manoeuvre. With the historical base so different and the evolving policy style so different, it is not ours to find a single best way to maintain and strengthen the unity option. Dominating the disciplinary and institutional imperatives that might otherwise promote a common course, opposite national settings are here in the driver's seat. Our differences are really very deep, very systemic.

References

American Council on Education (1989). *1989–90 Fact Book on Higher Education*. New York: Macmillan.

Becher, T. and Youll, P. (1988). Micro study: physics in Britain. Paper prepared for the UCLA Project on the Research Foundations of Graduate Education.

Ben-David, J. (1977). *Centers of Learning: Britain, France, Germany, United States*. New York: McGraw-Hill.

Carnegie Foundation (1987). *A Classification of Institutions of Higher Education*. Princeton, NJ: Carnegie Foundation for the Advancement of Teaching.

Clark, B. R. (1983). *The Higher Education System*. Berkeley and Los Angeles: University of California Press.

—— (1987). *The Academic Life: Small Worlds, Different Worlds*. Princeton, NJ: Carnegie Foundation for the Advancement of Teaching (ch. 1: 'The evolution of institutions').

Council of Graduate Schools (1989). *CGS Communicator*, April.

Farrant, J. H. (1987). Central control of the university sector. In Becher, T. (ed.) *British Higher Education*. London: Allen & Unwin.

Friedberg, E. and Musselin, C. (1987). The academic profession in France. In Clark, B. R. (ed.) *The Academic Profession: National, Disciplinary, and Institutional Settings*. Berkeley and Los Angeles: University of California Press.

Geiger, R. (1986). *To Advance Knowledge: The Growth of American Research Universities, 1900–1940*. New York: Oxford University Press.

Gellert, C. (1988). Research organization and the training of advanced scholars: the case of the Federal Republic of Germany. Paper prepared for the UCLA Project on the Research Foundations of Graduate Education.

Heyck, T. W. (1987). The idea of a university in Britain, 1870–1970. *History of European Ideas* 8(2): 205–19.

Hirch, W. (1982). Postgraduate training of researchers. In Oldham, G. (ed.) *The Future of Research*. At the University, Guildford: Society for Research into Higher Education.

Hofstadter, R. and Metzger, W. P. (1955). *Development of Academic Freedom in the United States*. New York: Columbia University Press.

Kogan, M. and Henkel, M. (1989). Research training and graduate education: the British macro-structure. Paper prepared for the UCLA Project on the Research Foundations of Graduate Education.

Maclure, S. (1987). The political context of higher education. In Becher, T. (ed.) *British Higher Education*. London: Allen & Unwin.

Stewart, W. A. C. (1989). *Higher Education in Postwar Britain*. London: Macmillan.

Trow, M. (1987). Academic standards and mass higher education. *Higher Education Quarterly* 41(3): 268–91.

—— (1988). Comparative perspectives on higher education policy in the UK and the US. *Oxford Review of Education* 14(1): 79–94.

Veysey, L. R. (1965). *The Emergence of the American University*. Chicago: University of Chicago Press.

Part 3

Prospects for Academic Research

12

Issues in American Science Policy

Robert M. Rosenzweig

As American science prepared to enter the 1990s, it faced an unusually difficult set of circumstances. Wherever one looks across the scientific horizon, one sees evidence of great creativity which has produced opportunities both for new discoveries and for greater exploitation of knowledge for human use. At the same time, one also sees evidence of unprecedented resource constraints imposed by the principal patron of modern science, the government, and what is perhaps even more troubling, one also sees signs that public confidence in the integrity and non-self-serving character of science and scientists has been shaken.

That is the setting in which science policy will be made in the years ahead. The more complicated and problematic the setting, though, the greater is the obligation to try to understand it, and by that test, our obligation at this meeting is high, indeed. So the best thing to do is to plunge ahead, finding order where it exists and sorting out disorder wherever possible.

I should make it clear at the outset that my main interest is in universities. As the suppliers of virtually all advanced technical, scientific and scholarly training and as the hosts to most of the fundamental research and much of the advanced applied research in the United States, they are clearly an important element in the total research enterprise. They are certainly not the whole of it; most applied research and virtually all development is done in industry and government labs. To overlook that fact is to miss an important part of the truth about research policy in the USA, namely that it embraces a large, dispersed and frequently disjointed enterprise. But an equally important part of the truth is that universities have come to hold the key to the success of the rest of the enterprise, and so to concentrate on university issues, while looking at the way government and industry interact with universities, is a useful way of understanding the whole.

At the usual risk of oversimplifying matters which are really more compli-cated, I shall address three classes of issues that seem to me to be at the core of current American science policy as seen through the university lens. First, not surprisingly, there is a set of resource issues that includes the simple question of how much money is available but also includes new questions about priorities that derive from the likelihood that however much money there is, it will not be enough. Second, I shall talk about an old American issue that has taken on new meaning as the justification for support of university research has moved in the direction of the purported contribution of research to economic development. I refer here to the shifting balance between the demands for widespread distribution of funds and the often conflicting goal of supporting the best science with the funds available. Finally, I shall address a number of matters affecting the climate in which research policy is made and the values of the universities in which research is done. Here, I have in mind such matters as fraud in research, issues raised by the potential commercial value of research, the animal rights movement, and what has come to be called in both countries 'NIMBY' (Not In My Backyard).

The funding of science

The Reagan Administration inherited a research enterprise that had suffered from the consequences of the Vietnam War and from a set of policies that began in Nixonian malice, improved marginally in the more benign atmosphere of the Ford Administration and had begun to change significantly in the last half of the Carter Administration. The evidence can be seen in the numbers. Total federal appropriations for R&D declined nearly 25 per cent in constant dollars from 1968 to 1975 – $40 billion to $31 billion. By 1982, the last year influenced by a budget of the Carter presidency, the total had grown to $36.5 billion – still short of the 1968 level but clearly moving in the right direction. Universities managed to hold their own during the period of decline. Their expenditures for R&D remained essentially stable in real dollars from 1968 to 1975, and during the inflationary years that followed, they managed a significant increase from $6 billion to $7.3 billion.

As always, the totals hide as much as they reveal. Beginning in about 1968, the government simply stopped investing in the capital structure of university-based research. Programmes in support of research facilities were ended, support of graduate students through fellowships declined precipitously, and the quality of research instrumentation was allowed to decline to an alarming degree. (In 1954, 1,600 fellowships and traineeships were available under government programmes. By 1969, that number had risen to 60,000; in 1986, the number was 12,800, slightly up from even lower years.) In fact, the policy of the government had become one of purchasing research outputs that were made possible by investments made in previous years. Any enterprise may face the need for such a policy as a short-term expedient, but if allowed to continue, it is a recipe for long-term disaster.

The Carter Administration had begun to see the problem and to formulate plans to deal with it when the electorate found other reasons to do without its services. Since national research policy until very recently has not reached the level of visibility in Presidential campaigns, it is no special criticism of the

Reagan Administration to report that it came to office without any. What it had instead was a set of pressures to deal with and a set of predispositions based largely on its view of the world and of the government's proper role in it. As Teich and Gramp (1988) have noted,

> The Reagan Administration did not come into office with a clear cut agenda for science and technology policy. Its early initiatives, in the Spring of 1981, which set the pattern for subsequent actions, were driven mainly by larger fiscal and policy choices. In civilian R&D, as in most other domestic areas, the budget drove policy, and cutting expenditures had an overriding priority. On the defense side, R&D rode the crest of increasing defense spending as the new President accelerated the military build-up that had begun in the last two years of the Carter Administration.
>
> In some areas, policy initiatives that went beyond budgetary considerations had major impacts on R&D. The first Reagan budget recommended deep cuts in energy R&D and demonstration programs, particularly on the non-nuclear side, as the President sought to fulfill his campaign promise to dismantle the Carter energy program and reverse its anti-nuclear tilt. R&D in the regulatory agencies, especially the Environmental Protection Agency, was also cut sharply as part of the Administration's deregulation thrust. And support for social science research and science education was reduced drastically for reasons that went beyond economy in government (Teich and Gramp 1988: 3).

The principal surprise of the Reagan Administration in this area as in others is the extent to which it succeeded in achieving its early goals. The energy programmes were virtually eliminated, social science research and science education programmes were sharply reduced and have recovered only slowly in subsequent years and, most important of all, defence R&D leaped forward with each increase in the defence budget. The most striking and perhaps the most important result of the Reagan years in R&D policy can be deduced from those early intentions. In 1980 the government spent about $1.10 in civilian R&D for every dollar spent on military R&D; in 1988 it spent about $2.20 in defence R&D for every dollar spent in the civilian sector (Teich and Gramp 1988: 7). That is as close to a policy revolution as one gets in a stable democracy.

The details of that change are additionally revealing. Within the defence R&D budget in those nine years, basic research increased only 11 per cent in constant dollars; applied research actually decreased by 7 per cent; and development, by which the military really means weapons testing, leaped ahead by a startling 99 per cent. The civilian side shows a decrease of 66 per cent in development, a decrease of 13 per cent in applied research, and an increase of 40 per cent in the support of basic research.

What one sees in those numbers is science policy as a derivative of much broader political, economic and social considerations. The military budget was driven by a powerful imperative to re-arm in a short period. Such a goal inevitably draws on existing technology because it cannot wait for new technology, much less new science. However, since even military budgets have limits, what can be deferred in the drive to accomplish the principal objective is put off. The science and technology base on which future progress depends was a principal victim of the rapid increase in military spending.

On the civilian side, the relatively large increase in spending for basic research is a bit misleading as a measure of Administration policy. There was, in fact, a disposition to support basic research as a distinctively national responsibility. The largest share of the increase, however – more than 40 per cent of it – came in funding for the National Institutes of Health, and much of that was added by the Congress over the Administration's objections. Moreover in the last several years, all of the increases in NIH have been directed to AIDS research, leaving other research areas no better off and in some cases worse.

The National Science Foundation (NSF) presents a special case. The first Reagan budget, that is to say, the Reagan revision of the final Carter budget, offered a reduction of 18.7 per cent for NSF. Much of that was to be taken from science education and research in the social and behavioural sciences, but there was no indication of affection or regard for any other aspect of the Foundation's work. That was the period, it will be recalled, when Milton Friedman, a guru whose acolytes occupied high positions, was arguing that neither research nor education was a proper responsibility of the federal government. In a remarkable turnaround, NSF, within a few years, became the darling of Administration science policy and the chief answer to critics who charged that the Administration had no science policy that was not directed by budgetary and national security interests.

The credit for the rise of NSF is shared (in proportions that I am unable to allocate) by its Director during those years, Erich Bloch, and the President's Science Adviser during most of the period, George A. Keyworth. Their argument had two parts. First, they argued that NSF, as the nation's principal instrument for the support of basic research in the physical sciences and mathematics, had been allowed to stagnate and that a large goal was required in order to draw attention to its importance. They proposed a doubling of the Foundation in five years. But merely to promise to do twice as much of the same things as in the past would not raise a flag around which political support would rally. Their answer was to build on to the Foundation's basic programmes of individual, investigator-initiated grants a restructuring of research activity into larger, interdisciplinary centres.

That proposal was supported by their second argument, namely that the scientific disciplines, as organized in universities, were obstacles to the performance of research in some new and exciting areas, including those with more direct connections to applications. They urged a change in the university culture away from tightly bounded disciplines defined by academic departments, to a more open cross-disciplinary form of organization as exemplified by the proposed new centres. It was their idea that organizing a significant fraction of new research in this way was intellectually necessary and that the new thrust would also have political appeal as the best way to connect basic research to economic productivity and the USA's international competitive position. Only by making that connection could the rest of the Foundation's activities be raised to the new, higher levels that they required.

Within the scientific community, this approach generated some support, but the opposition to it, ranging from scepticism to outright hostility, was louder, if not more numerous. Those whose work depended on the portion of the NSF budget allotted to investigator initiated grants never ceased to fear that more centres would mean fewer grants. The centres programme got off to a slow start because such fears were reflected in the Congressional appropriations committees. It should be said that before there was a penny appropriated for the programme, the first call for proposals produced about 400 elaborate, expensive proposals from universities. The centre idea had clearly taken hold. If further evidence of that proposition were needed, it is supplied by the Defense Department's (DOD) University Research Initiatives Program. DOD now funds more than one hundred university-based centres, each of which constitutes a node of political support for appropriations for the program.

It is hard to overstate the importance of the development of these larger aggregates for federal dollars. The rewards for winning one and the deprivation from failing to win, are far greater than those that attach to any ordinary research project. That is an invitation to political involvement in the allocation process. As the scale of science grows, so too does its value as a political good, with consequences yet to be seen.

With respect to NSF, the Bloch/Keyworth initiative shows once again that politics, including the politics of science, is full of ironies. It is surely ironic that Keyworth and Bloch won the argument with their hardest audience, the budget and policy barons of an Administration notably inhospitable to proposals to enlarge the size of government, but lost it in the ordinarily friendlier Congress. Notwithstanding repeated Administration requests for a five-year programme to double the budget of NSF beginning in the mid-1980s, the record from 1980 to 1988 showed an increase of 73 per cent in nominal dollars, and only 17 per cent in constant dollars.

The problem in the Congress is not so much hostility toward NSF, of which there is very little, but a collision between its needs and those of the other agencies with which it shares a common appropriations bill. However, the Foundation's cause has undoubtedly been hurt by the unwillingness of the Administration to bring its political guns to bear in its support. That problem has, in turn, been compounded by serious and vocal misgivings in parts of the scientific community about the direction in which the 'new' NSF would go. In part, that opposition arose from fear that the glamorous new centres would take money away from the small, investigator-initiated projects that have always been the heart of the Foundation's work. In part, it was the product of a related fear that the new thrust of the Foundation moved it away from basic science to a greater emphasis on engineering and development. The former is, of course, always debatable, and it is hard to debate people's fears. It is true that the core directorates of the Foundation, those which support investigator-initiated projects, have done less well than other parts of the Foundation. However, Congress's attachment to science education is at least as responsible for that result as the centre programme. In any case, the fears are real. The latter, however, is demonstrably true. The NSF has substantially augmented its engineering and technology programmes. Indeed, for the NSF to have failed to respond to the public and Congressional concerns about the erosion of the USA's technology base would have probably relegated it to a policy backwater that would have seriously damaged all its activities.

As someone who has testified regularly before Congressional authorizing and appropriating committees since the mid-1980s, I can offer personal witness to the intensity of those concerns. The inability of some of the United States' best scientists to grasp that fact does not speak well either for their political sophistication or for their ability to think beyond their next grant application. The inability of the Foundation's and the Administration's leadership to overcome the suspicions that nourished the underlying fears suggests a failure in those quarters, too.

In summary, then, the main features of the Reagan Administration in terms of science policy were its overwhelming commitment to military development and its comparative indifference to civilian research, save for an uncompleted effort to enlarge sharply the National Science Foundation. With the exception of some new money for research instrumentation, it showed no greater disposition to attack deficiencies in the research infrastructure than had its predecessors. It will not be remembered as an administration that was hostile to research, but neither was it especially thoughtful or systematic in its approach.

It might be argued that research policy in the USA is always the by-product of other policy concerns. Whether that is necessarily or always the case, the Reagan Administration provides further evidence in support of the argument. It is fitting, therefore, that the principal legacy to science policy of Mr Reagan's years has nothing at all to do with science. It is the fact that, while it took all of his predecessors a full 200 years to accumulate a national debt of $1,000,000,000,000, he managed the second trillion in just eight years. No wind will blow that cloud of zeros away, and its presence changes the way we must think about science policy. All resource questions for the foreseeable future will be decided in a context of budgetary stringency.

It is extremely difficult to have that fact taken seriously, and for good reason. The US political system does not reward those who make choices that give pain. The same President who preached small government and low taxes, nevertheless arranged to spend $17 billion on a Strategic Defense Initiative (SDI) that was, at best, problematic in scientific and technical terms. Bailing out the failed savings and loan companies is now estimated to cost $300 billion. Somehow the money will be found. Examples can be multiplied endlessly. So weak are the political incentives for facing the budgetary problem that the former director of the Congressional Budget Office, Rudolph Penner (1989) viewing the way in which the Administration and the Congress were conspiring to pretend to meet their agreed reduction was moved to say, 'I couldn't conceive in my wildest dreams how much cheating they'd engage in.'

What reason is there for anyone to think seriously about how to spend less when evidence of the unwillingness of others to do so is all around? The answer is that science is vulnerable. It does not profit materially from SDI and not at all from the savings and loans bail-out. Instead, large expenditures for such activities put greater pressure on the part of the budget that contains most of science, the so-called domestic discretionary element. There, science competes not only with itself but also with housing, veterans programmes, education, and many other social welfare activities that have important claims on public funds. That pressure will not go away. Even if the President were to propose to double the entire civilian science budget, the Congress would have its own views and its own constituencies to respond to, and somehow choices would need to be made, even at a higher budget level.

As a consequence, it will be difficult to avoid the dreaded 'P' word, priorities. Nobody likes the word, nobody wants to think about it, nobody really knows how to think about it. The National Academy of Sciences prepared a useful report on the subject for the Congressional Budget Committees. The report was solicited following a speech by Frank Press, President of the NAS (in the spring of 1988) in which he laid out clearly the claims of science in the context of the budget realities and urged that the scientific community begin to think about how to help the government decide among competing claims. The resulting report identified four classes of expenditures and suggested priorities among them. It was a useful beginning, but it remains to be seen what, if anything, will be made of it.

It is important to understand just how great a difference the consequences of the budget deficit make to science policy and to universities. For much of the post-war history of science funding, there was reasonable assurance that each year would bring larger appropriations than the year before. Not enough, perhaps, to fill everyone's wish list, but enough to sustain ongoing activities and start some new ones. Even when, as in the first half of the 1970s, that was not the case, it was easier to believe that the constraints were a temporary aberration rather than a new way of life. Moreover, the Carter Administration seemed to provide evidence to support that view.

The current situation is different. Most obviously, the budget agreement reached by the President and the Congress in 1990 limits increases in domestic discretionary spending to inflation or less for two years and limits total spending for another two. Thus the annual increases in total spending that supported the increases in science funding are no longer probable, or perhaps even possible. As a consequence, too, the rules of the Congressional appropriations process require that increases be made within the fixed limit of each appropriations category, so that increases in one programme must be balanced by offsetting decreases in others. Since, by definition, every programme in the budget has a constituency that was powerful enough to put it there, all offsetting decreases will be resisted by some politically potent group.

The prospect of scarcity has other kinds of consequences, as well. The Politics of Addition are different from the Politics of Subtraction, and nowhere more so than in coalitions. In the former, the members work together in the knowledge that in unity there is strength. In the latter, each member of the coalition is conscious of the fact that if a politically advantageous moment for it should arrive, the successes it may achieve are likely to come at the expense of a friend, and while it may be confident of its ability to withstand temptation, it has no such confidence in its friends. Conversely, any sign of favour directed toward one member of the coalition is likely to be converted into a demand by the others for their fair share. Subtraction breeds divisiveness, suspicion and tension, and that is at least one description of the current state of the overlapping coalitions of science and higher education today.

A recent, vivid example of the Politics of Subtraction can be found in the unhappy history of the Research Facilities Modernization and Renovation programme enacted as part of the National Science Foundation Act 1988. It is reasonably well understood, now that modern research has become a capital-intensive activity. Indeed, one useful definition of 'Big Science' is science in which capital costs exceed labour costs, a definition that now embraces most of the biological and physical sciences. It is also well documented that the failure of the government to attend to the capital needs of the institutions in which the research it sponsors is done has led to an overall deterioration of the capital stock and has imposed great pressures on universities to find ways to modernize their plant and equipment.

That underlying rationale was given political impetus by perceived connections between university-based research and increased productivity and competitiveness, and a receptive climate grew in the Congress in support of legislation to begin to address the problem. The moment that became apparent, battle lines were drawn, and they did not pit liberals against conservatives or big spenders against budget cutters, as might have been the case in earlier years. In this case, the adversaries were in the same coalition. The research universities, the originally intended recipients of the programme, were challenged by undergraduate colleges and historically black colleges, who, seeing a rare opportunity, were not going to let it pass. The resulting legislation created a small programme divided among so many classes of recipients and serving so many diverse purposes that, even if it were fully funded, it would do little of what it was intended to do in its conception.

But merely authorizing a programme is only the first step through the maze. As I have described, funding is yet another matter, and it brought still another set of interests into play. The President did not propose to fund the new programme in the 1990 budget, so an effort to have the Congress fund it would require an offsetting reduction, and the most likely place for it to be taken was in some other area of the National Science Foundation. As that became clear, the programme's adversaries came to include (1) the leadership of the National Science Foundation, who had worried all along that this very situation would arise; (2) scientists (university faculty) who depend on NSF for their support and who were understandably worried that funding for facilities would come at their expense; and (3) an increasing number of research university presidents, who had been among the chief proponents of the legislation as first conceived, but who now saw their universities and their faculties exchanging real and important research dollars for hypothetical and, in any case, minuscule facilities dollars. Those arguing for an appropriation now numbered only those who thought they had seen an opportunity for some easy money. In the event $20 million was appropriated in each of two years, at best a tiny place-holder for a large, unresolved problem.

Failure to think seriously about the subject of priorities has serious consequences. It is frequently argued that it is too difficult politically for members of a coalition to decide which of their goals belong at the top of the list and which are deferrable. That it is difficult is beyond question, but the case of the NSF Facilities Programme is evidence that one does not avoid political difficulty by avoiding hard questions.

One important reason why the priorities question is so difficult is because the argument always takes place over programmes and proposals that are so far advanced that their substantive justification is unassailable. The argument against the Superconducting Supercollider (SSC) is not that the science it will permit is unimportant or second class, but that it will take money away from activities of at least equal quality and importance – activities that are, moreover, incommensurable in any but dollar terms. The debate, therefore, is likely to take the form of 'My work is more important than your work', an assertion that, even if true, suffers from self-interest.

No doubt, it is important to have those discussions, and the NAS report gives us the categories to help us organize them and to avoid some glaring pitfalls. But the main problem with the priorities debate is that it always takes place within the confines of a critical, unspoken assumption, namely that the size of the scientific enterprise, as a whole, is a given; that it cannot contract; and that it must expand to accommodate newcomers. That has been the governing assumption of American science policy since the end of the Second World War. It was an assumption that took root in a time when resources were expanding to permit the system to expand. The effect was to render the concentration of the largest share of research funds at a relatively small number of institutions politically tolerable. Steadily increasing funding allowed demonstrated quality to be served and new aspirants to be admitted into the system at the same time. When, however, the assumption is not supported by increased funding, and if the assumption itself remains unchanged, then the result must be pressure for a redistribution of whatever money is available away from existing performers for the benefit of newcomers.

That is the issue that the budget deficit raises inescapably. Under the best of circumstances, it is a difficult issue in a representative political system. It is especially difficult in the American setting with all of its historical ambivalence about the competing values of merit and entitlement. And it has been made more difficult yet by the belief that having a thriving research institution in one's midst is more than a matter of mere prestige; it is the key to economic prosperity.

Sharing the pie

One of the most common and most vexing of all social phenomena is the unequal distribution among populations of benefits and obligations, successes and failures, rewards and penalties. Human abilities, intellectual and physical, are unequally distributed; income and wealth are typically more unevenly shared in capitalist than in socialist economies, but even in the latter, elite groups wind up possessing more of the things that wealth can buy; in politics, we may not be in the grip of Michel's Iron Law of Oligarchy, but few would argue that any real world political system distributes power and influence evenly; even in so trivial an activity as organized athletics, the same small number of teams in each sport seem to wind up at or near the top each year. Fortunately, it is not my task here to explain why the phenomenon is so pervasive across such a wide range of activities. I do, however, need to point out that the distribution of government research funds to universities is another example to add to the list.

From the beginning, there has been a demonstrable concentration of federal research dollars in a relatively small number of universities. That concentration began with the existing distribution of strength at the close of the Second World War and the need of the Department of Defense to build on that strength in its post-war research programmes. Some of those same universities had major medical schools and were well positioned to take advantage of the growth of NIH. That growth also brought additional institutions into the top group. The Johns Hopkins University is the paradigm case, with its huge Applied Physics Laboratory, wholly funded by DOD, and its eminent medical school putting it regularly at the top of the list of recipients of federal funds.

The facts about the concentration of funds are well known. What is less well known is that the identity of the institutions in the top group does change. Since 1970 four universities have displaced four others in the top twenty and nineteen edged another nineteen out of the top one hundred. It is hard to believe that one would want much more movement than that in a set of activities requiring large capital investments and in which stability and predictability have a high value. While that movement was taking place, the size of the universe was also expanding. At present, 125 universities receive more than $10 million a year in federal research funds.

By any measure, that is a large number of universities competing seriously to do advanced research. Why, then, does the pressure to distribute the money still more widely grow stronger? Extending the sports analogy one step further may suggest the answer. Notwithstanding the odds against being able to build a winning team, the competition for new franchises among promoters and the cities they represent is fierce and the bidding is high. The reasons are clear: it is widely believed that by owning a major league team and by having one in one's city, there is money to be made and glory to be won. Research universities are now in the class of major league sports franchises.

It is more accurate and fairer to say that research and development have become big business and universities, as key elements in the system, have become parts of that business. There has, of course, long been some connection between university research and industrial application. The field of chemistry has perhaps the longest history of that kind, but it has not been unknown in other fields as well. However, the growth of the computer industry and the birth of academic computer science marked a qualitative and quantitative change in the relationship, and those changes were reinforced by the invention in university laboratories of recombinant DNA technology with its host of potential applications. The story from that point on has been followed in the popular press and elsewhere, as well as any story involving universities ever has, with the possible exception of intercollegiate athletics. One early development involved the signing of a few large research agreements between companies and universities. In computers, IBM developed extensive connections with Carnegie Mellon, Brown, and several other universities involving the development and testing of software. In biotechnology, Monsanto funded Harvard and Washington University. Hoechst combined with Massachusetts General Hospital and a small number of other large contracts made the headlines. Meanwhile, the business of licensing patents arising from their faculties research grew from a rather arcane specialty engaged in by a few enterprising places to a rather larger and more aggressive activity in which a few have made some real money and many more are hoping to.

Another new stage appears to have been reached when universities which had refrained from investing in the commercialization of their faculties research began to find ways to do so. Some have been quite aggressive in that way; others, like Harvard, which had held back for reasons of academic principle, looked for and found instrumentalities that seemed to them to be less objectionable to those principles.

I shall have occasion to return to this subject later in another context. For the present, I shall point out only that the distribution of economic advantage has political consequences. As state legislators, governors and congressmen began to hear from their university leaders that there was gold in the form of money and jobs to be found in research, that actions of federal agencies determined who could enter the competition, and that the competition had been rigged to favour a few rich performers while excluding the worthy poor, the result was inevitable. The pressure to turn science policy into science politics became irresistible.

In a democracy, of course, politics are never wholly absent from policy, nor would we want them to be. Certainly in the area of science policy, large decisions have been shaped by political considerations both of the kind that are constituency-based and those that are more partisan in character. To a remarkable degree, though, political actors have been willing to defer to science professionals on decisions about what work will receive public funds. Although some possible explanations come to mind, it is not entirely clear why science should have been accorded such exceptional treatment, but it is clear that it has.

In 1983, the Congress took a sharp turn in a different direction when it voted, without reference to the cognizant agency or its own committees, funds for science buildings at Columbia University and Catholic University. Organized science and higher education responded with alarm and disapproval at this departure from the practice of competition judged by qualified professionals as the basis for the award of funds, but to no avail. The door had been opened by two highly respectable universities and through it came the release of pressures that had been building up for a decade and more. Three are of principal interest here. The first was the accumulated backlog of facilities needs to which I have already referred. The second was the accumulated resentment toward the large and successful universities that had for so long dominated the research system, and the third was the new political conviction that research was the key to economic growth and was, therefore, to be subject to a new set of distributional rules.

The interaction between the second and third of those forces has transformed the science policy scene. The economic argument gave new point to old hostilities. In the past, the periodic swing of the pendulum toward a more populist view of science and of universities was eventually overcome by arguments about the overriding importance of intellectual quality if funds for science were to achieve their intended purpose. Perhaps that will be the case once again, but it is important to recognize that we are no longer engaged in a debate about science policy, or even about national defence, space or public health. The current turn toward the politics of distribution is based on underlying arguments about the fair distribution of wealth across the nation, a force that in politics has its own historic logic and momentum.

There are signs that the growth of congressional direct appropriations for science may have its own self-limiting quality. Opposition to the practice has been growing within the Congress and has picked up some influential voices. It may be that the gaggle of claimants has become too large, too unwieldy, too difficult to deal with, and so some restraints may be imposed. That would be a happy development, but it would not make the central problem disappear. The connection between science and jobs has been fixed in the public mind and the arguments for distributing jobs fairly are of a very different force and character from the arguments for distributing science on the basis of intellectual merit.

We are perhaps learning again the old lesson that having one's representations ignored can be humiliating, but having them believed can be even worse. The connection between developments in science and economic growth has surely been oversold. In the long run, there is a connection between developments in science and fundamental technology and the creation of wealth, but it is not the crude one that is being so widely hawked today: if the science is done here, the wealth will be created here and stay here. With respect to basic science, it is nearer the truth to say that the nation that supports first-class science has the opportunity, if other economic and social policies are hospitable, to gain economic advantage from some lines of research. Viewed in that light, policies with regard to tax structure, incentives for saving, attitudes toward entrepreneurship, the cost of capital, the quality of education and training, to mention but a few, become the key elements of a national programme, the basis for translating knowledge into wealth. Treating science as if its distribution should be governed by the same principles as govern the distribution of economic opportunity will have the perverse effect of diminishing the quality of science and diverting attention from policies more directly relevant to the production of wealth.

We have not found a satisfactory way of dealing with the attention being lavished on science and advanced technology for reasons that produce policies that may, in fact, inhibit their development. Arguments on behalf of quality as the most important criterion for deciding who shall receive public funds are vulnerable to the charge that they are self-serving efforts to protect undeserved privilege. If we fail to find convincing ways of protecting the policies that helped to build such productive science in American universities – if, that is to say, constituency-based politics continue to grow in importance – then there are ample outlets for its practice, even if direct funding for facilities were to be limited. Most obviously, all of the laboratories for which funds have been appropriated since the early 1980s without regard to merit will come on line as competitors for project funds. Some will do well, but it is entirely predictable that others will not. The same arguments that produced their construction will surely be brought out again in support of the award of project funds to protect the investment already made. Perhaps the line between facilities funding and project funding will be strong enough to hold, but confidence can be based only on faith, not evidence.

We are at an important point in the history of science policy in the USA. One of the foundations of that policy since the 1950s has been the conviction that intellectual quality matters, that it ought to be supported wherever it is found, and that the best way to find it is through open competition that is judged by professionals in the relevant field. As I have argued here, growth of the system made that conviction work in practice. It provided room for new centres of quality and protection against institutional ambition that was not grounded in quality. The Congress helped to lay the foundation and it helped to protect it in practice by a combination of unusual self-restraint about allocation decisions and generosity in appropriations. The latter is hardly possible today and the former is in serious doubt. The 1990s will reveal much about the future quality of university-based science.

Matters of the soul

The heading of this section may seem a bit melodramatic, but it strikes me as altogether appropriate, because I turn now to a set of issues confronting research universities that do, in a very real sense, define their nature and are, therefore, matters of the soul. They constitute (in my view) a test of whether the changes that have been wrought in these institutions by their heavy commitment to research have changed their fundamental character and values or whether they are challenges that will be met by the application of traditional values to new circumstances. Specifically, I shall address an important change in the public climate for research, and with that as background, I shall take up the issues of fraud and misconduct and the commercialization of research.

It really is true that there once was a simpler time for science. Whether it was a better time, all things considered, is a more difficult question to answer, but that it was an easier one is beyond dispute. It was a time in which it was widely believed that science could do no wrong, that its imperatives were by definition those of the public's, as well. Generous public funding was the most visible symbol of that time, which can be dated from the Second World War; but what underlay the money was a belief in the totally benign quality of science, both in its conduct and in its consequences. It may not have been the Golden Age of Science, but it was surely the Golden Age of Scientists.

It should be said that this happy state did not last very long. While it is hard to date the beginning of the change from it with great precision, the movement for the protection of human subjects in the early 1960s is as good a marker as any. The political demand for the regulation of research using human subjects grew, it will be recalled, out of long-delayed revelations about medical experiments on prisoners dating back to the 1930s. Those revelations were followed by stories of other experiments, which, especially against the background of the concentration camp experiments of the Nazis, caused understandable discomfort.

Two things need to be said about the response of scientists to restrictions on the use of human subjects. The first is that they opposed them, arguing that they would interfere with research, that important findings would be lost, and that they, themselves, were capable of regulating their own behaviour. The second thing to be said is that they lost the argument and lost, too, a bit of the public confidence that all science was good science, that all science was good for people, and that scientists were always reliable arbiters of the public interest when their own work was at issue.

It is tempting to say that it was all down hill from there. It is certainly hard to find many public statements like that of Nobel Laureate David Baltimore to the American Association for the Advancement of Science (AAAS) in 1988:

> biology, or any science, will do its best and do the most if left free to establish its own priorities. This is one of our community's most deeply held beliefs: that all science progresses best autonomously, without external direction by the public, by administrators or by politicians.

Anyone who has had to operate in the public arena will recognize how far out of keeping with current reality such pure doctrine is. The environmental movement has taught the public that many of the problems for which science may be part of the cure were caused by uncritical application of earlier science. Nuclear power is far from the unmixed blessing that it once appeared to be; creating new organisms by recombining DNA, even if it is safe, is full of problems; very good research produces very bad waste products, whose disposal presents thorny problems; and as computers grow more powerful, so, too, do the variety of social controls they make available to the state and large commercial organizations. No polity could allow activities of such enormous concern to it to operate with unqualified autonomy.

In the usual way of such things, however, a necessary corrective has swung so far that it has, itself, become an evil to be guarded against. A healthy public scepticism about the claims of any group, including scientists and universities, has begun to turn into a well-financed negativism that plays on fear of the unknown and attempts to exploit public emotions rather than appeal to public intelligence. Just one year after David Baltimore's address to the AAAS, Donald Kennedy, Stanford's president, spoke to the same audience in San Francisco. He spoke of the growing feeling in Washington that universities and science are regarded as 'just another interest group'. He said:

> There is another and much more local manifestation. It takes the form of a generalized fear and mistrust of the perceived external costs of scientific work. You have come for this meeting to an unusually beautiful and admired part of the United States, and one that has an exceptional concentration of distinguished research universities. But I can say, speaking for the leadership of all of them, that you are also visiting the nation's capital of activist, single-issue, 'not-in-my-back-yard' politics when it comes to the externalities of politics.
>
> During the past two years, for example, facilities for the housing of research animals have been held up at the University of California, Berkeley and at Stanford by objections on the part of animal rights activists. The delays were accomplished by different means, challenge to a state legislative appropriation and lawsuits in one case, objections to the building permit at the county level in the other. The two together cost the universities in excess of two and a half million dollars. At Stanford the construction of a new animal facility designed to house rodents was held up for over a year by the delayed imposition of an environmental impact report – the first ever required for an academic building on campus. A similar delay was imposed on the construction of a new biological sciences building. In both Stanford cases, concerns about recombinant DNA research and toxic waste discharge were brought forward by objecting groups. But it is interesting to note that the leaders who used environmental concerns to force construction delay of the animal facility were the same ones who had earlier opposed its construction on animal rights grounds. I think it is fair to say that the real agenda was not the stated one.

All of this is to say that there is a growing concentration of well-financed, single-interest groups directed against key aspects of modern research in universities. In the Stanford case, there was an alliance between animal rights activists and the part of the environmental movement that has focused on the alleged dangers of recombinant DNA research. It is a dangerous development, and those who think it can be shrugged off by noting that these incidents happened in California should remember the number of times when a development in that strange state turned out to be not unrepresentative but prematurely representative, if I may coin a new political term.

The underlying point, however, is that these challenges would hardly have been taken seriously by political bodies in the mid-1970s. In the years since, the unquestioned belief in the virtue of universities and of science has been chipped away. There are political answers to political assaults, but even the most skilful politics cannot for long overcome a reality that is actually decaying. That is why the response of universities to the recent rash of cases of research fraud and misconduct and the way in which they manage the commercial spin-off from their research are so important. If handled badly, they can provide confirmation of a further fall from virtue. If, however, they are dealt with in ways that elicit confidence in their motives and their competence, they can help to alter the climate for the better.

Fraud and misconduct in research

It is not possible to know whether the incidence of fraudulent science has increased, decreased or remained about the same compared to any earlier period. One might reasonably conclude that, since there are more practising scientists today than ever before, and more science is being done, there must be more fraud in absolute, if not in relative, terms. Alternatively, one might observe that the pressures on scientists today are heavier than ever before – grants are hard to get, tenure is problematic, economic stakes are high – and so the temptation to cut corners in order to produce the right finding will lead more scientists into the path of sin. One might say that there has never been much fraud and there is not much now, because science protects itself through replication. Alternatively, one might say that replication is nonsense, very little work is ever actually replicated, and so the cases that come to light are only a small fraction of the ones that occur but remain hidden. None of those statements has been empirically verified, and so the recent controversy over the subject of fraud and misconduct in research has had a somewhat surreal air to it.

What is the argument about? If there is a lot of fraud, someone should prove it; if there is very little, let's stop the fuss and get back to work. The trouble is that the argument is really not about incidence; it is about confidence. What is at issue is not how often fraud occurs, but whether, when it is alleged to occur, the allegation will be dealt with expeditiously and guilt, if found, will be dealt with firmly. The policy questions that follow when the issue is understood in that way are: Who should be responsible for seeing to it that such a result is achieved? Should it be the institution in which the fraud is alleged to have occurred? Should it be the government? Or should it be some as yet non-existent third party that is neither university nor government?

It seems like a rather mechanical question; however, it is anything but. Rather, it is a question that goes to the heart of institutional responsibility.

Just what is a university responsible for? It is generally understood, for example, that universities are responsible for punishing students who are caught cheating. Therefore, most institutions have long had student disciplinary codes and judicial processes for enforcing them. In contrast, until very recently, most universities did not have clear codes of conduct for faculty and among those that did, still fewer had in place procedures for dealing with alleged violations. Most often, faculty misconduct, including fraud in research, was handled informally and quietly, using procedures made up for the occasion. At worst, at least until recently, it was not handled at all. In the last several years, a new category of 'worst' has been added. It consists of cases handled badly, which then become public.

The public airing in the press and in the Congress of a small number of cases in that last category has shaken public confidence that universities are able to warrant the integrity of the work that their faculty do. A poll conducted by the Gallup Organization for the American Medical Association in early 1989 reported that 17 per cent of the respondents in a national sample believe that 'a lot' of fraud is taking place and a further 41 per cent think that a 'fair amount' goes on. Those numbers suggest more than casual cynicism; they question the roots of faith in the entire process, and they should sound a loud alarm to those who care about the condition of American science. People who hold such views are unlikely to defend science against charges that it is cruel to animals and that it pollutes the environment or to believe that it is worth spending much money on.

There are encouraging signs that universities have seen the problem and are attempting to deal with it. Virtually all major universities now have policies and procedures for dealing with transgressions against accepted norms of research, and if they are not too late, they are not a moment too soon. It is, I believe, essential for universities to demonstrate that they have the will and the ability to deal fairly and efficiently with charges involving the integrity of research. Failure to act in ways that restore confidence would be to concede that they are little more than collections of individual faculty entrepreneurs held together by reason of administrative convenience but with no collective will or conscience.

Universities and commerce

Although the odds, and the weight of scientific opinion, now seem against it, in the end it may turn out that cold fusion will fulfil all of the claims made for it by Professors H. Stanley Pons and Martin Fleischmann and officials of the University of Utah. If so, it will be forgotten that this episode stands as one of the clearest cases yet of the pernicious effects of the intrusion of commercial values into research. That would be too bad, because there are important lessons to be learned if there is a will to do so.

The 17 May 1989 issue of the *Chronicle of Higher Education* captured the essence of the case in a brief story with the headline, 'Questions of Credibility:

Prospect of Commercial Gain from Unconfirmed Discovery Prompted Utah U. Officials to Skirt Usual Scientific Protocol'. The story read in part:

> If it had been entirely up to them, the two scientists who claim to have pioneered room-temperature fusion might have taken another year and a half to refine their research before announcing their findings. . . . But University of Utah officials, concerned that news of the research might leak out and jeopardize the prospects of commercializing its results, advised the scientists to scrap their schedule, prepare a preliminary paper on their work, and hold a press conference even before it was published.

It is as if those who most fear and resist any connections between universities and the world of commerce had been given the power to create the scenario that best made their point for them and to have it come true. It was all there; an ironic combination of premature exposure of a controversial finding because it had potentially great economic value, on the one hand, and great secrecy about what was actually being disclosed and how it had been done, on the other. In scientific terms, the result was to hide error and to inhibit the discovery of truth, whatever it turns out to be, for some indefinite period. In public terms, it did not take long for the press to turn on all of science with scorn and derision, seeming to feel that the physicists who derided the Utah work were as concerned about the protection of their stake in the continuation of support for hot-fusion research as they were for the truth of the matter.

To compound the problem, the Utah troupe, flushed with enthusiasm for the attention their announcement had received, appeared in Washington at a congressional committee hearing orchestrated by a high-powered – and expensive – lobbyist to ask for the down payment on a multi-million-dollar programme to exploit the as-yet-undisclosed and unconfirmed process which they had 'discovered'.

Thus, the headline, 'Questions of Credibility', went far beyond doubt as to whether the science was right to consideration of whether the process and the profession were right, or had become so infected with the acquisitive virus as to undermine confidence in their underlying integrity.

Obviously, if the Utah case were an isolated episode, it could be viewed as a regrettable curiosity. However, it is not. The term 'science by press conference' was coined in the 1970s. It grew out of some well-publicized cases in the area of biotechnology, and it is now a too-regular feature of scientific communication. More broadly, no topic of science policy has received more attention in the popular media than has the connection between science and business. It is an odd literature, compounded in roughly equal parts of cheerleading at the wondrous possibilities of this new alliance and worry about its dangerous consequences. Perhaps in this case, the popular media are speaking a popular wisdom.

It should be noted that the first development to catch the public attention as a problem has turned out not to be one. The fear that large corporations would, through a series of blockbuster grants to leading university departments, 'buy' the work of those departments, thus purchasing commercial advantage and corrupting the purity of science, was, in the event, exaggerated. It was not what industry wanted, and, in any case, science is too large and diffuse an enterprise reliably to yield such results to any sponsor.

The source of the real problems is the recognition, first, that some university science has the potential to create economic value, and second, the pressure to translate that value into economic return by moving scientific discoveries into the stream of commerce as rapidly as possible. But how shall that return be distributed? The government is satisfied to take its share in the form of tax revenues produced by greater business activity. The traditional form of return for industry is through profits. But universities believe that they are entitled to a share of the value they have helped to create and so, too, of course, do the faculty who are the creators. The stronger the pressure within universities to maximize return, the greater the potential for problems to arise. The difference between a university policy to aid in the patenting of inventions made by its faculty and a policy to encourage patentable inventions may be small in practice but enormous in its consequences for the kind of research that faculty undertake and the openness with which they do it. Similarly, institutional policies that encourage or discourage faculty entrepreneurship can produce very different patterns of faculty behaviour, stimulated by the prospect of financial gain rather than by the more traditional guides of research and teaching.

There are compelling reasons of public interest that argue for policies that move science into useful commercial application as rapidly as possible. Not the least of those reasons is to fulfil the scientist's and the university's obligation to provide benefits for the citizen who is paying the bill. But there is no blinking the fact that the drive to do that has changed the incentive structure in those fields of science that are closest to commercial applications and that the changes are not beneficial to such traditionally important academic values as openness and collegiality.

These changes, on the whole much desired by the public and by politicians, have, however, also produced suspicions that universities and their scientists are becoming harder to distinguish from more openly commercial enterprises. Those suspicions are hardened into certainty by episodes like the cold-fusion fiasco, and by revelations of quite blatant conflicts of interest, such as, for example, scientists who conduct clinical trials of drugs or new medical devices without disclosing that they have an economic interest in the company whose product they are testing.

There are hard problems here and few easy answers. The issues growing out of the commercialization of science and of universities are likely to be political issues of the 1990s. Whether the competing equities will be balanced properly is always hard to predict. It would be not merely ironic, but downright tragic, if the academic and scientific values at issue were left to politicians to defend while scientists and their universities were preoccupied with the protection of their new economic stakes. We may hope for something better, but we may be certain of nothing.

References

Penner, R. (1989). Congress is already hedging on deficit reduction plan. *Congressional Quarterly* 22 July: 1,840.

Teich, A. H. and Gramp, K. M. (1988). *R&D in the 1980s: A Special Report*. Washington, DC: American Association for the Advancement of Science.

13

Issues in British Higher Education Policy

Thomas G. Whiston

Three components

The problems, dilemmas or paradoxes (if you will) confronting British higher education policy and its attendant research component, centre upon three considerations: amount (level of resource), quality and accountability.

The 'amount' factor has to be viewed in the context of a possible decline in the *relative* totality of financial allocation in terms of international comparisons (Irvine *et al.* 1990). This can be seen as a problem of reallocation under conditions of contraction (Ziman 1987). The 'qualitative' factor is in one sense a derivative notion in as much as it is dependent upon the 'amount' and 'accountability' considerations. This is because the amount of finance available determines the scale of effort which can be reasonably expected (and, most importantly, the extent of infrastructural support which can be accorded to programmes and projects). While 'accountability' ultimately influences the nature, indeed the *raison d'être* of the research undertaken and the wider research agenda, a free hand to undertake curiosity or 'pure-discipline' based endeavour acts as its own stimulant to the creative process and the further development of knowledge.

In that sense 'accountability' strikes at the very essence of the research process. If the research process (and agenda) is deferential to government, to industry or the wider corporate framework then an inevitable shaping of the research-culture is implied. Thus the wider society, the educational and research establishment itself, the individuals who are themselves involved, have to judge the merits and faults of that shaping. The criteria of judgement remain in a state of fervent discussion and some flux. Some would take the view that educational independence, peer judgement and review, informed self-judgement, while often wasteful (running the danger of being self-serving, irreverent, nepotistic, and also lacking, in its sights, the strategic goals of a more centrally directive mode of operation), nevertheless offers the greatest opportunity of the 'creative leap'. The alternative, of increased societal accountability (seen in commercial and industrial terms), may lead to directive-strategic-coherence. It may even lead to greater absolute amounts of resources being directed toward the educational and research process. However, the process of *selection* of research priorities still remains a formidable problem, as do the deeper and more subtle requirements which determine the ongoing evolution of the educational and research system itself. Education and research are, at the end of the day, diverging explorative forces. To converge and conform, to be accountable to particular paymasters and to move to an increasingly converging agenda is essentially a process of closure. And with that 'closure' come many wider, and unseen, opportunity costs. This is not necessarily detected in terms of publication rate, citations or other more immediate performance indicators. The main requirement is therefore to ensure both a balance and a dialogue between what might be Caesar's and what might be God's.

In recent years in Britain, Caesar would seem to have been winning, but ultimately this may be at some cost to Caesar. One might therefore expect under contemporary circumstances that the Nobel-Laureate Index will decline, but that other levels of productivity will show increase. For a nation suffering industrial, manufacturing and applicative malaise, this is no bad thing. However, in a more universal, less parochial sense, the loss may have unwanted side-effects upon educational and research recruitment, motivation or 'timbre'. The question, then, will be whether particular forms of productivity gain will be maintained.

At this point in time the Japanese are urgently seeking ways of *introducing* or encouraging the 'creative process' into the enormous educational machine which they have meticulously constructed during the post-war era. There are lessons here for nations experiencing economic and industrial decline (who have previously painstakingly built up their own earlier educational empires). But beware: in a global economy where communication networks condense the world into a small community, a little bit of 'creativity' in one country can imply an awful lot of 'application' in another. Historically, Britain has often paid the price of that iniquitous equation. The continuing need therefore, and now an urgent one, is for Britain not only to balance research selectivity with more generous amounts of 'free rein' research, to restructure, but also to retain the best structural features; to consider the opportunity costs of its 'binary-divide'; to recognize the enormous economic *costs* of its relatively low participation rates in HE and FE. In short, to retain its creative excellence. That will require a much closer dialogue between Caesar and God, but not between Caesar and Aristotle.

The fundamental problems and paradox remain: how to encourage the expansion of higher education against a pattern of economic decline; how to encourage applicative and strategic research while not compromising the basic research agenda; how to conform with encroaching European (Federal) demands while retaining control of one's own backyard. Allocation of finances to Big Science, CERN, defence budgets, public and private ownership, are all part of that wider equation, problem and paradox.

Within that wider context there are more specific policy dilemmas. Table

13.1 provides a shopping list of some of the more major concerns. It is not exhaustive but, as I suggest later, there is an organic or even (possibly) sequential dependence to the concerns so listed. The tabulation permits, I believe, a means of exploring the decisions to be faced: scholasticism versus pragmatism, the interactive influence of research and teaching, the sense of direction of research and higher education, the choices of strategy under conditions of contraction, the importance and value of academic–industrial intimacy, and the need for a continuing dialogue between academe, state and commerce.

A listing of policy and structural problems or concerns

Table 13.1 Difficulties, concerns and problematics regarding British higher education policy and the related research agenda

---

1. Derivation of the total spend (especially the 'science vote') together with the stability of the planning cycle.
2. Allocation of the spend to areas and 'levels' of research (for example: the relative allocation to 'basic, strategic and applicative' endeavour; the spend on 'Big Science'; the internal decisions by subject area).
3. The pattern of concentration: the extent to which excellence is concentrated through some form of 'tiering' and the ways in which the central policy process explicitly encourages such concentration.
4. The means of establishment of goals and priorities.
5. Empirical monitoring and evaluation of both performance and the efficacy of new institutional structure and arrangements.
6. The means of linking 'monitoring and evaluation' to established goals and priorities; and the debate, or uncertainties, or risk, surrounding new institutional arrangements.
7. The best, or most appropriate, means of linking academe and commerce; the nature of the funding-reliance emerging from an increased coupling.
8. The continuance of 'scholarship'.
9. The importance and nature of academic independence.
10. The relative strengths and weaknesses of 'directive' modes of funding versus the 'responsive' mode.
11. The demography of higher education and the further development of the research-agenda.

An organic dependence

In listing the eleven concerns in the way that I have I would suggest that there is a pattern of dependency, a certain logistical flow of concern which is worthy of consideration at both national and institutional level. In that respect it is dangerous to overclaim deterministic dependency, but nevertheless useful to examine linkage. Here, I shall briefly signal what I have in mind regarding such linkage; my intention then is to highlight a few of the concerns and in so doing signal the particular policy dilemmas which will have to be faced in coming years.

Undoubtedly the first consideration is the level of total spend on higher education in general and the research component in particular. Despite the protestations of government there is evidence of relative resource decline (Irvine *et al.* 1990). Within the context of a diminishing (or at least non-expanding) pot of gold there immediately arise questions as to allocation, selectivity and concentration. Who is to do this and according to what criteria or guidelines? How is continuity and coherence of research effort to be maintained, without the now long-lost stability of quinquennial planning horizons; or with the uncertainties of possibly temporary academic-industrial financing arrangements? Undoubtedly it is necessary to explore new financing and structural or institutional arrangements. But it is equally important to ensure that the monitoring, evaluation, analytic consideration of those new arrangements be themselves as fully developed as possible *and linked back* into the policy *formulation* process itself. At present so much is done on faith and a prayer.

Within the context of formulating a new Higher Education and Research Agenda, several important perspectives have been put forward; and not a few false starts. The earlier considerations and analysis put forward by the Advisory Board for the Research Councils (ABRC), under the chairmanship of Sir David Phillips, may be seen as seminal (ABRC 1987). The further arguments and position explored by Professor John Ziman (1987) synergize with the ABRC perspective. ABRC considered the appropriateness or otherwise of 'tiering' of universities, possible allocation into a three-layered system of research, teaching and combinatorial endeavour (the *R*, *T*, *X* system). While this was not explicitly followed or accepted by the nation at large, *de facto* forces suggest a semblance of its existence. For a few universities predominate in the research stakes. Additionally location of new institutes, of multimillion pound 'interdisciplinary research centres' can compound the *de facto* tiering. Ziman explored the needs of concentration and selectivity which inevitably derives from a no-growth scenario. Such thoughts necessarily take us, then, to the means of establishment of preferred goals and priorities, the monitoring and evaluation of performance (including the finer development of performance indicators – Phillimore 1989) as a means of both guiding and legitimizing the selectivity process. The satisfactory linking of evaluation to the formulation of policy is no easy matter. Gross inadequacy may even fundamentally compromise the ongoing research process. To say that is not to abandon evaluation, but to point to the need of the most subtle institutional mechanisms on the policy apparatus.

Moving to other areas of concern, one might posit that despite the undoubted high international reputation of many features (and institutions) comprising the British higher education system, there are many faults. An early elitism of intake (as well as its location) has as many detractors as plaudits. Thus critics might point to comparatively low social participation rates; a self defeating binary-divide (of which more later); a lack of sufficient linkage between academe and commerce; a suspicion regarding the importance of the 'applicative'. The agenda of the 1980s has, in part, addressed some of those matters. But much remains unresolved: concentration and selectivity may be meritocratic but can also sow the seeds of a new elitism. Also the increasing applicative and strategic nature of research may come to be more fully appreciated with the furtherance of academic–industrial linkage and collaboration, but at what cost to a more fundamental-remit so valued by many?

Thus the New Agenda has begotten a fistful of developments each separately (and hopefully combinatorially) seeking to maximize the utility of the allocated research budget and to direct that utility toward a greater commercial good. The mechanisms are various. They include a much greater reliance upon a *directive mode* of research allocation, rather than reliance upon the 'responsive' mode, the development of a national agenda (Martin and Irvine 1989) to formulate that directive-mode; to some degree a move away from peer-review (academic self-creditization) toward more public indices of performance; an exchange of the earlier high academic representation of the University Grants Committee (UGC) into the smaller UFC (together with greater industrial representation) – academic buffer between government and university thereby being replaced by a slightly more singular perspective; the creation of new 'interdisciplinary research centres'; encouragement of greater academic–industrial collaboration through a variety of mechanisms (science parks; the need to fund research through private sources; sponsored chairs; *mutual* design of training and research programmes by academe and industry (Whiston 1988a; 1988b). The overall pattern is not difficult to discern. Its effectiveness, sufficiency and perhaps unwanted side-effects or research opportunity – costs remain upon the debating-table (Whiston 1988a; 1989).

I shall consider some of those difficulties a little later, but first let us complete our brief survey of the concerns listed in Table 13.1, where the final entry referred to the 'demography of education' and the further development of the research agenda. In order to anticipate future problems it is necessary to incorporate several ingredients into that 'demographic soup': the nature and level of future student participation rates (and the knock-on effects into postgraduate education, research and faculty composition); the effect of lowered morale and lack of independence on academic recruitment; the continuance (or curtailment) of the 'binary-line' tradition; the importance of independence in ensuring creativity. Let us briefly consider those ingredients.

In the last few years there have been calls by government for academe to increase significantly its total student intake. For a nation which selects and specializes early and maintains a low social-participation rate that is undoubtedly a 'good thing'. Unfortunately there have not been resources to match. The 'Dutch auction' of competitive bidding (by universities) would have appeared to have failed. The unit of resource remains compromised. Student grants/loans remain an ongoing debate and concern. As a consequence, British higher education remains in the doldrums regarding pressure on resources and uncertainty regarding academic prospects and its graduate-feeder-line. Ultimately, though a few years later, associated infrastructural stretching seriously compromises the faculty body and the research capability. Morale and recruitment, conditions of service and the *quality* of recruitment all then become circumspect. Of utmost importance to the future demography of British higher education is resolution of the problems of the 'binary-divide'; that continuing and famous divide between the two major components of the British higher education system. Erosion of that line there has been, but the wall still remains. Preliminary steps to dismantling the wall (or divide) include the translation of the National Advisory Board (NAB) into PCFC; the corpora-tization of the polytechnics; the creation of professorial posts in the public sector . . . but the greater integration of the wider academe is some time away. There are two deep-rooted concerns relating to a continuance of the binary-divide. First, universities gobble up the lion's share (95 per cent) of the Higher Education research budget. Yet the polytechnics' interests are (to date) in the applicative and commercial arena, hence a potential high national research opportunity – cost. Second, with complete erosion of the binary-line will the 'public-sector institutions' become *de facto* the bottom tier of a strongly striated HE sector? If so, at what ultimate cost to the nation? Again we see the possibility of a compromised future research agenda. The history of the earlier Colleges of Advanced Technology (the CATs) and their subsequent transformation into universities at some great applicative opportunity–cost might be borne in mind.

And as to my third ingredient of the demographic soup – 'the role of independence in ensuring creativity' – what of that? There are several subcom-ponents here: the increasing dependence upon industrial funding may *direct* research where it is presently needed but also comprise wider, freer endeavour; the tendency of Research Councils to devote more and more of their funds to centrally directive modes of funding ensures concentration of effort, but cur-tails many areas of exploration, generated by the 'responsive mode'; the pendulum-like swings in adherence to an applicative, strategic or basic research programme compromises an unswerving academic loyalty.[1] In com-bination creativity while not killed, nor perhaps even mortally wounded has certainly had its wings clipped. The question surely is how best to maintain a balance of academic excellence, academic endeavour, scholarship and scien-tific and social critique with the understandable increasing societal and applic-ative problems of a nation in industrial and possibly deep-seated economic malaise.

Each of the problems to which I have so briefly referred separately compro-mise that balance. But, as I hinted earlier, those 'separate problems' are in fact intimately bound together. Failure with respect to any one of them has wider ripple or derivative consequences. It is therefore essential for the British higher education system to be viewed holistically. That is not a too onerous task. In contrast to the USA's 'three thousand institutes' of higher learning (Carnegie Council . . . 1980), Britain possesses fifty or so universities and a smaller number of polytechnics. The policy-making circles, the CVCP, the Research Council structure, comprise a comparatively small population – not homogenous but interconnected in a way which could permit considerable coherence. The deeper requirement is that the 'academic-circle' sufficiently intertwines with government (DES) and industry, maintaining the fullest communication lines while carefully considering its independence.

Major dilemmas and challenges

Judged against the backdrop of the above problems and concerns I list *seven* major dilemmas (and therefore challenges) confronting the British higher education system and its associative research agenda. These are

1. the problem of maintaining a *sufficient level* of *resource allocation* (while not conceding *independence* to a degree which compromises the fullest possible exploration of academe's research frontiers)
2. the satisfactory *linking* of 'output measurement' or empirical monitoring and *evaluation* with a fuller assessment and *definition* of the new and developing institutional structures
3. fuller assessment of the most appropriate *Research Council structures* (in relation to the determination of research priorities and the allocation of funds)
4. fuller assessment of the academic and research implications (both short-term and long-term) of the *post-1992 European environment*
5. more careful elucidation of the *teaching–research dependency* and mutually interactive influences
6. greater clarification of higher education's *research-role*
7. derivation of a robust, but not rigid, *time-scale agenda* with regard to future HE policy.

Let us consider each of these in a little more detail as to why I consider those seven dilemmas or challenges to be so important.

The level of resource allocation and the maintenance of research independence

The allocation of funds to 'Big Science' may contract somewhat; reliance upon industrial sources of funding will undoubtedly increase; dependent upon Britain's economic performance in future years (as well as the political climate) increasing inroads to 'public expenditure' may ensue. Within that context directive modes of funding, selectivity and accountability will almost certainly increase. Whither then academe? 'Accountability' becomes a code-name for externally located directing of research horizons, thereby increasing the need for the maintenance of a high proportion of academic independence. That independence has to be used wisely. Most likely it implies a need to maintain and encourage academic-pluralism: a multiplicity of parallel uncontrolled endeavours which *open up* new frontiers of knowledge; new openings; new ideas, theories and possibilities. Such pluralism requires that academe puts them on the table for society to decide later as to whether or not it will foot a much greater bill. The challenge and the skill will be in developing transparency of assessment, equity in judgement regarding what is taken further and what is temporarily held back. Maintenance of research independence can apply only to those early stages. As the cost-development stage escalates societal selection and prioritizing is inevitable, essential and legitimate.

The linking of monitoring and evaluation to the assessment of new and developing institutional structures

Increasing reliance is being placed upon new institutional structures, 'new arrangements'. 'Big is beautiful' has returned with a vengeance; concentration is the order of the day; 'interdisciplinary research centres' are being developed; early retirement and 'new blood' schemes encouraged; directive-modes of research funding demand more of total resources; departments merge, new links are formed; science parks evolve. . . . Out of all of this it is essential that myth is separated from reality; that empirical validation measures of untested, untried or preconceived approaches are linked as fully as possible back into the sources and seed-beds of policy formulation. Already the value of 'size' (in terms of productivity) has been queried (Hicks and Skea 1989); some of the difficulties (despite the enormous challenges) of interdisciplinary management detailed (Whiston 1986). Some of the steps being taken will fundamentally determine the structure of British higher education for decades; empirical validation of their efficacy is a major requirement; linkage of such acquired evaluatory knowledge to future policy-making is essential.

Research Council structures

At present the UK relies upon five Research Councils (SERC, MRC, NERC, AFRC and ESRC) to distribute its research budgets across academia. It is the second arm of the dual-support system. To some degree conflict of interests – for example in Biotechnology – develop which may be helpful or unhealthy (Senker and Sharp 1988). 'Total coherence' through complete merger has been rejected; partial merger (e.g. NERC–AFRC in environmental issues) might make sense. Some councils are to some degree divesting themselves of parts of their own institutional empires and directing more resources to academe, for example AFRC (Whiston 1987). The dilemma and challenge which remains is how to obtain inter-council coherence without over-collusion; how to arrive at socially justifiable highly resourced 'directive programmes' without maintaining (purely) the special interests of the individual research council. As governments choose to transfer more funding from the UFC purse to Research Council sourcing as a means of increasing the accountability index (and the directive mode) the problems of best means of determining, justifying and allocating the directive-mode capital become increasingly urgent.

The post-1992 European environment

As Britain contracts, Europe expands. The influence of each constituent member of the European Community (EC) post-1992 is still to be mapped. Higher education will no doubt be subjected, ultimately, to radical changes. Harmonization of degree requirements; student-placements; terms of reference of faculty; IPR rights; multi-national collaborative programmes; the interlacing of Big Science projects with local endeavour will require the most careful analysis and assessment. Pan-European programmes at their present levels (for example European Strategic Programme for Research and Development in Information Technology (ESPRIT), Community in Education and Training for Technology (COMETT) – European Commission 1989) are no doubt only trial runs for greater federal initiatives in forthcoming years. The opportunities for rationalization of research endeavour – multi-informational networking and linking possibilities – grow each day. Necessarily the concentration and selectivity of research referred to earlier then has to be seen in a much wider international context: planning, analysis, research priorities and ranking will come to face dilemmas of proprietorial knowledge not yet encountered. The challenge is enormous; the centralist, conformist and bureaucratic problems formidable.

The interdependency of teaching and research

Research funds are increasingly concentrated upon particular areas, departments and individuals. The separation of the teaching and research functions has been gaining pace. Conventional wisdom argues that the research and teaching functions are, or should be, synergetic – each gaining from the other. In that way both student and faculty gain. Empirical validation of the conventional wisdom is certainly difficult, if not impossible other than at the anecdotal or subjective level. Validation of the thesis often requires the benefit of hindsight stretching over many years, if not decades. To be taught by Einstein (or Newton) may not require personal contact; for stimulation may come from the written source and by their example. Even so the mutual rubbing of shoulders of research-teacher and student brings to life one of the main planks of higher education's remit. This raises enormous questions in the wake of 'concentration' as to how best expose the student to the vitality of good (or bad) research. Visits? Temporary access? Advanced audio-visual media input?

Intercalated semesters? The possible menu knows no bounds once the recognition of need is ascertained.

Greater clarification of higher education's research-role

The relative allocation of effort toward basic (fundamental), strategic and applicative research remains a battleground and an enigma. Oscillations (or outright reversal) in governmental policy are not unknown. Previously the applicative was emphasized only to be followed by an argument that industry should fund 'near-market' endeavour. Senior industrialists argue that academe should do what it knows best and that in moving toward the applicative (which 'industry does best') the goose that lays the golden egg may be killed (Kenward 1986). But a counter-argument notes that as the academic picks up the 'applicative' gauntlet a new breed of student, a new culture, emerges of value and importance to the nation. Again, as with so many other areas, the need is not for absolutism, but balance. Students, faculty, institutions will find their *métier*. The establishment of that 'balance of roles' still requires much debate, exploration, testing: above all pluralism of both *attitude* (as to intent) and of institutional *structures*.

Time-scale agenda

British higher education is in the throes of both much dismantling and much construction. To what extent policies are piecemeal, on the hoof, or conform to a more robust well-thought-out, organic long-term agenda is not clear.[2] Educational structures take decades to develop and mature: witness the history of polytechnics, CATs, the new universities, and so on. However, the existent can be destroyed in a much shorter time-scale. One worries that government notes, decides, tinkers and moves on, to new pressures on the economy. Ministers come and go. . . . Short-termism and pragmatism – strong features of the UK commercial-market – are poor bedfellows in such a delicate arena as education, academic research, within which it can require years, a decade or two, to bring concepts, approaches, intentions to maturity. Vice-Chancellors and college Principals no longer have the luxury of quinquennials, or demographic surety of intake. Combinatorially, therefore, both from without and within, the need is for deeper consideration of the organic development of Britain's higher education system. The system so examined has to be seen in holistic terms, stretching down into secondary education and across the binary-divide. Research council institutes; pan-European initiatives; science park and academic–industrial liaison must all be considered in the wider blueprint. Adhocracy, piecemeal localized planning, free-market merger, undoubtedly herald, if there is not to be a profound nervous breakdown, the need for the most imaginative examination of intent, purpose and requirement: across the dimensions I have so briefly and inadequately signalled here. And across so much more. Above all a careful consideration of time-scale, of the years it necessarily takes to bring new structures to maturity; of the long-term response requirements to evolving demographic changes must be incorporated into overall policy-making if coherence and robustness is to ensue.

Note

1. At one stage (in 1988) the Chief Scientist (Cabinet Office) transmitted to Research Councils the need to move toward strategic and applicative work. Shortly after applicative near-market work was seen as industries' responsibility.
2. Martin Trow explores 'uncertainty in transition' in Chapter 14.

References

ABRC (1987). *A Strategy for the Science Base*. London: Advisory Board for the Research Councils.

Carnegie Council on Policy Studies in Higher Education (1980). *Three Thousand Futures: The Next Twenty Years for Higher Education*. San Francisco: Jossey-Bass.

European Commission (1989). *Evaluation of the COMETT Programme*. Brussels: SPRU-Coopers and Lybrand (UK).

Hicks, D. and Skea, J. (1989). Is big really better? *Physics World* 2(12): 31–4.

Irvine, J., Martin, B. R. and Isard, P. A. (1990). *Investing in the Future: An International Comparison of Government Funding of Academic and Related Research*. Aldershot: Edward Elgar (and Brookfield, Vermont).

Kenward, M. (1986). On ivory towers, muck and brass. *New Scientist* 17 July (1,517): 46–50.

Martin, B. R. and Irvine, J. (1989). *Research Foresight: Priority-Setting in Science*. London and New York: Pinter.

Phillimore, A. J. (1989). University research performance indicators: a critical review. *Research Policy* 18: 255–71.

Senker, J. and Sharp, M. (1988). *The Biotechnology Directorate of the SERC: Report and Evaluation of its Achievements 1981–87*. Science Policy Research Unit, Brighton: University of Sussex.

Whiston, T. G. (1986). *Management and Assessment of Interdisciplinary Training and Research*. Paris: UNESCO-ICSU Press.

—— (1987). *The production and effectiveness of the AFRC Corporate Plan*. Confidential Report to the AFRC, University of Sussex, Brighton.

—— (1988a) *Restructuring and Selectivity in Academic Science*, SPSG Concept Paper no. 5. London: Science Policy Support Group.

—— (1988b). Co-ordinating educational policies and plans with those of science and technology: developing and Western developed countries. *Bulletin of the International Bureau of Education* 247: 1–129 (whole issue) Geneva.

——. (1989). Higher education and research in Britain – a quasi independence? In Kruger, H. (ed.) *Fundamental Problems of Research and University Organisation*. Bonn, Germany: Wissenschaftsrecht Wissenschaftsverwaltung Wissenschaftsforderung.

Ziman, J. M. (1987). *Science in a 'Steady State': The Research System in Transition.* SPSG
    Concept Paper no. 1, London: Science Policy Support Group.
—— (1989). *Restructuring Academic Science: A New Framework for UK Policy.* London:
    Science Policy Support Group.

14

Uncertainties in Britain's Transition from Elite to Mass Higher Education

Martin Trow

This chapter was read as the 'summary' paper at the end of the Anglo-American conference held at York University, 10–14 September 1989. I have not changed it substantially, editing only for sense and clarity. I have not tried to bring the paper up to date by discussing developments in British higher education during the year and a half which elapsed between the conference and the decision to publish the papers read there and have allowed 1991 to correct 1989 only in a few footnotes. Superficially much has occurred: Mrs Thatcher no longer heads the government, and the ministers who were then responsible for government policy for higher education (Kenneth Baker and Robert Jackson) have also assumed other duties. Sir Peter Swinnerton-Dyer is no longer Director of the Universities Funding Council; the government has put in place a modest student loan scheme in the face of strong resistance from students and banks alike; the first efforts to create a competitive market for students among the universities, managed by government, failed in the summer of 1990. All this and more would require a substantial revision of the paper. But while the details of the relationship between British higher education and the state have changed, my impression is that the basic climate of uncertainty that I wrote of, within which Britain made its first hesitant moves toward mass higher education, is still in place.[1]

It is something of a cliché that Britain is moving from a system of elite higher education to something like mass higher education.[2] The former is characterized by high and common standards of entry and exit, up to about 14 or 15 per cent of the age grade, in a system of relatively expensive units of resource allowing relatively low rates of attrition, rather personalized relationships between students and staff, a genuine focus on undergraduate education, and the education of leaders of the various institutions in society. British universities not only have traditionally focused on the transfer of knowledge, but also have tried to shape character, and socialize students to the belief that they are or can be leaders, developing in them high levels of expectation and aspiration. The United Kingdom is moving toward a system marked by greater diversity in which elite forms will survive alongside less expensive forms, more variable standards of instruction and performance, and the education of a rather broad professional stratum who will not all be (or be educated to be) the leaders of society.[3]

Now, this transition from elite to mass higher education has been observed in a number of societies, and it always generates problems. In the course of this transition, patterns of governance, finance, cost, the articulation with secondary education, the curriculum, the relations with government, student recruitment, careers, the academic profession – all of these are affected by changes in the size of the system, as well as in other respects that are associated with size. And some of these difficulties can be predicted, at least in broad, general terms.

But different strategies of transition generate different orders of difficulty. The strategy, if we can call it that, that seems to have been adopted in the UK seems almost to have been designed to create very high levels of difficulty. The strategy adopted in the UK is one marked by a very high level of uncertainty about the future, and very unclear, and indeed, conflicting expectations on the part of nearly all the participants in the system. British academics, on the whole, find themselves exposed to contradictory incentives and disincentives marked by unclear signals from central government about where it's going or what it wants.

The result, at least to American eyes, is profound uncertainties within this system in transition, uncertainties shared by many actors within it. And these uncertainties create an extraordinary political, normative, economic environment for the responsive units – for the institutions, for departments and for individual academics. This environment, in turn, generates high levels of anxiety, frustration, and anger among the members of the system.

This climate of uncertainty, its pervasiveness throughout the system, has effects on British higher education and on its members – Vice-Chancellors, deans, chairmen, teachers and students independent of any of its components. Its most visible effects are coping mechanisms, strategies for short- and long-term survival, which themselves have unknown consequences for teaching and learning in universities.

I want to reflect briefly on some of these 'macro-system' uncertainties which together define this climate of uncertainty.

First, what are enrolment targets for the near and medium future? So many aspects of higher education are driven by the size of the system, notably its structures of governance and finance. Britain is currently at the upper limit of elite higher education, with 14 per cent of the age grade enrolled in degree-granting institutions of higher education. But how far and how fast does it mean to expand? Kenneth Baker and Sir Peter Swinnerton-Dyer have referred to a possible doubling of enrolments by the year 2000. But what is the nature of such a statement? Is that a policy, leading to a plan? Is it a prediction, as it might be in the USA, based on demographic projections and other considerations affecting guesses about how many people will enrol, leading to the plans and policies designed to respond to that anticipated demand, or to possible errors in the prediction? Or is it a wish, on the order of 'Britain would be a happier and richer country if it enrolled twice as many students in its colleges and universities as it now does.' I have come to believe that the references to doubling are more a wish than a policy. At the conference (at which this paper was first delivered) York University's Vice-Chancellor dealt with it as if it were just such a casual remark when he said, 'No, I don't think there will be a doubling. I wouldn't be surprised if it were 50 per cent or 40 per cent.' The Vice-Chancellor's estimate was not, I believe, based on any serious studies of demand that he had in his pocket, but merely something anyone might say casually, counterposing to government's hopes a different guess about growth.

Second, there are many uncertainties about the way British Higher Education will grow and how fast, alongside equal uncertainties about how growth will be achieved, and where. For example, will entry requirements be modified? Will academic standards become more variable? At this conference, British academics were both uncertain about the answers, and differed on what they ought to be. And that disagreement on so basic an issue is considerable evidence of the deep uncertainties I spoke of earlier. Will the polytechnics take the bulk of whatever growth occurs? Again, differences of opinion. And if the polys and colleges offer to do so, will that be acceptable to whatever powers determine such things? Moreover, will there be any provision by the state for any capital investment to accompany any wished-for growth? Up to now the answer is pretty clearly 'No'. Indeed no one, in government or outside it, appears to have given capital investment much thought. The very fact that nobody apparently has thought about capital investment in relation to growth is itself strong evidence that growth is as yet a wish and not yet a policy, and certainly not a plan.

Third, associated with (and perhaps underlying) these uncertainties are fundamental contradictions in the political philosophy of central government agencies. The Director of the new Universities Funding Council, Sir Peter Swinnerton-Dyer, holds rather strong *dirigiste* views, side by side with a rather market-oriented Chairman, Lord Chilver. The very leadership and composition of that important new body is still uncertain, and the flat prediction has been made that they cannot both continue in these posts for more than a year.[4] Moreover, the internal structure and operation of the UFC below the top management is itself problematic. There are confused relationships between the Director and his support staff which cannot help but increase the uncertainty of its outcomes.

Fourth, the survival of the binary distinction itself is uncertain. It is known that the two funding councils, for the universities and for the polytechnics and colleges, will share a building in Bristol, and that leads to predictions of a merger within a year or two. But whether the two systems are made one, or continue a separate development, has large consequences for the future, and for thinking about the future. For example, will the bulk of the growth be taken by the polytechnics, or will all institutions simply compete for students (if they so choose) on roughly equal terms, a competition marked by a convergence of the 'unit of resource' in the two systems? Put differently, will whatever incentives and rewards created by central government for growth be applied to both sectors equally – a question which would be settled if the two sectors merge into one. So far as I can see, the future of the binary system, and all that implies, remains highly uncertain.

The uncertainty felt throughout the system stems at least in part from a fundamental ambivalence about the future of higher education within the Conservative government. At the heart of government are ministers such as Robert Jackson committed to a free-market conception of higher education and deregulation; in this sense he is an ally of Lord Chilver. On the other side, officials of the Department of Education and Science appear to be rather more managerialist, concerned with rationalization as sketched in the Jarratt Report, pressing for more accountability and micro-management. And these attitudes (habits of mind, really) exist side by side with the more market-oriented philosophy of politicians in the Thatcher government and their direct appointees. And it is not at all clear to either the academics or the civil servants where this will come out. One guess is that central government will find a way to reconcile a market orientation with *dirigisme* and try to create markets or market-like mechanisms that achieve predetermined outcomes – that is to say, managed markets.[5]

Fifth, the character of the internal differentiation within the university sector, what institutions go where, is still uncertain. There has been some talk by government officials of the separation of the universities into three tiers on the bases of their past and current record of research activity: Tier One, a group of internationally recognized research institutes; Tier Two, a group of universities of national distinction, emphasizing research and teaching equally; and Tier Three, a group of regional universities emphasizing teaching primarily. But while the initial assignments would be made on the basis of the aggregated assessments of component departments, it remains quite uncertain whether those initial assignments of institutions to one or another tier are immutably fixed; if not, how their functions (and assignments) would be allowed to change over time; and how their levels or forms of support would differ. The issue is especially difficult for institutions of mixed functions; the internal pressures on them to try to 'advance' to Tier One would be immense. The implications of a formal internal differentiation of function within the university sector would be very broad. Would Tier Three, or 'teaching' universities, tend to recruit weaker students? Will they be characterized by lower staff–student ratios, poorer capital provisions, poorer amenities, poorer libraries and labs? What, in fact, will be the concomitants of relegation to the third league?[6]

With respect to the polys, will they all be relegated to Tier Three, or will they be allowed to be promoted through the ranks? There were very sharp differences among the conference participants on that issue. The issue of internal differentiation, whether achieved by governmental policy or by the play of the market, has large consequences for all institutions and remains a main contributor to the general climate of uncertainty. A formal and recognized differentiation of function among universities, as well as between universities and polys, and among polys, is a step toward mass higher education, and toward the recognition that substantial growth in enrolments carries with it a greater diversity of student talent and motivation, as well as the necessity to provide access to higher education at lower average per capita costs. Differentiation of function, whether the result of public policy or the market, or some combination of the two, reflects an effort to preserve elite forms of higher education – high academic standards, low student–staff ratios, and so on – alongside a growing mass sector. And this is true whether the differentiation occurs between institutions and sectors, or within institutions.[7]

Sixth, what about staff and student mobility? Diversity of institutions implies a certain measure of career mobility to sort out talent and interests. But in the past, certainly, mobility between institutions has not been permitted to students, nor greatly encouraged on the part of staff. That seems to me a matter of a proposed policy (of differentiation) carrying with it implicit attitudes and values directly at odds with strongly held traditional attitudes regarding the nominal and formal equality of universities with one another. Differentiation and mass higher education imply marked differences between institutions, in the academic quality of students, the research achievement and promise of teaching staff, and average costs of instruction – roughly, the 'unit of resource'. The government has made clear that it wants to reduce its contribution to the costs of higher education, but has not made explicit a belief that average per student costs from all sources will have to come down if enrolments are to grow substantially.[8] We still find in government pronouncements the vague suggestion that the universities can make up the shortfall from private sources, and perhaps even gain permission to raise (and keep) the tuition payments of home students in the future. But all this remains uncertain.

Differentiation implies also the easy mobility of academics with different talents and interests from one kind of institution to another more closely matched to their own interests and talents. Mobility across the binary line is still very rare; in addition, the maintenance of national salary schedules still inhibits (though it does not wholly prevent) the mobility of academics between universities. Markedly different pay for people of the same rank within the same institution, along with inducements for mobility across institutions, are all part of an active academic labour market, implying a sharp competition among scholars and scientists for rank and compensation. This is not something the academic guild in Britain is accustomed to or welcomes. It comes in slowly, but like the policy regarding institutional finance and student recruitment, remains uncertain.

Seventh, with respect to funding, what unit of resource can institutions look forward to in the different tiers? If the three tiers are characterized by different units of resource, does not an institution run risks in accepting more students which run down its unit? The evidence suggests that the present government believes substantial enrolment growth can be achieved at current levels of public expenditure. But to what extent will central government exploit efforts by institutions to raise money themselves? There have been expressions of cynicism at this conference about what would happen if an institution increased tuition; the next time a salary plea came in from staff, would not the government say, 'Well, you can raise the money'. This constitutes a profound uncertainty for a Vice-Chancellor (VC) about the consequences of any managerial decision that he makes.

Correlated with that, who is actually going to negotiate academic salaries? Is it going to be the VCs, institution by institution, the CVCP, the UFC, or government directly? Or, as in the latest exercise, some peculiar and uncertain combination of these? It must be an extremely unsettling question for university administrators to not know how these matters will be dealt with in the future.

Eighth, there seems to be occurring a transformation of institutional roles. One would expect this in a movement from elite to mass forms. In many universities, though not everywhere, Vice-Chancellors are moving toward the model of American university presidents. They are increasingly in a more entrepreneurial situation. They have to be able to make decisions, seize opportunities, be innovative, exercise power regarding the allocation of resources, reshape their external relations, and so forth. This has obviously gone further in some institutions than in others. But increasingly, Vice-Chancellors have to be leaders rather than chairs of committees representing powerful guilds. And they must be political and administrative leaders, and not just in their symbolic and academic roles. As the role of VC changes, it also changes the role and power of the senates and of the administrative staffs that support Vice-Chancellors (and especially the role of registrar). But this all happens unevenly in different institutions and challenges traditional and conventional relationships throughout the university. This itself is a source of new frictions and uncertainties for all, academics and administrators alike, a set of uncertainties I believe inherent in the transition to mass higher education.

Structural sources of uncertainty

There are two rather different sources of uncertainty in British higher education, one arising out of what are widely defined by academics as unwise political policies regarding the transition to mass higher education, and another arising out of the transition itself, which every society would be facing if it were moving from where the UK started to where it may be heading. An example of the first is the deep uncertainty about the relative weight to be placed on market forces and governmental decisions in the move toward mass higher education. An illustration of the second is in the changing roles of university councils and of council chairmen. We hear of a nascent force, the relatively new Committee of Chairmen of University Councils (CCUC), who will be meeting with Lord Chilver, Chair of the UFC. It is rather important that he chooses to meet regularly with this new association of university council chairs rather than with Vice-Chancellors. In the course of meeting together inevitably the conceptions of the roles of council chairs will be changed, and one wonders how that will shape the character and functions of this body two or three years down the line.[9] Its members may in fact begin to think about national higher education policy, not just their own universities. Council members, and especially chairs, tend to be powerful people who are accustomed to making decisions. They are not drawn from academic life, but have independent bases of power. Their collective experience as an organization, with access to the UFC, may be a very heady one, and I suspect that it will affect their relationships with their Vice-Chancellors in uncertain directions. This is yet another uncertainty for Vice-Chancellors to face, as if they didn't have any others.

The Vice-Chancellors themselves may begin to break along the new tiered lines. Any one VC will certainly have more in common with VCs in other universities in the same tier than with VCs across the tier lines. I think Vice-Chancellors within the new first tier group may become a far more influential group than the CVCP has been in the past because of the inherent conflicts that exist in that institution between the stronger and the weaker institutions. If there were fifteen to twenty universities in Tier One, their vice-chairs meeting together, would constitute a very important and powerful body; as home to the bulk of academic research and scholarship in the country, it certainly would have a powerful collective voice and constitute a key segmental organization that hasn't existed in the UK between universities and central government.[10]

I'm here merely pointing to some areas of uncertainty that arise in part out of the problems of market and management, basic contradictions that are part of the inevitable transitions to mass higher education. First, all of this is going on in a political climate marked by official secrecy. Second, the environment and its political institutions are marked by a weak analytical capacity and the absence of forward planning exercises setting forth models of change with cost estimates of alternative futures, models which would be the focus not of plans in the narrow sense, but of normative and technical discussions out of which future plans might arise. There is also the absence of arenas for serious discussion of higher education issues, discussions made meaningful by real numbers attached to enrolments and financial support. Add to that the university tradition of court politics, depending on personal relationships, shared values and assumptions, high levels of trust, and common expectations regarding the future that characterized British higher education when I first came to view it in 1960. In the United Kingdom of the early 1960s I found an academic world profoundly different from the one I knew in the USA. That has changed fundamentally, although many academics (if fewer Vice-Chancellors) act as if the old verities were all still in place.

And yet if the old court politics of 'the great and good' meeting with politicians and senior civil servants in the Athenaeum has gone, universities have not entered the realm of real politics. As I was reminded the other day, the Vice-Chancellors and Principals have not begun seriously to discuss the future with the new association of council chairs. That would be the beginning of real politics, but it hasn't yet happened. *Why* it hasn't is not so clear to me. It may be a manifestation of Thorstein Veblen's insight about a 'trained incapacity' to respond to new problems and circumstances arising out of a long experience of successful and rewarding solutions to older problems which have changed.[11] The slowness to move to real politics is the result partly of this trained incapacity to deal with the new, and also part of a romantic belief that the old world will return with the next election.

The environment for British higher education I've been describing is one of high uncertainty, low levels of trust, internal contradictions in government policy and philosophy, changing roles, and unpredictability of various kinds. This environment must affect every aspect of the universities – their research plans, whether basic or applied, their size, curriculum and staffing. And the effects of these factors on university leadership and administration, with some notable exceptions, must lead them to defend strength, accept the inevitable, and hunker down until the signals from government are clearer. There may be little energy or enthusiasm for innovations which inevitably introduce further uncertainties.

What are some of the responses of individual academics to the prospects of growth in an atmosphere of uncertainty, where growth means more deprivation, a threat to academic standards, a decline in studies and leisure and close relations with colleagues and students? One, of course, is clinical denial: people going on as if nothing were happening, in so far as they are able. Among those for whom denial is not possible, we see the development of high levels of cynicism, and a retreat to privatization. On the department level, energy is going into the systematic falsification of departmental research plans, and other documents of 'accountability'. I suspect that we could develop lists of social pathologies on the individual and departmental level that arise as responses to the climate of uncertainty and anxiety.[12] On the institutional level the most common response is to search for alternative resources in the private sector, to try to maximize government resources, or some combination of those. British universities are just beginning to discover the moral and intellectual problems associated with new and close relations with business and industry.

Perhaps the most important questions are: to what extent does this climate of uncertainty affect the quality of thought and work done in universities? And to what extent does it affect the quality of recruitment to the academic profession and to its leadership?

More generally, what is likely to be the range of responses to the kinds of uncertainties I have sketched, and how stable can this climate of uncertainty be? Are tendencies visible to resolve some of these questions? What might resolve them? Can we anticipate the emergence of forward planning, of frameworks for development, which are not in place today? Can we imagine some genuine decisions by government (including cost estimates and commitments) about the size and shape of the system in the future?

As I ask those questions, and almost assume they must be answered, I remind myself that if there is no political consensus regarding the future of higher education in Britain, the most destabilizing element, the dream of the coming of a White Knight, a post-Thatcher government remains. Because no matter what decisions are taken by government now, academics and administrators can continue to hope (and act on the hope) that everything associated with the Thatcher revolution in higher education will be swept away, and the old order of elite higher education (but a bit larger) will be restored.[13] I can't imagine anything more destabilizing than that widespread hope and belief, one that may persist in some parts of the system unless a broad consensus about the future of British higher education emerges and is accepted by all parties.

Matters in the United States, at least compared to the UK, are much less interesting, except to those like myself and the other Americans who are professionally fascinated by them anyway. But the United States shows a profound stability in the basic character of its system of higher education: its diversity, its mixture of liberal, graduate and professional education, its broad access, market orientation, patterns of mixed state and private finance, and of federal research support and student aid. The fundamental structure of governance and finance has been in place since the turn of the century. But despite enormous growth, there have been very few fundamental changes in American higher education since the 1880s and 1890s.[14] That doesn't mean that we don't generate a lot of problems having to do with the finance and governance of our institutions, and other problems associated with the politicization of access and the curriculum. Problems also arise as we move toward a system of universal access, where the boundaries between higher education and the society at large become extremely fuzzy and permeable. The question then arises: how can we defend the identity and integrity of the institutions of higher education themselves as they become more deeply implicated and involved in private business, in government programmes, in the socialization of immigrants, in the mobility of minorities? Universities and colleges in the United States take on ever broader societal functions and those impinge on the core functions. We have been very good at managing internal diversity and insulating elite from mass from universal functions, within and between institutions. But today we see very great strains on those insulation mechanisms which endanger some of the core functions of American higher education, and threaten the integrity of its institutions. But while those are central and important problems, they are of a different order of urgency, I think, than those facing British higher education.

Conclusion

My series of questions (together with others to which I did not refer) characterize the climate of uncertainty in which British higher education currently operates. This climate is of greater importance than any of the elements which enter into it; moreover, that climate is so pervasive it is scarcely noticed or recognized by British academics who have lived with some variant of it for over a decade. The future will see at least some of these questions answered, either by deliberate policy or by drift and the market. What the answers will be, and how they are made, will determine the character of British higher education for the next few decades as it struggles to make the transition to mass higher education.

Notes

1. I am grateful to Dr Oliver Fulton of Lancaster University for his comments on an early draft of this paper, and especially for his comments on developments since the York Conference.
2. The York Conference was concerned primarily with the universities and thus this paper gives scant attention to the 'public sector' in the UK.
3. But most British academics are still committed to high common standards of instruction and performance; in my view they have not yet drawn the full implications of mass higher education.
4. Sir Peter Swinnerton-Dyer resigned as Director of UFC as of April 1991.
5. This was the case in relation to the abortive effort by the government to create an auction for student places in 1990, an effort defeated by the creation of a university cartel.
6. At the time of the York Conference this issue – of an explicit differentiation among universities – was very much on people's minds, involving as it would a sharp break with previous policy. Protests and arguments prevented its formal adoption; it may, however, emerge informally as a consequence of changes in funding patterns.
7. The UK, with its smaller institutions, will probably opt for differentiation between institutions; the big state universities in the USA and some European countries are differentiated both among and within themselves. But some measure of internal differentiation is already visible in some UK universities, as a result of sharply different disciplinary ratings.
8. By 1991, as Oliver Fulton notes, the universities were feeling much sharper pressures for 'efficiency gains', that is more students for less money. 'In other words the "unit of resource" is now [Spring 1991] being more openly and less apologetically shrunk' (personal communication). The uncertainty survives in people not knowing how far this will go.
9. As of Spring 1991, very little has been heard of this body, though it has met. If I exaggerated the role of this (then) new committee, it may be because from an American perspective it was an obvious new instrument for the defence of universities in their changing relationships with government. It has not yet begun to play a major role in British higher education. That may well illustrate the reluctance of British academics and administrators to engage in 'real' (versus 'court') politics, and to use the non-academic actors and pressure groups (businesses, alumni and parents) that that implies. Even that may now be changing, but more slowly than I imagined.
10. The decision to allow these 'tiers' to emerge informally rather than by governmental decision has slowed all these tendencies; but I believe has *only* slowed and not reversed them.

11. See Thorstein Veblen (1973). *The Theory of the Leisure Class*. Boston: Houghton Mifflin, pp. 145–64. See also R. K. Merton (1949). *Social Theory and Social Structure*. Glencoe, Ill: The Free Press, pp. 153–55, and Kenneth Burke (1935). *Permanences and Change*. New York: New Republic, pp. 150ff.

12. One is reminded of the work of social psychologists who have learned to drive rats mad by giving them conflicting signals. When the rats have learned to perform in a way that earns pellets, they get electric shocks instead. Gradually they give up trying to behave as expected, and huddle in the corner of their cage with their fur standing on end. As I write, a Conservative post-Thatcher government has arrived, but the questions remain.

13. Oliver Fulton suggests that this dream is fading 'among Vice-Chancellors if not AUT members' (personal communication).

14. This view is developed in my essay (forthcoming). American Higher Education: exceptional or just difficult. In Byron Shafer (ed.) *Still Different? A New Look at American Exceptionalism*. Oxford: Oxford University Press.

Index

The Society for Research into Higher Education

The Society for Research into Higher Education exists to stimulate and co-ordinate research into all aspects of higher education. It aims to improve the quality of higher education through the encouragement of debate and publication on issues of policy, on the organization and management of higher education institutions, and on the curriculum and teaching methods.

The Society's income is derived from subscriptions, sales of its books and journals, conference fees and grants. It receives no subsidies, and is wholly independent. Its individual members include teachers, researchers, managers and students. Its corporate members are institutions of higher education, research institutes, professional, industrial and governmental bodies. Members are not only from the UK, but from elsewhere in Europe, from America, Canada and Australasia, and it regards its international work as amongst its most important activities.

Under the imprint SRHE & Open University Press, the Society is a specialist publisher of research, having some 30 titles in print. The Editorial Board of the Society's Imprint seeks authoritative research or study in the field. It offers competitive royalties, a highly recognizable format in both hard- and paper-back and the world-wide reputation of the Open University Press.

The Society also publishes *Studies in Higher Education* (three times a year), which is mainly concerned with academic issues, *Higher Education Quarterly* (formerly *Universities Quarterly*), mainly concerned with policy issues, *Abstracts* (three times a year), and SRHE NEWS (four times a year).

The Society holds a major annual conference in December, jointly with an institution of higher education. In 1990, the topic was 'Industry and Higher Education', at and with the University of Surrey. Future conferences include in 1991, 'Research and Higher Education in Europe', with the University of Leicester, in 1992, 'Learning to Effect', with Nottingham Polytechnic, and in 1993, 'Governments and the Higher Education Curriculum' with the University of Sussex. In addition it holds regular seminars and consultations on topics of current interest.

The Society's committees, study groups and branches are run by members. The groups at present include:
Teacher Education Study Group
Continuing Education Group
Staff Development Group
Excellence in Teaching & Learning
Women in Higher Education Group.

Benefits to members
Individual

Individual members receive:

- The NEWS, the Society's publications list, conference details and other material included in mailings.
- Reduced rates for *Studies in Higher Education* (£9.75 per year – full price £72) and *Higher Education Quarterly* (£12.35 per year – full price £43).
- A 35% discount on all Open University Press & SRHE publications.
- Free copies of the Proceedings (or Precedings) – commissioned papers on the theme of the Annual Conference.
- Free copies of *Higher Education Abstracts*.
- Reduced rates for conferences.
- Extensive contacts and scope for facilitating initiatives.
- Reduced reciprocal memberships.

Corporate

Corporate members receive:

- All benefits of individual members, plus
- Free copies of *Studies in Higher Education*.
- Unlimited copies of the Society's publications at reduced rates.
- Special rates for its members, e.g. to the Annual Conference.

Subscriptions August 1991–July 1992
Individual members

standard fee	£ 47
hardship (e.g. unwaged)	£ 22
students and retired	£ 14

Corporate members

a) teaching institutions		
under 1000 students		£170
up to 3000 students		£215
over 3000 students		£320
b) non-teaching institutions	up to £325	
c) industrial/professional bodies	up to £325	

Further information: SRHE, 344–354 Gray's Inn Road London WC1X 8BP, UK Tel: 071 837 7880
Catalogue: SRHE & Open University Press, Celtic Court, 22 Ballmoor, Buckingham MK18 1XW. Tel: (0280) 823388